DATE DUE

DEMCO 38-296

Dedicated to

Mr. Larry Yarwood of Crewe
and
The Late Mr. Ron Haynes of Hythe Road

A Phantom III Hooper Limousine de ville, 3CM29. It was photographed at Castle Ashby, England by Mr. Klaus-Josef Rossfeldt.

The Directory and Register

Of The

ROLLS~ROYCE

Phantom III

Motor Car

Published by

The Phantom III Technical Society

R. D. Shaffner, F.PIII.T.S.,
Chairman

M. N. Estridge, M.D., F.PIII.T.S.,
Editor-Publisher

Mark Tuttle, F.PIII.T.S.,
Associate Editor

Based on Compilations by

Steve Stuckey, F.PIII.T.S.

Third Edition
1994

San Bernardino, CA 92405

The Society expresses our thanks to Rolls-Royce Motors, Ltd. for use of their trademarks and other copyrighted material. We also thank them for valuable technical and other support during the years of our existence.

Library of Congress Catalogue Card Number: 93-86793
ISBN: 0-9638988-4-1

Robert D, Shaffner, F.PIII.T.S., Chairman
Phantom III Technical Society
515 Fishing Creek Road
Lewisberry, PA 17339
Phone: (717) 932-9900
Fax: (717) 932-9925

M. N. Estridge, M. D., F.PIII.T.S., Editor-Publisher
989 West Marshall Boulevard
San Bernardino, CA 92405
Telephone: (909) 883-9339
Fax: (909) 886-4259

Table of Contents

Specifications for the Phantom III Car

THE Phantom III was the last new chassis design begun by Henry Royce. First envisioned in 1930 to meet the competition of American and European eight, twelve and sixteen cylinder luxury cars, it was a giant leap ahead of the technology of the Phantom II.   A V-12 engine was the logical choice for the aero engineers of Rolls-Royce; they coupled it with a superb independent front suspension inspired by a General Motors design. Unfortunately, Henry Royce did not live to see this last creation; he died in April, 1933. A. G. Elliot was subsequently appointed to head the team that brought the magnificent Phantom III to reality.

Engine:

Configuration: V-12 set at 60 degrees; light-alloy block and head with cast-iron wet liners. Single camshaft with pushrods and hydraulic tappets (solid tappets from 1938). Fork and blade connecting rods on seven-bearing crankshaft.

Dimensions: 3.125 in. x 4.5 in. (448 c.i.); 82.5 mm x 114.3 mm (7,338 cc).

Ignition: Dual coils and dual point twin distributors. Two spark plugs per cylinder.

Carburation: Single Stromberg type dual downdraft. Dual electric fuel pumps.

Cooling System: Centrifugal pump, thermostatically controlled radiator shutters.

Compression ratio: 6:1

Horsepower: (Estimated) A,B,C Series: 180.

Transmission and Differential:

Clutch: Single dry plate.

Gearbox: Separate from engine on rubber mounts with cardan shaft and flexible coupling.

Intermediate gears: Four speeds; ratios: 3:1, 1.98:1, 1.32:1, 1:1. Synchromesh on 2nd, 3rd and top (Overdrive fourth gear from 3DL172).

Drive shaft: Open, with lubricated universal joints and needle roller bearings.

Final drive: Fully floating, hypoid rear axle.

Final drive ratio: 4.25:1.

Chassis:

Type: Pressed steel , ladder type cruciform.

Front Suspension: Unequal wishbone type with encased helical springs and dampers.

Rear suspension: Live axle; semi-elliptical leaf springs.

Dampers: Hydraulic. Controllable, front and rear.

Road Wheels: Well-base wire type.

Tires: 700 X 18.

Steering: Marles cam and roller.

Turning circle: 48 feet.

Turns: Lock-to-lock: 3.

Brakes: Servo-assisted mechanical on all four wheels. Independent hand brake to rear wheels.

Fuel Capacity: 33 Gals. (Imp.) 39.6 Gals. (U.S.)

Consumption: 10 mpg (average).

Lubrication: Centralized system to all points by firewall-mounted foot pump.

Jacking System: Built-in hydraulic by hand pump.

Weight: Less spare wheels, lamps, tools: Approximately 4060 lbs.; with limousine coachwork, typically, 5500 lbs.

Performance:

(1936 Autocar Test, Park Ward limousine)
Second gear: 44 mph; Third gear: 73 mph.
0-50: 12.6 seconds.   0-60: 16.8 seconds.
Best timed speed over 1/4 mile: 91.84 m.p.h.

The Compilation of the Register Information

 N the early 1970s, a friend and I were passing one of the great colonial houses in suburban Sydney, when we noticed a collection of Rolls~Royce cars lined up. We were in my Mazda RX3 rotary - these were my little boy racer days - but stopped to have a look. As I wandered the rows of cars, I was almost scared out of my wits by a very loud horn going off nearby. Mere inches behind me was the first Phantom III car I had ever seen. Its engine was so noiseless that I had, of course, not heard it approach. Thinking back on it, the car was probably 3DL146, the splendid H. J. Mulliner sedanca owned by Bruce Ross, a great man and friend of R~R in Australia, now departed.

It was the beginning of a fascination with the Phantom III, more so than with any other of the great cars produced by the Company. This enchantment I cannot explain other than to say that once you have seen a number and driven a few, it is easy to be smitten.

As an historian by education and an archivist by profession, I began to collect information about this car. I went to the UK in 1976 and saw more, in private hands, at rallies, in dealer's places. Then in 1979 I bought a copy of John Fasal's book on the Twenty - a book that I still judge all other single-marque or single-model books by. I decided to write something similar on the Phantom III and started on a Register, using it to teach myself how to use a personal computer. The 1979 version of the Phantom III Technical Society's Directory was an enormous help. My Register has gone through a number of modifications as more and more information has become available, and one version has been used as a basis for this publication by our Society.

I continue to prepare the book on the model, and by the time you read this it will be well advanced. It will include much information gained from original sources used during my trip to the UK in 1991. It will have a history of the 727 Phantom III cars made. Many owners have given invaluable help to me, and there are too many of them to list here; they will be mentioned in the book. The model engenders enthusiasm and friendship amongst its fans, and I now treasure many of the contacts I have made through this mutual fascination. Amongst those who are the most knowledgeable, enthusiastic and inspirational to me are Bob Shaffner and Ned Estridge of the Society. We all owe them enormous gratitude.

The Phantom III is in my humble opinion the greatest car of all times. It epitomizes all that is great in engineering, and was clothed by the height of the coachbuilders' art. It deserves our respect and admiration, but was made for our enjoyment. I hope that in some small way we as a group can continue the model's rehabilitation after some years of neglect and criticism.

The book that I am writing, along with this Directory, will place the Phantom III where it should be in the story of motorcars. It will include, not just technical details, but also the fascinating post-production files. There will be much of the subsequent histories of the individual cars and some of the famous coachwork placed on the chassis. The book will be profusely illustrated.

Steve Stuckey, F.PIII.T.S.
7 Pindari Gardens
Condell Street
Belconnen ACT 2617
Australia

Nearside view of the engine.

Offside view of the engine.

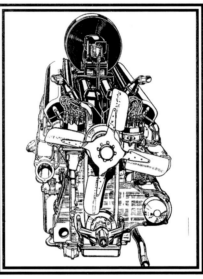

Drawing of the engine from the sales catalog.

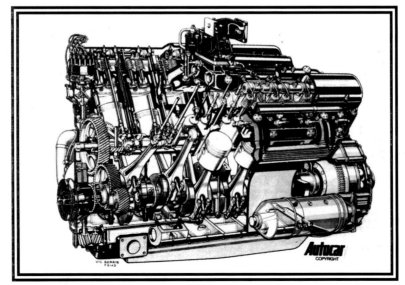

Cutaway drawing of the V-12 engine.

The Chairman's Preface

THIS product in your hands is the hard work of Dr. Ned Estridge, the Co-founder and Editor of The Phantom III Technical Society since 1971—all the years we have been in existence.

An updated PIIITS Directory with photographs of the cars of the members seemed a relatively straightforward project. It became anything but when Ned took on the challenge of accompanying the car data with as many photographs of Phantom IIIs as could be found.

The task has taken literally years longer than planned and Ned's full-time efforts, assisted by Mark Tuttle. Working from David King's previous Directory and Steve Stuckey's comprehensive compilation, this book is the long-awaited result.

All those who added their photographs to those of Ted Reich's, John de Campi's and the Society to make this newest Directory possible should find it worth the wait.

Ned and I are very proud of this publication . We hope you enjoy it.

R. D. Shaffner, F.PIII.T.S., Chairman
Post Office Box 25
Mechanicsburg, PA 17055

About the Photographs

NCLUDING the ten experimental chassis, 727 Phantom III cars were constructed from 1934 to 1939. This directory has a photograph depicting more than five hundred of them. Many of the contributors are identified in the captions; they may or may not be the actual photographer. Where a photograph has been computer scanned from a publication, the source is noted. We have many to thank for this visual treasure.

Steve Stuckey must head the list. He made his large collection of Phantom III photographs and sources available to the Directory, the result of years of research and contacting owners, organizations and publications.

The Rolls-Royce Owner's Club Foundation, The Sir Henry Royce Memorial Foundation and The Rolls-Royce Enthusiast's Club of England generously assisted from the start. Eric Barrass, Peter Baines and Bunny Austin of the RREC have been of great help to Steve Stuckey and to this Directory; the RREC Photo Library and the pages of the RREC *Bulletin* became essential sources. We were able to scan many photographs from the RROC's *The Flying Lady,* an invaluable archive.

A number of publishers and authors generously waived all fees, enabling us to borrow from their works when other sources could not be found. Lawrence Dalton gave us invaluable access to his well-known books, "Those Elegant Rolls-Royce", "Coachwork on Rolls-Royce, 1906-1939" and, with Roy Brooks and the ever-helpful RREC, "The Derby Phantoms". Ian Rimmer fearlessly loaned the original photographs from his "The Rolls-Royce and Bentley Experimental Cars". The late W.J. Oldham had given us the use of the "The Rolls-Royce 40/50: Ghosts, Phantoms and Spectres". "Rolls-Royce in America" author, John deCampi, gave us valuable access as did the publishers of *Automobile Quarterly.* Rolls-Royce Ltd. opened their archives and the pages of their historic *Bulletin.* Monty Bowers, the son of R.M. Bowers, who photographed a number of the cars when new, allowed us the use of his father's work as well.

Other authors and publishers who are waiving the usual charges for this highly not-for-profit effort are: Tom Clarke for "The Rolls-Royce Wraith"; Paul Woudenberg for "The Rolls-Royce and Bentley Buyer's Guide"; IPC Press for "Rolls-Royce, From the Pages of Autocar", and Edward Eves for "Rolls-Royce: 75 Years of Motoring Excellence". The *Illustrated London News* and *Country Life* kindly allowed us to reprint from their pages and the Quadrant Picture Library gave us material from *Autocar.*

The Science Museum of London and the National Motor Museum at Beaulieu, England, forgave their usual reproduction charges and made possible the inclusion of many photographs from their historic collections which were otherwise unavailable. We also had the use of John deCampi's, Bill Dobson's and Ted Reich's extensive Phantom III photo collections, along with the Society's and Bob Shaffner's picture files (The deCampi and Shaffner photos were inadvertently combined and appear above the contributor's credit, 'D.S. Archives').

A number of dealers in classic motorcars helped us: Frank Dale & Stepsons, The Baron Motor Co., Coys of Kensington, Porters In Kensington, The Real Car Co., Sotheby's; also Mssrs. Tom Barrett, Rance Bennett, Ivor Bleaney, Charles Bronson, Charles Crail, Glyn Morris - all are appreciated for supplying photographs of cars that have passed through their establishments.

Especially helpful were European enthusiasts André Blaize, Hans Enzler, Andrew Pastouna and Klaus-Josef Rossfeldt. These good gentlemen opened their files to us and went out of their way to track down photographs and sources.

Far from last in importance, our gratitude goes to the many individuals who contributed photographs of their own and other Phantom III motorcars. Their contributions make up the majority of the pictures supplied and provide a fascinating view of the cars as they are today - whether awaiting restoration or on the road.

To every contributor, to those mentioned above and to the few, who, in the complexity of this effort have inadvertently not been given proper credit, the Society and all those who appreciate the Phantom III are in your debt.

Guide to Picture Sources

Auto Quarterly	**Automobile Quarterly, Vol. XVII. No.2. 1979; Vol. XIX, No. 3. 1981**
B	The **Bulletin** of the Rolls~Royce Enthusiast's Club of England
Bennett	**Rolls~Royce: The History of the Car** by M. Bennett, OUP, 1983
Bird	**The Rolls~Royce Motor Car** by A. Bird and I. Hallows, Basford, 1964, 1966, 1972
Bishop	**Rolls~Royce** by G. Bishop, Colour Library Books, 1982
Bolster	**The Upper Crust** by J. Bolster, Follett, 1976
Brookland	**Rolls~Royce Cars 1940—1950** by R. M. Clarke (Ed.), Brookland Books, 1972
BA	**Advertiser** Supplement of the RREC Bulletin
Car	**The Car, Vol 7, Part 84** by D. B. Wise, Orbis, 1986
Christie	**Chrtistie's Catalogue,** Melbourne, 11 June 1991
Christie Frey	**Christie's Catalogue, Tony Frey Collection,** 2 June 1980
Clarke	**The Rolls~Royce Wraith** by T. C. Clarke, Fasal, 1986
CORR	**Coachwork on Rolls~Royce, 1906—1939** by L. Dalton, Dalton Watson Ltd., 1975
deCampi	**Rolls~Royce in America** by J. W. deCampi, Dalton Watson Ltd., 1975
Drehsen	**The Schlumpf Automobile Collection** by W. Drehsen, Verlag, Schrader, 1979
Eves	**Rolls~Royce: 75 Years of Motoring Excellence** by E. Eves, Books for Pleasure, 1980
FL	**The Flying Lady** of the Rolls~Royce Owner's Club of America
Garnier	**Rolls~Royce: Seven Decades of Descriptions, Reports and Road Tests in Facsimile, Compiled from the Archives of Autocar** by P. Garnier and W. Allport, Hamlyn, 1978
Harvey-Bailey	**Rolls~Royce: The Pursuit of Excellence** by A. Harvey-Bailey and M. Evans, SHRMF, 1984
Hughes	**Rolls~Royce Enthusiasts' Club Royal Silver Jubilee Souvenir** by C. Hughes, Acanthus, 1977
Hugo	**Private Motor Car Collections of Great Britain** by P. Hugo, Dalton Watson Ltd., 1973
Jubilee	**The Historic Vehicle Silver Jubilee Tribute** by L. Dalton (Ed.), Lavenham, 1977
Kobayashi	**Rolls~Royce: The Prewar Period** by S. Kobayashi, Interanto, 1977
Oldham	**The Rolls~Royce 40/50: Ghosts, Phantoms and Spectres** by W. J. Oldham, Foulis, 1974

(Continued)

Guide to Picture Sources (Cont'd)

Oliver	**Rolls~Royce: The Best Car in the World** by G. Oliver, Haynes, 1988
P	**Praeclarum,** Journal of the Rolls~Royce Owner's Club of Australia
P3TS	**Newsletter** of the Phantom III Technical Society
Phantoms	**Rolls~Royce: The Derby Phantoms** by L. Dalton, RREC, 1991
R&T	**Road & Track on Rolls~Royce and Bentley,** Brookland Books, 1984
Rimmer	**The Rolls~Royce and Bentley Experimental Cars** by I. Rimmer, RREC, 1986
Robinson/'79	**Classic Car Investment Review** by M. Robinson, Vintage & Historic, 1979
Robinson/'81	**Collector Car Price Review, 1981** by M. Robinson, Vintage & Historic, 1981
Robinson/'82	**Collector Car Price Review, 1982** by M. Robinson, Vintage & Historic, 1982
Roscoe	**75 Years: A Commemorative Album** by D. Roscoe for Rolls-Royce Motors, 1977
Rossfeldt	**Rolls~Royce und Bentley** by K-J Rossfeldt, BLV Verlagsgesellschaft, 1989
Shoup	**Rolls~Royce: Fact and Legend** by C. S. Shoup, RROC. Inc., 1979
Smith	**Vanden Plas Coachbuilders** by B. Smith, Dalton Watson Ltd., 1979
Sotheby/'89	**Sotheby's Catalogue,** Paulerspury, 1989
Sotheby/'90	**Sotheby's Catalogue,** Paulerspury, 1990
Sotheby/'91	**Sotheby's Catalogue,** Castle Ashby. 1991
Stuhlemmer	**The Coachwork of Erdmann & Rossi** by Rupert Stuhlemmer, Dalton Watston Ltd., 1979
TERR	**Those Elegant Rolls~Royce** by L. Dalton, Dalton Watson Ltd., 1972
Tubbs	**The Rolls~Royce Phantoms** by D. B. Tubbs, Hamish Hamilton, Ltd., 1964
Ullyett	**The Book of the Phantoms** by K. Ullyett, Max Parish, Ltd., 1964
Wood	**Great Marques: Rolls~Royce** by J. Wood, Octopus, 1982
Woudenberg	**The Illustrated Rolls~Royce and Bentley Buyer's Guide** by P. Woudenberg, Motorbooks International, 1984

The Fellowship Awards

Criteria for Award and Roster

ROLLS~ROYCE published very little about the Phantom III. It was intended that the car be returned to the maker for any major work. Many of us who bought these cars as a hobby and fell in love with these exquisite machines, found ourselves very much on our own when we wanted to maintain or restore them.

By the time the 1970's rolled around, Rolls~Royce had other problems. Their interest was directed toward the sale of current models, and the Phantom III quickly became a near-orphan. With the passing of years, more and more of the Rolls~Royce personnel who designed and built these cars passed away or retired, making our problem even more difficult.

The purpose in forming the Phantom III Technical Society in 1971 was to gather and publish technical and historical information specific to this car while the original builders were still around. It quickly became evident that there was another equally important source—owners who had done research or restoration and maintenance work themselves. Some of this work was clearly equal to Rolls~Royce standards, and they shared their knowledge so as to benefit us all. We have established a special PIII.T.S. award to honor those whose contributions will benefit the Phantom III forever. The Award was borrowed from the medical community—the naming of a Fellow. To date there have been fifteen awards of Fellowship.

1. **M. N. Estridge, M.D.** Born 1919. Neurosurgeon by profession. The story of his car, 3BT5, appears in his preface here. Co-founder and Editor of the Society. He has written many Spectre issues from personal experience and research. Interviewed, visited and corresponded with many Rolls~Royce personnel who designed and built Phantom III cars. Reproduced many no longer available parts. Reads and advises on the Society *Newsletter*.

2. **R. D. Shaffner.** Born in 1937. President, Flight Systems, Inc. He has owned 3DL66, 3CM92, 3DL198, 3BU36, 3DL88, 3AZ146, 3BU8, 3AX197, 3CM183. Currently, 3AX163. He has written several Spectre issues from personal experience and research, interviewed, visited and corresponded with many Rolls~Royce personnel who designed and built the Phantom III. Reproduced many no longer available parts. Edits the Society *Newsletter*.

3. **W. J. Oldham.** Born circa 1922, died 1987. Historian by profession. Owned 3AZ146. Researched and authored two major books on Rolls~Royce cars: "The Hyphen in Rolls~Royce" and "The Rolls~Royce 40/50 hp: Ghosts, Phantoms and Spectres". It was his exhaustive research and the more than 80 pages devoted to the story of the Phantom III in the latter book that earned John Oldham his Fellowship.

4. **R. A. York.** Born 1937. Vice President/Chief Engineer, Flight Systems, Inc. Owned 3AZ134, 3DL88. Authored *Spectre* No. 22 on the Starting System. Reverse-engineered and meticulously documented all winding data. Re-created drawing for producing obsolete parts, and other items.

5. **D. King.** Born 1947. Real estate Manager. Collected the data for the first edition of the "Register and Directory" of the PIIITS. He still provides historical material to the Society.

6. **N. H. Allen.** Born 1905, Died 1990. Attorney. Owned 3DL86, 3AZ154. Engineered and perfected the installation of an epicyclic overdrive on the Phantom III, which reduced the engine RPM at road speed. This greatly reduces engine wear, fan noise and petrol consumption. About 30 Phantom III cars currently have the Norris Allen-engineered overdrive installed.

7. **D. H. Parker.** Born circa 1925. First discovered the relationship of oil level in the cam nest to cam and follower wear. At a time when extensive and expensive modifications to the cam system with roller tappets were being recommended by professional restorers, Donald's research cured the cause, not the effect. This, at a fraction of the effort and cost.

8. **L. Yarwood.** Born 1910. Worked at Crewe 1939-1979. Spent most of his career as a Technical Service Representative. Authored many of the original PIII Depot Sheets. Authored *Spectre* No.30 and 31 on the Gearbox. Gave much advice to the Editor and reviewed pending publications for accuracy.

9. **J. Dennison.** Born 1929. Professional Restorer. Owns 3DL70. Even though John is in the business, he has volunteered his time and experience to help Phantom III owners solve technical problems without compensation. Authored *Spectre* Issue No. 28 on the Bijur system. He took over Ned's headache of reproducing carburator bowls.

10. **J. Star.** Born 1916. Electrical Engineer. Owned 3AZ92. The tool tray is one of the most interesting and elaborate features of the PIII. Joe is the most knowledgeable person in the United States (and possibly the world) on Phantom III tool tray items. Authored *Spectre* Issues 25 and 26 on the Phantom III tool tray.

11. **C. Black.** Born 1941. Manager, High HP Engines, Cummins Engine Co. Maintained 3DEX204; rebuilt 3BU180. Researched and made special tools for restoring drive train components for all series of Phantom III cars. Co-Authored *Spectre* No. 32 on the differential.

12. **G. Pollard.** Born 1954. Engineer. Owns 3CM101, 3BU28. Authored *Spectre* issues 33 and 34 on the Braking System.

13. **S. Stuckey.** Born 1950. Information Manager/Archivist. Recompiled and corrected the record of each original chassis, tracing the survivors to date. This major work took several years to complete. It forms the basis for this publication.

14. **K. Karger.** Born 1943. Co-editor/Photographer: *The Flying Lady.* Owns 3DL122. Has provided top quality photographs which have appeared in *Spectre* and the *Newsletter* over the past 20 years. He wrote the section in this publication on photographing the cars.

15. **M. Tuttle.** Born 1935. Television/film writer. Has owned 3BT93, 3DL66, 3DL134. Currently owns 3BU92, 3BT23, 3CP12, 3CP20, 3CM39, 3CM106. Author of articles extolling the Phantom III and the forthcoming RROC Phantom III Technical Manual. Associate Editor of the Directory.

Acknowledgements

THIS publication owes many debts.   My thanks to the many persons who made it possible.

First, my appreciation to Bob Shaffner, for his idea of producing a photographic edition of the Directory and providing the basic materials to begin. He laid out the general plan and provided the entire bank account of the Society to start it.   Thanks also to the Rolls-Royce Owner's Club and Foundation for their general support and photographs and to Ken Karger, Co-Editor of *The Flying Lady* for his help. Eric Barrass and Peter Baines provided the assistance of The Rolls-Royce Enthusiasts Club of England and also published requests for owners to send us pictures.   They, and the Sir Henry Royce Memorial Foundation, were a great help.   Ian Rimmer of Rolls-Royce Ltd. was also generous with assistance.   To the many owners who con- tributed, especially the members of the Australian Owner's Club, who were the best at sending photographs, my thanks.

I made many friends abroad during the course of this project.   Hans Enzler of Switzerland scrounged pho- tographs where none were thought to exist.   Matti Schumacher of Switzerland provided many prints.   Klaus-Josef Rossfeldt of Germany was a big help.   André Blaize of France not only provided pictures but his database of the cars, with many details to help identify unknown chassis numbers. Phantom III spares supplier John Little of Great Britain surprised me with a donation for the publication.   I must also mention a long-time British friend, Larry Yarwood, who has provided technical and moral support for a number of projects of mine over the years, includ- ing this one.

I want to thank my instructors who taught me Quark Xpress®, and Photoshop®. Also, Myrna Esparza, my part-time typist; she entered much of the data and made up the cross indices and members list.   Kwaku Boeting did the image-setting and taught me, an old IBM fan, to use the MacIntosh computer.   He helped in the layout and production of the work.   Frank Klein assisted with the printing.   Robert Stauffer of Stauffer's Bindery gave much help on planning the book and did the final binding.   Also appreciated is Garry Ellerman of The Ellerman Report who donated an ad for the Directory.

I'm very grateful for the help provided by Steve Stuckey.   He supplied the car data, accumulated by him over a search of many years, and many photographs from his collection for use here. He also identified many pho- tos and did a final proofing to be sure the right picture ended up with the right car.

The most help was from Mark Tuttle, the Associate Editor. He contributed in every way, from writing to providing his extensive library and checking each Directory page for alignment, grammar and content countless times. Although seventy miles apart, we were in contact almost daily by visit, phone, fax or mail for nearly two years. The more enjoyable meetings were in Los Angeles where, over lunch and a bottle of vintage French wine, we went over the problems and material. At times I wanted to abandon the project, but Mark's encouragement kept me at it .

Finally, I must thank the members of the Society, without whom there would have been no need for this publication. I hope that the two years of full time work and the many years of effort by Steve Stuckey have been worth the effort. The data is stored on optical disks and could be reprinted later, quite easily; however. I am depending on you for corrections. If you find some inaccurate information or a photograph of your car missing from these pages, please send me a photo or correction for the archives and any future publications. I am running a database on these cars and changes regarding them must be sent to me if it is to be kept up to date.

M. N Estridge, M. D., F.PIII.T.S.,
Editor and Publisher,
Spectre, The Journal of The Phantom III Technical Society,
989 West Marshall Boulevard,
San Bernardino, CA 92405,

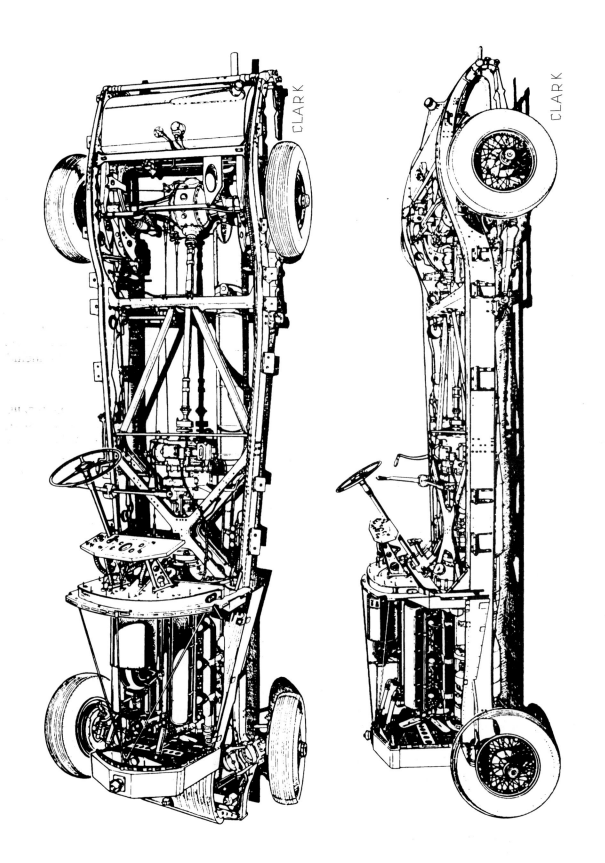

Chassis Drawing from the Phantom III Catalogue.

The Editor-Publisher's Preface

 N 1963, when I bought my Phantom III, 3BT5, I found that an English used car salesman is the same as one in the United States. I had answered an advertisement in *Car and Driver* regarding used Rolls-Royce cars. I wrote to the late "Bunty" Scott-Moncrieff and he sent me a list of his stock. The most desirable one seemed to be a Phantom III. He assured me that the car was in perfect condition, "a jewel in every hole". He said that the car was so good that it should not be shipped without crating. This would cost me another $200, but I agreed.

Some six weeks later, I was advised that the car had arrived. I rented a 1 1/2 ton truck and loaded it with friends and family. I took five gallons of gas as the tank was drained prior to shipping. I also took various tools and a chain, in case I had to tow the car.

After visiting Customs, I was ushered to the gigantic crate. It had been made of 3/4 inch plywood on a 4x4 frame, nails driven in and clinched on the inside. It was almost impossible to get inside. After hours of chopping, a hole was finally made. A fork-lift operator slipped a blade inside and lifted off the crate. The car was dirty, tires almost flat, and generally a disappointing mess. I reconnected the battery, put in the five gallons of gas, which didn't even register on the gauge, and tried to start it up. It turned over so sluggishly that I knew it would never start. (All Phantom III owners recognize this as normal.)

The Customs Inspector came back, checked the boot and was about to release us but, while walking away, noted mud under the rear wing. This was English mud and we were required to have an agricultural inspection. It was now 6:00 PM. We called them and they willingly sent an inspector. He took a sample of the mud and released us but advised us to have the car steam-cleaned underneath as soon as possible. We started towing it but the tires gave out. I tried to start it again, but no luck. We changed the tires, after some problem learning about the hub spanner. The jacks worked, and the spare tires were in good shape. I later learned that they had been swapped for the voyage. Now someone passing the car reported a funny noise inside – I never knew how long the engine had been running.

We started out and quickly found a service station that would lift the car and steam-clean the underneath while we went across the road for an excellent meal. When we returned, the car looked much better. With a fresh 40 gallons of gas, we climbed in and flew off to San Bernardino, some 60 miles away. We got there with all the dash warning lights flashing, but we made it.

The next day I took the car to a friend who ran a garage and owned a 20/25 Rolls-Royce. I asked him to do a general check of the car for safety. He was going to remove a brake drum to check the lining, but I stopped him when he brought out a cold chisel to remove the nuts. It was apparent that I would have to learn to care for the car myself.

Shortly afterwards, the engine quit because of a sheared-off timing gear, meaning a major job. I was guided through this by Ron Haynes, of Hythe Road, and Marshal Merkes, both now gone.

After about a year, the engine was back together. I took the car to many meets and always won some prize. I made three cross-country trips, with little problem. Then it needed another engine overhaul. My shop was too low to lift the car to allow easy access to the underside. While working on it one day, Arthur Nisson walked in and admired it. The heads and oil sump were off. After several visits, he offered me a fair price, so it was sold.

During this time, I had published several articles about my experiences in *The Flying Lady*. I was appointed a RROC Phantom III expert. Once, I was sent a manuscript written by Bob Shaffner. It was good and was published. Shortly afterward, Bob visited me and this became the first meeting of *The Phantom III Technical Society*. Bob would run the business and publish a Newsletter and I would publish a Shop Manual: *Spectre*. When we had published all our information and all the reproducible blueprints given to me by Rolls~Royce, Ltd., we shut *Spectre* down. The yearly or appropriately timed Newsletter will continue as long as the members consider it valuable.

This Directory will be a continuing effort, with updates as new items come to light. **Please keep me informed as to sales, work done, etc.** We have a database on all cars, which you will need to keep updated. Any mistakes in this publication should be reported and anyone with better or missing photographs, should send them.

M. N. Estridge, Editor–Publisher
989 West Marshall Boulevard, San Bernardino, CA 92405
Phone: (909) 883-9339, Fax: (909) 886-4259.
May 1994.

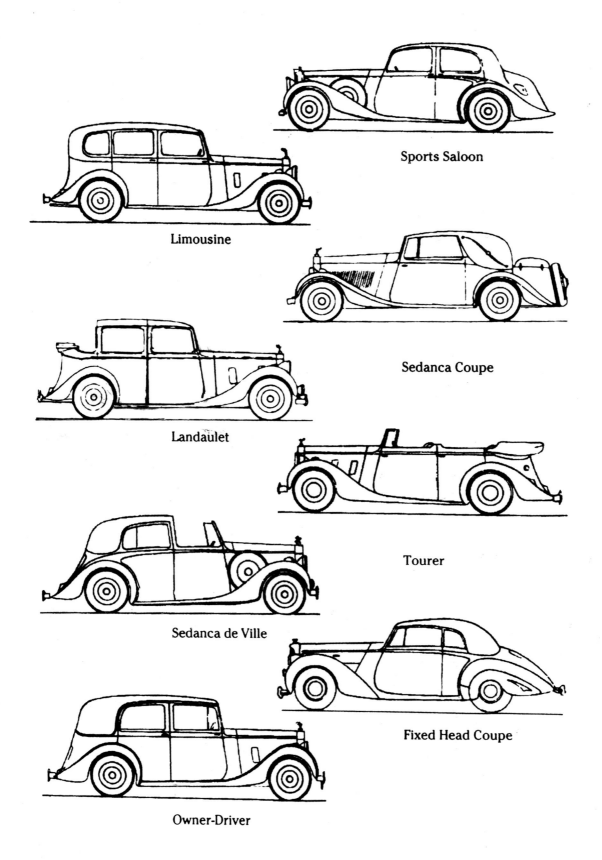

Sports Saloon

Limousine

Sedanca Coupe

Landaulet

Tourer

Sedanca de Ville

Fixed Head Coupe

Owner-Driver

Some types of coachwork fitted to Phantom III cars.

The Experimental Series
of
Phantom III Cars

The Experimental Series consisted of 10 cars,
numbered consecutively from 30EX thru 39EX.
All but two of these cars were eventually
renumbered and sold.

The Experimental Cars

THE achievements of the Phantom III brighten, its failings become more understandable, when one considers that the invention of the most complex automobile chassis developed by Rolls~Royce during the pre-WWII era took only about four years, from vision to highway. This, from a relatively small company struggling through a global depression and the death of its founder and guiding light, long before CAD/CAM and computers. The entire road testing program fell to just ten experimental chassis, only a few of them on the road during the crucial pre-production period.

Development of the company's first V-12 motor car began in 1930; the initial test example, 30EX, met the road in November, 1934. This was a scant eleven months before the Phantom III introduction at Olympia and helps to explain why many of that show's coachbuilt offerings were mounted on dummy chassis.

Coming from the continental test courses of Chateauroux and the Alpine passes, the first testing driver's reports must have caused many a sour stomach at Derby.   The inaugural chassis, 30EX, fighting its complement of four balky carburetors, was soon recalled to have its body removed and a dynomometer test begun to explain its poor performance.   In early 1935 the second experimental car, 31EX, was sent to France for a 10,000 mile wring-out - and promptly lost its big end bearings. Soon after, it claimed a life in a mismatched tangle with a French cyclist.

A Park Ward touring saloon bearing the chassis number 32EX was next sent across the Channel in May 1935. Its driver's reports have been excerpted by W. J. Oldham in his book, "The Rolls-Royce 40/50 hp: Ghosts, Phantoms and Spectres", and send a familiar chill through today's Phantom III enthusiast. Complaints of boiling, tappet problems, oil leaks and the maddening inaccessabilty so dear to our hearts were all there at the beginning.

Fortunately, the promise of the car was showing as well. Fixes and improvements were coming forth. Then, a Park Ward limousine, 34EX, was pulled from the sales department to make an amazing run to Nairobi and back across a 5,500 mile North African obstacle course. With relatively minor modifications, it finished the ordeal in record time, the water it began with still in the radiator. Its biggest problems were a rock-damaged prop shaft and tires which couldn't begin to match the strength of the chassis.

In following the story of the Phantom III experimental cars, the little written about the test driver/mechanics cannot conceal their contribution. Forcing the machines to reveal their design flaws was the mission, but cars had to be kept running to accomplish it. Five day overhauls are dismissed in as many words. Field repairs and modifications that must have exhausted resources and patience are reported as routine.

The brief descriptions of 30EX through 39EX that follow barely hint at the history each holds - the first examples of a most extraordinary Rolls~Royce.

*(Unless otherwise indicated, the Experimental Cars
photographs were supplied by Mr. Ian Rimmer.)*

30EX. The first Phantom III on a test run.

31EX. Before the accident shown below.

31EX. Instant tourer, from the collision.

32EX. (Now 3DEX202).   *(Photo: Mr Griffiths).*

Coachbuilder:	Park Ward.	**30EX.**
Engine:		1, then 3, then 4.
Off Test:		1934.
Body Style:		Limousine.
Registration:		RC 2406, RC 3054.
First Owner:		Never sold.
Present Owner:		**Scrapped.**

Pictures: Oldham/208g, Rimmer/62.
Comments: The first 12 cylinder Rolls~Royce car ever built. It was used in local driving tests. The body was removed in Nov. 1937 for better access during testing. The car was scrapped in 1939.

Coachbuilder:	Park Ward.	**31EX.**
Engine:		2, then 10.
Off Test:		1935.
Body Style:		Limousine.
Registration:		RC 3055, RC 2406.
First Owner:	F. F. Thompson, (10/45), UK.	
Present Owner:		Unknown.

Pictures: Oldham/184h, Rimmer/63.
Comments: While on tests in France, the car was involved in the accident shown. It was thought to be irreparable and was shipped home for dismantling. Ron Haynes told Oldham it had been rebuilt and used as a company car until sold to Mr. Thompson of Liverpool in 1939. There is a Company record of a repair to the electrical cutout in 1939. The car was last heard of in October, 1945.

(Left) The accident caused by a French cyclist. Damage to the car was from collision with a tree during the event. The cyclist was killed, the car's passenger suffered a broken arm, but the driver was unharmed.

The top of the car was torn off and there was major damage to the front suspension. The rear axle was knocked back and the frame badly bent.

Coachbuilder:	Park Ward.	**32EX.**
Engine:		13.
Off Test:		1935.
Body Style:		Continental touring limousine.
Body No:		4034.
Registration:		RC 2545, DMJ 600, JTA 500 (Vic).
First Owner:	Mr. Messinger, UK. (1940).	
Present Owner:		**H. J. Griffiths, Australia.**

Pictures: Oldham/208a, P102, B146/54, B154/41, Rimmer/66.
Comments: In May, 1938, after 67,000 miles, the car had an overdrive gearbox installed and was renumbered 3DEX202. It has been in Australia since 1965.

33EX.   Coachbuilder: Park Ward.
Engine: 6.
Off Test: 1935.
Body Style: Continental touring limousine.
Body No: 4085.
Registrations: RC3168, GF9500
First Owner: James Cadman, (6/38), UK.
Present Owner: Unknown, Canada.

Pictures: Oldham/208b, FL/608 (Shown).
Comments: The car was renumbered 3AEX33 before sale to James Cadman in 1938. It was last known to be in Canada.

33EX. When owned by George Farr.

34EX.   Coachbuilder: Park Ward.
Engine: 7.
Off Test: 1935.
Body Style: Limousine.
Body No: 4100.
Registration: RC 3169.
First Owner: L. A. Nelson (5/38), UK.
Present Owner: **J. E. Little, UK.**

Pictures: Ullyett 53, B146/55, Rimmer/67, Oldham/208b (Shown).
Comments: This is the car that made the fabulous trip across Africa to Nairobi. It was later fitted with a Hooper limousine body, 8966 (10/37) and renumbered 3AEX34 prior to sale.

34EX. Prior to the trip across Africa. Humfrey Symons (l) and Hoppy Hamilton stand alongside.

35EX.   Coachbuilder: Park Ward.
Engine: 8 then 11.
Off Test: 1935.
Body Style: Saloon with division.
Design No: 4101.
Body No: RC 3170, RB 4600.
First Owner: Lt. Col. Gerald Osborn (10/42), UK.
Present Owner: Unknown.
Pictures: CORR/259, B146/56, B79/5, B159/48, Oldham/208d
Comments: Colin Black inspected 35EX in Rhodesia. It was in poor condition and missing the overdrive gearbox fitted by the factory before its initial sale.

35EX. As delivered new, renumbered 3DEX204.

36EX.   Coachbuilder: Hooper.
Engine: (Original) 8.
Off Test: 1935.
Body Style: Limousine.
Design No: 6273.
Body No: 8475.
Registration: RC3695.
First Owner: E. C. Eliot-Cohen, (5/38), UK.
Present Owner: **Donald Wetzel , U S.**

Pictures: Rimmer/72, Car.
Comments: Displayed at the 1935 Olympia show, R~R stand. Renumbered 3AEX36, engine D54W was fitted before sale. Mr. Wetzel recently donated the car to the RROC Foundation.

36EX.   *(Photo: Mr. Wetzel).*

37EX. Renumbered 3AEX37.   *(Photo: Mr. McKee).*

Coachbuilder:	Park Ward.	**37EX.**
Engine:		9.
Off Test:		1935.
Body Style:		Sedanca de ville.
Body No:		4098.
Registration:		RC 4090.
First Owner:	Mrs. Clare S. Quinn, (8/41), US.	
Present Owner:		**Mark T. McKee, US.**

Pictures: Bird, Oldham/208a, FL/334.

Comments: Olympia show, 1935, Park Ward stand. Mark writes that the car is in good condition outside, but the interior is a bit shabby.

38EX. At the R~R School of Instruction.

Coachbuilder:	Park Ward.	**38EX.**
Engine:		(Original) 15.
Off Test:		1936.
Body Style:		Limousine.
Body No:		4529.
Registration:		DGT 367.
First Owner:	Seborn Perry, (1940), US.	
Present Owner:	Mahy Collection, Belgium.	

Pictures: Clarke/27. Clarke/141.

Comments: The only long wheelbase Phantom III. Renumbered 3AEX38 prior to sale, it was used as a R~R School of Instruction car for a time. It came to the US, returned to the UK in 1940 and ended up in Belgium, where Steve Stuckey found it. A Dodge engine replaces the original.

39EX. The photograph was very poor and required much computer manipulation to be presentable.

Coachbuilder:	Hooper.	**39EX.**
Engine:		Not listed.
Off Test:		1936.
Body Style:		Touring limousine.
Registration:		RC 4922.
First Owner:		Never sold.
Present Owner:		**Scrapped.**

Pictures: Oldham/208a, Rimmer/74.

Comments: This car was to be the first of a series of Continental Phantom III cars with lighter weight for better performance. Poor sales led to abandoning the project. The body was removed (later fitted to 3DL152) and in 1938, with only 4,527 miles on the odometer, 39EX, the last experimental car, was scrapped.

Page 20

PLEASE NOTE

Exhaustive efforts have been made to obtain a coachwork photograph for each Phantom III chassis number. Where the 'Missing Photo' design occupies the box, none could be found.

The Society hopes to keep this Directory ongoing. As missing car photos become available, pressure-sensitive adhesive prints of them will be periodically supplied to members for insertion in the appropriate picture boxes. Updates to the factual information on a particular car may also be provided.

The success of this updating depends on you. Should you be able to supply a now-missing photo or correct the particulars on a car, please contact the Editor.

AN OWNER'S NAME IN BOLD FACE TYPE DENOTES A MEMBER OF THE PHANTOM III TECHNICAL SOCIETY.

The AZ Series of Phantom III Cars

The AZ Series was the first group of production cars, numbered even, 3AZ20 through 3AZ238, plus two odd-numbered cars, 3AZ45 and 3AZ47. All AZ Series cars were delivered in 1936.

3AZ20.

Coachbuilder:	H. J. Mulliner
Engine:	A54A.
Delivered:	8/11/36.
Body Style:	Saloon with division.
Design No:	Drawing 5749.
Body No:	4353.
Registration:	1000 RK (France).
First Owner:	H. M. Blackmer, France (10/38).
Present Owner:	L. C. Pivron, France.

Pictures: B121/4, RRB12.37/28.
Comments: Rolls-Royce French Trials. Paris Salon, 1936. Phantom II 11SK used as trade-in by Blackmer. See Gallery pages for 3AZ20's fate.

3AZ20.   *(Photo: RREC Photo Library.*

3AZ22.

Coachbuilder:	Hooper.
Engine:	(Original) Z14A.
Delivered:	8/2/36.
Body Style:	Limousine.
Design No:	6402.
Body No:	8534.
Registration:	CYP 921
First Owner:	H.W. Winsbury-White, UK (12/38).
Present Owner:	M.T. Palfreyman, UK.

Pictures: B152/51, Oldham/208g .
Comments: Rolls-Royce Trials to 1938. Phantom I 85EH used as trade-in. Later engine Z28D ex 3CM31, then B80 engine.

3AZ22.   *(Photo: Mr. Palfreyman).*

3AZ24.

Coachbuilder:	Barker.
Engine:	A64A.
Delivered:	9/4/36.
Body Style:	Sedanca de ville.
Registration:	DGH 2.
First Owner:	Ernest T. Thornton-Smith, UK (6/38).
Present Owner:	R.A. Stitzer, US.

Pictures: TERR/51.
Comments: Barker & Co. Trials.

3AZ24.   *(Photo: D. S. Archives).*

3AZ26.

Coachbuilder:	Thrupp & Maberly.
Engine:	A24A.
Delivered:	7/21/36.
Body Style:	Sports saloon.
Design No:	Drawing SLF.1067.
Body No:	6201.
Registration:	CYV 781.
First Owner:	Henry Herbert, 6th Earl of Carnarvon, UK (6/37).
Present Owner:	A. F. Bennett, Canada.

Pictures: CORR/313, B142/11.
Comments: Rootes Ltd. Trials.

3AZ26.   *(Photo: Mr. Bennett).*

3AZ28.   *(Photo: Mr. Twomey).*

Coachbuilder:	H. J. Mulliner.	**3AZ28.**
Engine:		A84A.
Delivered:		8/7/36.
Body Style:		Saloon with division
Design No:		Drawing 5741.
Body No:		4354.
Registration:		JB 9999, AJB 127, KOL 888.
First Owner:		C. J. MacKay, UK 93/37).
Present Owner:		V. H. Twomey, UK.

Pictures: Eves/171. Phantoms/361.
Comments: Jack Barclay Ltd. Trials.

3AZ30.   *(Photo: Mr. Robertson).*

Coachbuilder:	James Young.	**3AZ30.**
Engine:		A14A.
Delivered:		8/20/36.
Body Style:		Sedanca de ville.
Registration:		Not listed.
First Owner:		Colonel E, Roseveare, UK, (4/37).
Present Owner:		M. Robertson, Australia.

Pictures: TERR/260, P/98, P/1460, Garnier/108.
Comments: Pass & Joyce Trials. To Australia 1949.
Featured in *The Autocar*, 27 November 1936.

3AZ32.   *(Photo: Mr. Rusnak).*

Coachbuilder:	Gurney Nutting.	**3AZ32.**
Engine:		A74A
Delivered:		9/10/36.
Body Style:		Sports sedanca de ville.
Registration:		DGP 500.
First Owner:	Doris, Viscountess Castlerosse, UK.	
		(5/37).
Present Owner:		**A. C. Rusnak, US.**

Pictures:
Comments H. R. Owens Ltd. Trials.

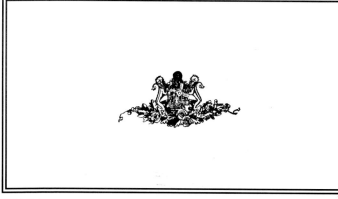

3AZ34.

Coachbuilder:	H. J. Mulliner.	**3AZ34.**
Engine:		A44A.
Delivered:		9/10/36.
Body Style:		Saloon with division.
Body No:		4351.
Registration:		LL 1111, FLH 575.
First Owner:		R. W. FitzAucher, UK. (10/37).
Present Owner:		**Dismantled. J. Little, UK.**

Pictures: Schrader/102.
Comments: Car Mart Ltd. Trials (Major R. S. Grigg).
Owned by Kenneth Ullyett, 1961. This car has been
dismantled by Mr. Little for spare parts. 3BT65
bears a similar body.

3AZ36. Coachbuilder: Hooper.
Engine: A94A.
Delivered: 9/9/36.
Body Style: Sports limousine.
Design No: 6542.
Body No: 8593.
Registration: CYY 2.
First Owner: Mrs. S. H. Prince, UK (8/37).
Present Owner: J. Zamot, M. D., US .

Pictures: Robinson/79, TERR/120.
Comments: Hooper & Co. Trials (G. L. Slater-Booth).
Featured in *The Motor*, 15 September 1936. Engine
later to 3BT23.

3AZ36.   *(Photo: D. S. Archives).*

3AZ38. Coachbuilder: Barker.
Engine: A34A.
Delivered: 7/28/36.
Body Style: Touring limousine.
Design No: Drawing E11195.
Registration: CXU 976.
First Owner: Stanley E. Sears, UK (2/38).
Present Owner: D. A. L. Dwyer, UK (1950).

Pictures: R. Clarke/40, Oldham/208g, Roscoe/35.
Comments: Rolls-Royce Continental Trials. Road
tested by *The Motor*, 29 September, and *The Autocar*,
2 October 1936.

3AZ38.   *(Photo: D. S. Archives).*

3AZ40. Coachbuilder: Windovers.
Engine: Z14B.
Delivered: 7/1/36.
Body Style: Sedanca de ville.
Registration: Not listed.
First Owner: Lionel, 6th Earl of Portarlington,
UK.
Present Owner: **J. K. Goodman, US.**

Pictures:
Comments: Windovers Ltd Trials. Body at Scottish
Show, 1935, Windovers stand. Owned by Captain R.
L. Jolliffe, who owned, new, 3CM153.

3AZ40.   *(Photo: Mr. Goodman).*

3AZ42. Coachbuilder: Rippon.
Engine: Z54A.
Delivered: 11/3/36.
Body Style: Limousine.
Registration: BWU 999.
First Owner: Ernest Waddilove, UK (1/37).
Present Owner: G. T. Thunelius, US.

Pictures: FL/1570 (Shown).
Comments: Rippon Bros. Trials. Olympia Show,
1936, Rippon stand. Mr. Thunelius bought the car
from Rippey's Veteran Car Museum, drove it home
and stored it in a warehouse where it is inaccessible
for photographing.

3AZ42.

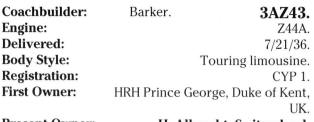

3AZ43.

Coachbuilder:	Barker.	**3AZ43.**

Engine: Z44A.
Delivered: 7/21/36.
Body Style: Touring limousine.
Registration: CYP 1.
First Owner: HRH Prince George, Duke of Kent, UK.

Present Owner: H. Albrecht, Switzerland.

Pictures: Garnier/115, B146/55, Oldham/208g (Shown).
Comments: Ordered without mascot.

3AZ44.   *(Photo: Mr. Enzler).*

Coachbuilder:	Abbott.	**3AZ44.**

Engine: Z84A.
Delivered: 8/7/36.
Body Style: Limousine.
Design No: 3591.
Registration: CYP 922.
First Owner: Rt. Hon. David Lloyd George, OM, UK.

Present Owner: H. Enzler, Switzerland.

Pictures:
Comments: Taken over by his son when Lloyd George died in 1950.

3AZ46.   *(Photo: Mr. Meserow).*

Coachbuilder:	H. J. Mulliner.	**3AZ46.**

Engine: Z24A.
Delivered: 8/17/36.
Body Style: Sedanca de ville.
Design No: Drawing 5804.
Body No: 4394.
Registration: CYX 437.
First Owner: Edward Partington, 3rd Baron Doverdale, UK.

Present Owner: F. P. Meserow, US.

Pictures: CORR/194.
Comments:

3AZ47.

Coachbuilder:	Hooper.	**3AZ47.**

Engine: Z24B.
Delivered: 7/16/36.
Body Style: Limousine.
Design No: 6419.
Body No: 8594.
Registration: Not listed.
First Owner: Viceroy, Victor, 2nd Marquess of Linlithgow, India.

Present Owner: P. Bhogilal, India.
Pictures: Bird, Phantoms/363 (Shown).
Comments: The oddly-shaped tall body was to accomodate the cocked hats used by passengers during its Vice-Regal duties in India.

3AZ48.
Coachbuilder:	H. J. Mulliner.
Engine:	(Original) D54W.
Delivered:	10/30/36.
Body Style:	Saloon with division.
Body No:	4398.
Registration:	Not listed.
First Owner:	Arthur Sainsbury, UK.
Present Owner:	Garrard, US.

Pictures: Garnier/108, FL/3050 (Shown).
Comments: Sainsbury also owned 3CP96. Engine fitted to 3AEX36, May 1936.

3AZ48.

3AZ50.
Coachbuilder:	Gurney Nutting.
Engine:	Z74A.
Delivered:	9/7/36.
Body Style:	Drophead sedanca coupé.
Registration:	Not listed.
First Owner:	HM King Carol II, Romania.
Present Owner:	Unknown.

Pictures: Phantoms/363 (Shown).
Comments: King Carol also owned 3CP34. The similar Gurney Nutting sedanca coupé, 3AZ158, has flap-type bonnet ventilators and no belt molding.

3AZ50.

3AZ52.
Coachbuilder:	Park Ward.
Engine:	Z34B.
Delivered:	8/18/36.
Body Style:	Touring Limousine.
Design No:	Drawing 12141.
Body No:	4196.
Registration:	BH 44.
First Owner:	Lionel Nathan de Rothschild, UK.
Present Owner:	S. R. Schneider, US.

Pictures: Eves/106.
Comments: Phantom II 33MW used as trade-in. Body to 3BT157 by Park Ward (7/46). Rebodied with Windovers sedanca de ville.

3AZ52. The Windovers body.   *(Photo: Mr. Glyn Morris).*

3AZ54.
Coachbuilder:	Crosbie & Dunn.
Engine:	Z64A.
Delivered:	9/9/36.
Body Style:	4-light saloon.
Body No:	141.
Registration:	AWD 578.
First Owner:	F. Lonsdale Allen, UK.
Present Owner:	E. Cobb, UK.

Pictures: CORR/60, B168/61.
Comments:

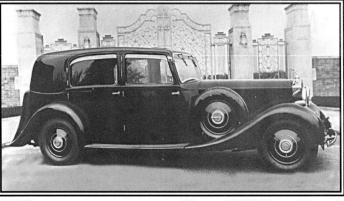
3AZ54.   *(Photo: RREC Photo Library).*

3AZ56.   *(Photo: Mr. Hooke).*

Coachbuilder:	Thrupp & Maberly. **3AZ56.**
Engine:	Y44B.
Delivered:	10/16/36.
Body Style:	Sedanca de ville.
Design No:	Drawing SLF.1070.
Body No:	6239.
Registration:	JHO 11 Not listed.
First Owner:	Isabel, Mrs. Alfred Michael Nicholas, Australia.
Present Owner:	**J. A. L. Hooke, Australia.**

Pictures: P/97, P/99, P/1290, FL/425, FL/1314.
Comments:

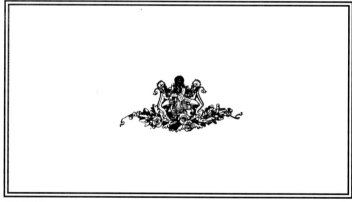

3AZ58.

Coachbuilder:	H. J. Mulliner. **3AZ58.**
Engine:	D44W.
Delivered:	9/21/36.
Body Style:	6-light saloon.
Design No:	Drawing 5815.
Body No:	4413.
Registration:	Not listed.
First Owner:	Sir (Griffin Wyndham) Edward Hanmer, Bart, UK.
Present Owner:	C. Dukehart, US.

Pictures: FL/907 (Not reproducible).
Comments: Phantom II type instruments fitted.

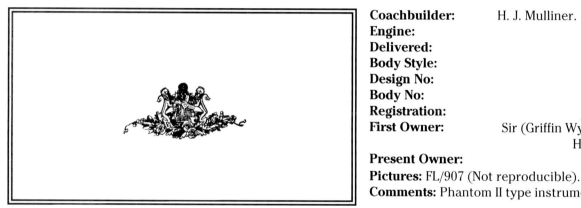

3AZ60.

Coachbuilder:	H. J. Mulliner. **3AZ60.**
Engine:	D34W.
Delivered:	9/16/36.
Body Style:	Fixed-head sedanca coupé.
Body No:	4396.
Registration:	AGH 10.
First Owner:	S. F. Raphael, UK.
Present Owner:	Unknown.

Pictures:
Comments:

3AZ62.

Coachbuilder:	Gurney Nutting. **3AZ62.**
Engine:	Z34A.
Delivered:	10/4/36.
Body Style:	Sedanca de ville.
Registration:	DGO 3.
First Owner:	Hon. (John) Seymour Berry, UK.
Present Owner:	W. McNally, US.

Pictures: B68/23 (Shown).
Comments: Berry's father, Baron Camrose, owned 3BT41.

3AZ64.
Coachbuilder: Allweather.
Engine: Z94A.
Delivered: 10/5/36.
Body Style: Limousine.
Registrations: DUL 507, LU 35707 (Swiss).
First Owner: Alec Lionel Rea, UK.
Present Owner: H. Bieri, Switzerland.

Pictures: B176/34.
Comments: Rea's brother owned 3AZ226.

3AZ64. *(Photo: Mr. Bieri).*

3AZ66.
Coachbuilder: Hooper.
Engine: D14W.
Delivered: 8/22/36.
Body Style: Sports limousine.
Design No: 6420.
Body No: 8592.
Registration: ASR 114.
First Owner: Mrs. Margot Fyfe-Jamieson, UK.
Present Owner: M. O. Johnson, US.

Pictures: FL/3720, Phantoms/264 (Shown).
Comments:

3AZ66.

3AZ68.
Coachbuilder: Freestone & Webb.
Engine: D74W.
Delivered: 8/28/36.
Body Style: Sports saloon.
Design No: 1700.
Body No: 1199.
Registration: DGH 7.
First Owner: Sir John Leigh, Bart., MP, UK.
Present Owner: W. A. Lockley-Cook, UK.

Pictures: TERR/80, Hugo/130, Woudenberg/47.
Comments: Sir John Leigh also owned 3BU136, 3BT99 and 3DL154.

3AZ68. *(Photo: Mr. Rossfeldt).*

3AZ70.
Coachbuilder: Park Ward.
Engine: (Original) D64W.
Delivered: 9/8/36.
Body Style: Limousine.
Body No: 4148.
Registration: DGJ 28.
First Owner: W. Wallach, UK.
Present Owner: A. M. Courtney, UK.

Pictures: BA104/10 (Shown).
Comments: Olympia Show, 1936, Park Ward stand. Owned by the actor (later, Sir) Michael Redgrave, 1948. Later fitted with six cylinder Bedford engine, subsequently replaced by a R-R B80 straight eight.

3AZ70. *(Photo: The Real Car Co.).*

3AZ72.

Coachbuilder:	Windovers.	**3AZ72.**
Engine:		D84W.
Delivered:		9/10/36.
Body Style:		Saloon with division.
Body No:		6378.
Registration:		CYX 523.
First Owner:		Alfred Sainsbury, UK.
Present Owner:		M. M. H. Lips, Netherlands.

Pictures:
Comments:

3AZ74.   *(Photo: Mr. Dia).*

Coachbuilder:	Barker.	**3AZ74.**
Engine:		K34P.
Delivered:		10/17/36.
Body Style:		Allweather.
Registration:		Not listed.
First Owner:		Miss E. W. Thomson, UK.
Present Owner:		**A. M. Dia, US.**

Pictures: Oldham/208g, FL/1690.
Comments: Ordered without mascot. Miss Thomson also owned 3DL126.

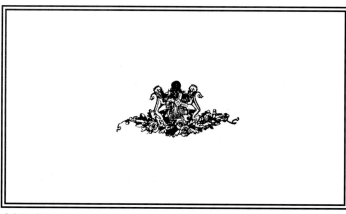

3AZ76.

Coachbuilder:	Allweather Mtr. Bod.	**3AZ76.**
Engine:		D24W.
Delivered:		9/10/36.
Body Style:		Cabriolet.
Registration:		CYP 930.
First Owner:	George Leveson-Gower, 5th Duke	
	of Sutherland, UK.	
Present Owner:		R. B. Honeywill, US.

Pictures: Bird, CORR/373, Woudenberg/51 (Shown).
Comments: Ordered without mascot.

3AZ78.

Coachbuilder:	Barker.	**3AZ78.**
Engine:		D94W.
Delivered:		10/30/36.
Body Style:		Landaulette.
Design No:		Drawing C9368B.
Registration:		DGF 998.
First Owner:		Leopold Sutro, UK.
Present Owner:		Unknown.

Pictures:
Comments: Phantom I 62DC used as trade-in.

3AZ80.
Coachbuilder:	Mann Egerton.
Engine:	K44P.
Delivered:	10/30/36.
Body Style:	Touring saloon.
Registration:	BAH 717.
First Owner:	H. A. Green, UK.
Present Owner:	M. Engelberg, Canada.

Pictures: CORR/156, FL/1554.
Comments:

3AZ80. *(Photo: Mr. Engelberg).*

3AZ82.
Coachbuilder:	Rippon.
Engine:	K64P.
Delivered:	10/14/36.
Body Style:	Fixed-head coupe.
Registration:	BTD 149.
First Owner:	Richard Edwin Hattersley, UK.
Present Owner:	Brian Classic, UK.

Pictures: Phantoms/364 (Shown).
Comments: Rippon Bros. Trials (Major A. Seymour Mead).

3AZ82.

3AZ84.
Coachbuilder:	Barker.
Engine:	K54P.
Delivered:	10/28/36.
Body Style:	Saloon.
Registration:	DGX 3.
First Owner:	Henry Brandon, UK.
Present Owner:	D. W. E. Kyle, UK.

Pictures: Phantoms/365 (Shown).
Comments:

3AZ84.

3AZ86.
Coachbuilder:	Arthur Mulliner.
Engine:	K74P.
Delivered:	10/16/36.
Body Style:	Coupé cabriolet.
Registration:	DGP 715, PUF 3.
First Owner:	Hon. Alexander Crighton Nivison, UK.
Present Owner:	D. Z. de Ferranti, Ireland.

Pictures: Oldham/208h.
Comments: Ordered without mascot. Nivison's brother, Baron Glendyne, owned 3AZ156.

3AZ86. *(Photo: Mr. de Ferranti).*

3AZ88.

Coachbuilder:	H. J. Mulliner.	**3AZ88.**
Engine:		K14P.
Delivered:		10/22/36.
Body Style:		Saloon with division.
Design No:		Drawing 5798.
Body No:		4393.
Registration:		DGO 750.
First Owner:		Captain Woolf Barnato, UK.
Present Owner:	(Engine only) Smithsonian Inst., US.	

Pictures: FL/721, Phantoms/365 (Shown).
Comments: Engine only remains, after display at New York World's Fair, 1939.

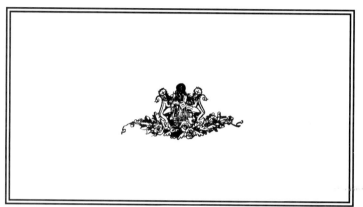

3AZ90.

Coachbuilder:	Windovers.	**3AZ90.**
Engine:		K24P.
Delivered:		10/1/36.
Body Style:		Saloon with division.
Body No:		6371.
Registration:		Not listed.
First Owner:	Thomas Octave Murdoch (TOM) Sopwith, CBE, UK.	
Present Owner:		Unknown.

Pictures:
Comments: Sopwith was the developer of the famous Sopwith Camel airplane, used in WW1. He died in 1994, over 100 years old.

3AZ92.   *(Photo: Mr. Star via RROC).*

Coachbuilder:	Barker	**3AZ92.**
Engine:		K84P.
Delivered:		10/5/36.
Body Style:		Sedanca de ville.
Registration:		DGK 43.
First Owner:	David Field, 2nd Earl Beatty, UK.	
Present Owner:		Unknown.

Pictures: Oldham/208g, TS/34.
Comments: Beatty's brother owned 3DL118. PIIITS Fellow Joe Star writes that he sold the car years ago to someone who wishes to remain anonymous.

3AZ94.   *(Photo: Mr. Mausolf).*

Coachbuilder:	H. J. Mulliner.	**3AZ94.**
Engine:		K94P.
Delivered:		11/28/36.
Body Style:		Saloon with division.
Design No:		4399.
Body No:		DLA 762.
Registration:		Walter Samuel, 2nd Viscount
First Owner:		Bearsted, UK.
Present Owner:		E. G. Mausolf, US.

Pictures: FL/1720.
Comments: Original order by K. A. Wagg. Viscount Bearsted's son owned 3AZ154.

3AZ96.

Coachbuilder:	Thrupp & Maberly.
Engine:	Y64B.
Delivered:	9/7/36.
Body Style:	Saloon.
Design No:	Drawing SLF.1159C.
Body No:	6468.
Registration:	DGP 300.
First Owner:	Count Curt Haugwitz-Reventlow, UK.
Present Owner:	Unknown.

Pictures: CORR/313 (Shown).
Comments: The Countess Haugwitz-Reventlow owned the nearly identical 3BU200.

3AZ96.

3AZ98.

Coachbuilder:	Gurney Nutting.
Engine:	Y14B.
Delivered:	11/6/36.
Body Style:	(First) Sedanca de ville.
Registration:	DJJ 6.
First Owner:	J. S. Emanuel, UK.
Present Owner:	P. W. Hackett, US.

Pictures: Phantoms/409 (Shown).
Comments: Rebodied with H. J. Mulliner saloon with division, probably body 4642, ex 3DL102.

3AZ98. With the first body.

3AZ100.

Coachbuilder:	Hooper.
Engine:	Q14J.
Delivered:	9/29/36.
Body Style:	Landaulette.
Design No:	6428.
Body No:	8596.
Registration:	Not listed.
First Owner:	Edward Stanley, 17th Earl of Derby, UK.
Present Owner:	M. P. Koeplin, US.

Pictures: Oldham/232a.
Comments: Ordered without mascot. Used by Lord Mayor of Manchester, 1948.

3AZ100. *(Photo: Mr. Koeplin).*

3AZ102.

Coachbuilder:	Hooper.
Engine:	Y94B.
Delivered:	8/29/36.
Body Style:	Limousine.
Design No:	6273.
Body No:	8609.
Registrations:	CYP 927, 800 HRY, LYU 822.
First Owner:	J. H. Jacobs, UK.
Present Owner:	T. Talbot, U.K.

Pictures:
Comments: Phantom I 93EF used as trade-in. Shortened chassis only, 1981.

3AZ102.

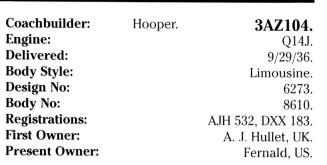

3AZ104.

Coachbuilder:	Hooper.
Engine:	Q14J.
Delivered:	9/29/36.
Body Style:	Limousine.
Design No:	6273.
Body No:	8610.
Registrations:	AJH 532, DXX 183.
First Owner:	A. J. Hullet, UK.
Present Owner:	Fernald, US.

3AZ104.

Pictures:
Comments: Olympia Show, 1936, Rolls-Royce stand. 20/25 GLR22 used as trade-in.

3AZ106.   *(Photo: Mr. Brotherus).*

Coachbuilder:	Park Ward.
Engine:	J44Q.
Delivered:	11/10/36.
Body Style:	(First) Limousine.
Body No:	4194.
Registration:	A 351.
First Owner:	Henry Gage Spicer, UK.
Present Owner:	I. J. Brotherus, Finland.

3AZ106.

Pictures:
Comments: In USA from 1960's to 1990. The top of the car has been cut away. The owner is not sure whether it should be rebuilt or left as a tourer. (I advised the latter — Ed).

3AZ108.   *(Photo: Mr. Browne).*

Coachbuilder:	Windovers.
Engine:	J14Q.
Delivered:	Limousine.
Body Style:	11/10/36.
Body No:	6357.
Registration:	DGT 393.
First Owner:	W. Riley-Smith, UK.
Present Owner:	A. V. Browne, UK.

3AZ108.

Pictures:
Comments: Car severely damaged in accident, 1960's.

3AZ110.

Coachbuilder:	Windovers.
Engine:	J54Q.
Delivered:	9/5/36.
Body Style:	Sedanca de ville.
Registration:	CYX 525.
First Owner:	Benjamin Guinness, UK.
Present Owner:	**J. R. Rossum, US.**

3AZ110.

Pictures: CORR/359 (Shown).
Comments: Guinness also owned 3AZ150 and 3DL98.

3AZ112. Coachbuilder: H. J. Mulliner.
Engine: Q64J.
Delivered: 10/31/36.
Body Style: Sedanca de ville.
Body No: 4425.
Registration: EMF 929.
First Owner: John Dibble, UK.
Present Owner: S. K. Schumann, Germany.

Pictures: Bird, Phantoms/365.
Comments: Olympia Show, 1936, H. J. Mulliner stand. Later owned by Lord Astor, and Ian Hallows in 1961.

3AZ112. *(Photo: RREC Photo Library).*

3AZ114. Coachbuilder: Hooper.
Engine: Q74J.
Delivered: 2/11/37.
Body Style: Sports limousine.
Design No: 6542.
Body No: 8710.
Registrations: DXB 211, PPW 807, WSU 604.
First Owner: D. Stoner Crowther, UK.
Present Owner: N. D'Schaetsen Brienen, Belgium.

Pictures:
Comments: Originally ordered by C. A. Cochrane. Car reimported to the UK in 1989 after some years in the USA.

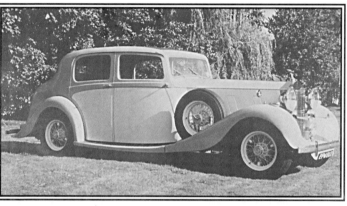

3AZ114. *(Photo: Stuckey Collection).*

3AZ116. Coachbuilder: Barker.
Engine: J84Q.
Delivered: 11/5/36.
Body Style: Limousine.
Registration: DLA 136.
First Owner: Sir William John Firth, UK.
Present Owner: Brookes Auctions, UK (1974).

Pictures: Phantoms/366.
Comments:

3AZ116. *(Photo: RREC Photo Library).*

3AZ118. Coachbuilder: Thrupp & Maberly.
Engine: Q34J.
Delivered: 10/6/36.
Body Style: Limousine.
Design No: Drawing SLE.1072E.
Body No: 6377.
Registration: DHL 888.
First Owner: Sir Edmund Davis, UK.
Present Owner: C. H. Dyer, US.

Pictures:
Comments: Olympia Show, 1936, Thrupp & Maberly stand.

3AZ118. *(Photo: Mr. Dyer).*

3AZ120.   *(Photo: RREC Photo Library).*

Coachbuilder:	Park Ward.	**3AZ120.**
Engine:	(Original) Q44J.	
Delivered:	10/26/36.	
Body Style:	Touring saloon.	
Body No:	4151.	
Registration:	CBP 889.	
First Owner:	Colonel Evelyn William Margesson CMG, UK.	
Present Owner:	M. L. Peveler, US.	

Pictures: Phantoms/366.
Comments: Margesson also owned 3CM185. Later fitted with American V8 engine.

3AZ122.   *(Photo: Science Museum, London).*

Coachbuilder:	Hooper.	**3AZ122.**
Engine:	J74Q.	
Delivered:	10/12/36.	
Body Style:	Sports limousine.	
Design No:	6537.	
Body No:	8622.	
Registration:	Not listed.	
First Owner:	Mme. Olga Clare de Romero, UK.	
Present Owner:	E. T. Campbell, US.	

Pictures:
Comments: Hooper Body Book says original order by L. A. Hordern.

3AZ124.   *(Photo: Mr. Mason).*

Coachbuilder:	Barker	**3AZ124.**
Engine:	(Original) J94Q.	
Delivered:	11/4/36.	
Body Style:	Touring limousine.	
Design No:	Drawing E11195.	
Registration:	DGT 361, 454 YKR.	
First Owner:	H. O. Short, UK.	
Present Owner:	T. Mason, UK.	

Pictures: BA112/31 (Shown).
Comments: Short also owned 3BU138. Used by Rolls-Royce Inspection Department, 1937-1942. Engine to 3AZ150, later engine Q78K ex 3BU138.

3AZ126.

Coachbuilder:	Lancefield.	**3AZ126.**
Engine:	A14Z.	
Delivered:	12/3/36.	
Body Style:	Limousine.	
Registration:	Not listed.	
First Owner:	Lt. Colonel G. W. Parkinson, UK.	
Present Owner:	Lt. General Sir C. King, UK, (1954).	

Pictures: TERR/287 (Shown).
Comments: Ordered without mascot.

3AZ128. Coachbuilder: Park Ward.
Engine: A24Z.
Delivered: 11/10/36.
Body Style: Limousine.
Body No: 4150.
Registration: DLD 580.
First Owner: Jonas Wolfe, UK.
Present Owner: **Dismantled.**

Pictures:
Comments: John Little dismantled this car for spare parts. He says the car was a 'D' back design.

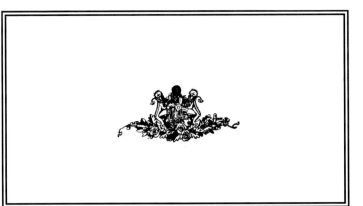
3AZ128.

3AZ130. Coachbuilder: Windovers.
Engine: A34Z.
Delivered: 11/17/36.
Body Style: Limousine.
Body No: 6370.
Registration: Not listed.
First Owner: George Bonar, UK.
Present Owner: Unknown.

Pictures:
Comments:

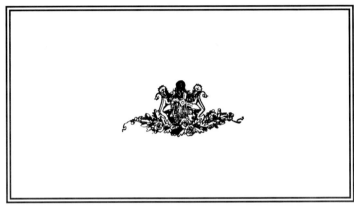
3AZ130.

3AZ132. Coachbuilder: H. J. Mulliner.
Engine: A44Z.
Delivered: 11/23/36.
Body Style: Drophead coupé.
Design No: 5709.
Body No: 4335.
Registration: TL 5947, HLT 1.
First Owner: Vincent Hemery, UK.
Present Owner: P. Swenden, Belgium.
Pictures: Oldham/232a, FL/962, Woudenberg, Phantoms/366,
Comments: Phantom II 149TA used as trade-in. From USA to Belgium, 1991.

3AZ132. *(Photo: Coys of Kensington).*

3AZ134. Coachbuilder: Arthur Mulliner.
Engine: A54Z.
Delivered: 10/24/36.
Body Style: Limousine.
Registration: CTA 646.
First Owner: Miss (1937: Dame) Violet Edith Wills, UK.
Present Owner: A. Ayres, UK.

Pictures: Oldham/232a (Shown).
Comments: Ordered without mascot.

3AZ134.

3AZ136.

Coachbuilder:	H. J. Mulliner.	**3AZ136.**

Engine: A64Z.
Delivered: 11/9/36.
Body Style: 4-light saloon.
Design No: Drawing 5814.
Body No: 4410.
Registration: DJJ 180.
First Owner: Hon. Philip Henderson, UK.
Present Owner: J. A. Young, UK.

Pictures: B82/36, CORR/195 (Shown).
Comments: Henderson also owned 3CM167. Owned by Sir John Blunt 1938-1949. Car in Sweden for some years.

3AZ138.   *(Photo: Mr. Gary Wales).*

Coachbuilder:	Hooper.	**3AZ138.**

Engine: A74Z.
Delivered: 11/3/36.
Body Style: (First) Limousine.
Design No: 6545.
Body No: 8650.
Registrations: DJJ 401, 170TU.
First Owner: F. H. Bailey, UK.
Present Owner: Estate of Amherst-Villiers, UK.

Pictures:
Comments: Rebodied with Brockman replica, 1980's, and fitted with twin turbo-chargers, overdrive and center gearchange.

3AZ140.   At Paris Salon, 1936.

Coachbuilder:	Binder.	**3AZ140.**

Engine: Y84B.
Delivered: 10/26/36.
Body Style: Touring saloon.
Registration: Not listed.
First Owner: Alfred Benhaim, France.
Present Owner: P. H. Gee, UK.

Pictures: Phantoms/367 (Shown).
Comments: Paris Salon, 1936, Binder stand.

Coachbuilder:	Barker.	**3AZ142.**

Engine: A84Z.
Delivered: 10/13/36.
Body Style: Limousine.
Registration: DGK 45.
First Owner: Arthur Nall-Cain, 2nd Baron Brocket, UK.
Present Owner: A. T. Midgley, UK.

Pictures:
Comments: Offered for sale in August 1981, *PIIITS Newsletter*, with rebuilt engine.

3AZ142.   *(Photo: National Motor Museum, England).*

3AZ144.
Coachbuilder: Hooper.
Engine: P24K.
Delivered: 11/12/36.
Body Style: Limousine.
Design No: 6308.
Body No: 8597.
Registration: DLU 985.
First Owner: Martin H. Benson, UK.
Present Owner: C. Wright, US.

Pictures: Oldham/232b (Shown).
Comments: Ordered without mascot.

3AZ144.

3AZ146.
Coachbuilder: Hooper.
Engine: P14K.
Delivered: 10/16/36.
Body Style: Limousine.
Design No: 6469.
Body No: 8600.
Registration: CLJ 600 (to 1965), J 376.
First Owner: Miss Harriet R. Maconochie, UK.
Present Owner: **H. T. Treworgy, US.**

Pictures: TERR/122, Oldham/232c, B81/13, B86/27.
Comments:

3AZ146. *(Photo: Mr. Treworgy).*

3AZ148.
Coachbuilder: Barker.
Engine: Q28J.
Delivered: 11/2/36.
Body Style: Limousine.
Registration: Not listed.
First Owner: Sir Pomeroy Burton, UK.
Present Owner: Unknown.

Pictures: Oldham/232c.
Comments: Olympia Show, 1936, Barker stand.
Body removed from chassis, Feb. 1941.

3AZ148. *(Photo: D. S. Archives).*

3AZ150.
Coachbuilder: Windovers.
Engine: (Original) Q84J.
Delivered: 1/14/37.
Body Style: Limousine de ville.
Body No: 6356.
Registration: CYK 731.
First Owner: Benjamin Guinness, UK.
Present Owner: W. S. Ries, US.
Pictures:
Comments: Windovers Trials (Lord Portarlington).
Olympia Show, 1936, Windovers stand. Guinness
also owned 3AZ110 and 3DL98. Used by Lord
Killearn, UK Embassy, Cairo, 1944. Later fitted with
engine J94Q ex 3AZ124.

3AZ150. *(Photo: Mr. Ries).*

3AZ152.   *(Photo: Mr. Johnson).*

| Coachbuilder: | H. J. Mulliner. | **3AZ152.** |

Coachbuilder: H. J. Mulliner.   **3AZ152.**
Engine: W64D.
Delivered: 12/2/36.
Body Style: Saloon with division.
Design No: Drawing 5798.
Body No: 4438.
Registration: DUL 591.
First Owner: J. B. Snow, UK.
Present Owner: A. W. Johnson, US.

Pictures: B170/7, FL/251, FL/300, FL/1426.
Comments: Original order by Sir Adrian Baillie, Bart. Phantom II, 119 RY used as trade-in. To USA 1939. For sale 1992.

Coachbuilder: Gurney Nutting.   **3AZ154.**
Engine: P34K.
Delivered: 11/12/36.
Body Style: Sedanca de ville.
Registration: Not listed.
First Owner: Hon. Marcus Richard Samuel, UK.
Present Owner: J. R. Cleveland, US.

Pictures: FL/885 (Shown).
Comments: Samuel's father, Viscount Bearsted, owned 3AZ94.

3AZ154.

Coachbuilder: Park Ward.   **3AZ156.**
Engine: W84D.
Delivered: 12/30/36.
Body Style: Sedanca de ville.
Body No: 4222.
Registration: DLK 959.
First Owner: John Nivision, 2nd Baron Glendyne, UK.
Present Owner: R. J. King, UK.

Pictures:
Comments: Ordered without mascot.

3AZ156.   *(Photo: Stuckey Collection).*

Coachbuilder: Gurney Nutting.   **3AZ158.**
Engine: P44K.
Delivered: 12/11/36.
Body Style: Drophead sedanca coupé.
Registration: GO 45.
First Owner: Albert Primrose, 6th Earl of Rosenbery, UK.
Present Owner: Blackhawk Collection, US.

Pictures: TERR/94, Bennett/37, P/103.
Comments: Car in Australia, 1950's-1960's, owned by Owen Bailey.

3AZ158.   *(Photo: RROC Foundation).*

3AZ160.

Coachbuilder:	Hooper.
Engine:	P54K.
Delivered:	11/9/36.
Body Style:	Sports saloon.
Design No:	6525.
Body No:	8619.
Registration:	Not listed.
First Owner:	(Edward) Graham Guest, UK.
Present Owner:	K. J. Russell, Australia.

Pictures: P/102, P/875.
Comments: To Australia 1950.

3AZ160. *(Photo: Mr. M.E. Belfield).*

3AZ162.

Coachbuilder:	Hooper.
Engine:	H94S.
Delivered:	11/25/36.
Body Style:	Limousine.
Design No:	6273.
Body No:	8611.
Registration:	DLB 450.
First Owner:	Axel Johnsson, Sweden.
Present Owner:	Unknown.

Pictures:
Comments:

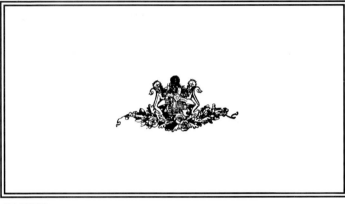

3AZ162.

3AZ164.

Coachbuilder:	Hooper.
Engine:	Q94J.
Delivered:	1/1/37.
Body Style:	Sedanca de ville.
Design No:	6606.
Body No:	8642.
Registration:	BSV 993.
First Owner:	Mrs. Beatrice Violet Chotzner, UK.
Present Owner:	H. D. Case, UK.

Pictures: Phantoms/367, B165/39.
Comments: Olympia Show, Hooper stand. Scottish Show, 1936. Original order by Nubar S. Gulbenkian. Later fitted with landaulette opening. Car in South Africa for some years.

3AZ164. *(Photo: Mr. Case).*

3AZ166.

Coachbuilder:	Barker.
Engine:	P84K.
Delivered:	12/4/36.
Body Style:	Touring saloon.
Registration:	DLB 1.
First Owner:	D. A. Sursock, UK.
Present Owner:	H. J. Cowan, South Africa.

Pictures: B87/6, FL/350 (Neither reproducible).
Comments: To South Africa 1957.

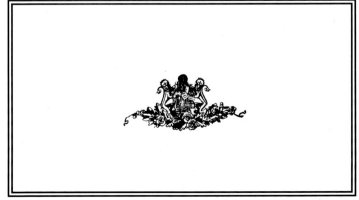

3AZ166.

3AZ168.   *(Photo: Mr Hans Enzler).*

Coachbuilder:	Gurney Nutting. **3AZ168.**
Engine:	P94K.
Delivered:	12/29/36.
Body Style:	Sedanca de ville.
Registration:	DLY 380.
First Owner:	Sir Herbert Smith, Bart, UK.
Present Owner:	H. Dursteller, Switzerland.

Pictures: TERR/93.
Comments: Sir Herbert also owned 3BT81, 3CM31, 3DL104.

3AZ170.   *(Photo: Mr. Ken Batchelor).*

Coachbuilder:	H. J. Mulliner. **3AZ170.**
Engine:	P64K.
Delivered:	11/20/36.
Body Style:	Sedanca de ville.
Design No:	Drawing 5779.
Body No:	4384.
Registration:	DLA 133.
First Owner:	Hugh R. Leonard, UK.
Present Owner:	Unknown, UK.

Pictures: BA60/13 (Shown)
Comments:

3AZ172.

Coachbuilder:	Thrupp & Maberly. **3AZ172.**
Engine:	H14S.
Delivered:	12/10/36.
Body Style:	Allweather.
Design No:	Drawing SLE.1154B.
Body No:	6466.
Registration:	DLB 5.
First Owner:	Sir Norman James Watson, Bart, UK.
Present Owner:	E. H. Green, US.

Pictures: Jubilee/56, FL/1724, CORR/314 (Shown, miscaptioned 3DL26).
Comments:

3AZ174.   *(Photo: Mr. Norris Allen via RROC).*

Coachbuilder:	Freestone & Webb. **3AZ174.**
Engine:	W54D.
Delivered:	1/12/37.
Body Style:	Drophead sedanca coupe.
Design No:	1774.
Body No:	1225.
Registration:	DUC 314.
First Owner:	A. Markham, UK.
Present Owner:	**R. A. McIninch, US.**

Pictures: Oldham/232d, Auto Quarterly/154, FL/352, FL/568 (Shown).
Comments: Mr. McIninch's father owned the car previously.

3AZ176.
Coachbuilder: H. J. Mulliner.
Engine: H24S.
Delivered: 11/30/36.
Body Style: Sedanca de ville.
Design No: Drawing 5812.
Body No: 4419.
Registration: DYR 620, RTR 1.
First Owner: Lady Maud Irene Buckland, UK.
Present Owner: J. Schofield, UK.
Pictures: TERR/153 (Shown).
Comments: Lady Buckland also owned 3BU92. For sale 1957 for £1,000.

3AZ176.

3AZ178.
Coachbuilder: Barker.
Engine: H34S.
Delivered: 11/21/36.
Body Style: (First) Limousine.
Registration: CS 2.
First Owner: A. J. Coppinger, UK.
Present Owner: H. C. Boucher, UK.

Pictures:
Comments: Ordered without mascot, and lamps painted black. Rebodied 1937 with Thrupp & Maberly drophead coupe for use by Maharajah of Darbhanga.

3AZ178. *(Photo: Mr. Boucher).*

3AZ180.
Coachbuilder: Arthur Mulliner.
Engine: J24Q.
Delivered: 10/30/36.
Body Style: Limousine.
Registration: Not listed.
First Owner: C. W. Batten, UK.
Present Owner: Unknown.

Pictures:
Comments: Olympia Show, 1936, Arthur Mulliner stand. Car last seen, 1990.

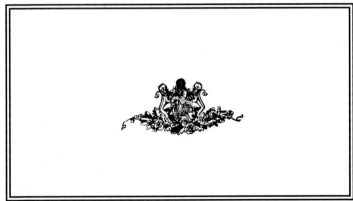

3AZ180.

3AZ182.
Coachbuilder: Gurney Nutting.
Engine: H64S.
Delivered: 12/12/36.
Body Style: Sports saloon with division.
Registration: 7904 PE.
First Owner: Peter F. Jackson, UK.
Present Owner: W. E. Wetzel, US.

Pictures: TERR/93.
Comments:

3AZ182. *(Photo: Ted Reich Archives).*

3AZ184.

Coachbuilder:	James Young.	**3AZ184.**
Engine:		P74K.
Delivered:		11/9/36.
Body Style:		Saloon with division.
Registration:		DOF 474.
First Owner:		W. Brice, UK.
Present Owner:		E. Johnston, UK (1954).

Pictures: B133/45 (Shown).
Comments: Ordered without mascot.

3AZ186.   *(Photo: Mr. Wilcock).*

Coachbuilder:	Freestone & Webb.	**3AZ186.**
Engine:		W24D.
Delivered:		11/27/36.
Body Style:		Saloon with division.
Design No:		1760.
Body No:		1222.
Registration:		DGY 1, 5545 RH, DGY 1.
First Owner:		Frederick Wilcock, UK.
Present Owner:		F. M. Wilcock, UK.

Pictures: Oldham/232d, Phantoms/368.
Comments: Used as Government VIP car during WW II. To Malaya 1956, back to UK 1963. Now owned by original owner's grandson.

3AZ188.

Coachbuilder:	Gurney Nutting.	**3AZ188.**
Engine:		W44D.
Delivered:		12/18/36.
Body Style:		Sedanca de ville.
Registration:		DLR 797.
First Owner:		A. S. Fuller, UK.
Present Owner:		Estate of the late Mr. E. M. Heath, US.

Pictures: FL/1884 (Shown).
Comments:

3AZ190.   *(Photo: Mr. Everett Pauls).*

Coachbuilder:	Inskip.	**3AZ190.**
Engine:		W74D.
Delivered:		2/2/37.
Body Style:		5-Passenger limousine.
Registration:		Not listed.
First Owner:		E. W. Bill, US.
Present Owner:		C. Wells, US.

Pictures: FL/166.
Comments: For sale 1952 for $3,500.

3AZ192.
Coachbuilder: H. J. Mulliner.
Engine: (Original) H44H.
Delivered: 11/14/36.
Body Style: Saloon with division.
Design No: Drawing 5814.
Body No: 4417.
Registration: DLR 137.
First Owner: Cecil Moores, UK.
Present Owner: M. L. Peveler, US.

Pictures: Phantoms/368.
Comments: To USA 1964. Later fitted with US V-8 engine.

3AZ192. *(Photo: Stuckey Collection).*

3AZ194.
Coachbuilder: Barker.
Engine: A94Z.
Delivered: 12/9/36.
Body Style: (First) Touring limousine.
Design No: Drawing E11195.
Registration: Not listed.
First Owner: Philip Dakin Wagoner, US.
Present Owner: W. C. Donoghue, US.

Pictures: deCampi/160, FL/50 (Shown).
Comments: US Trials. Rebodied with Inskip sedanca de ville. Inskip charged $22,000 for the car afterwards, complete. Barker body to 3BT53, June, 1947.

3AZ194. *The Inskip sedanca de ville.*

3AZ196.
Coachbuilder: Gurney Nutting.
Engine: W34D.
Delivered: 1/22/37.
Body Style: Sports sedanca de ville.
Registration: Not listed.
First Owner: Arthur Smith-Bingham, UK.
Present Owner: Musée de l'Automobile, France.

Pictures: Drehsen/167.
Comments:

3AZ196. *(Photo: Mr. Hans Enzler).*

3AZ198.
Coachbuilder: Hooper.
Engine: N74M.
Delivered: 12/3/36.
Body Style: Limousine.
Design No: 6273.
Body No: 8666.
Registration: Not listed.
First Owner: C-in-C Delhi, General Sir Robert A. Cassels, India.
Present Owner: S. V. Dongre, India.

Pictures: B89/368, B149/11.
Comments: Allied Motors Ltd. Trials.

3AZ198. *(Photo: Mr. Dongre).*

3AZ200. At the Hotel Baur au Lac, 1940.

Coachbuilder:	H. J. Mulliner.	**3AZ200.**
Engine:		N24M.
Delivered:		12/8/36.
Body Style:		Limousine.
Design No:		6370.
Body No:		8653.
Registration:		Not listed.
First Owner:		Dr. Jean-Jacques Brodbeck Sandreuter, Switzerland.
Present Owner:		**Scrapped.**

Pictures: *(Photo shown from Mr. Hans Enzler).*
Comments: Scrapped about 1961 after being used from 1940s as a hotel limousine by the Hotel Baur au Lac, Zurich.

3AZ202.   *(Photo: Stuckey Collection).*

Coachbuilder:	Gurney.	**3AZ202.**
Engine:		W94D.
Delivered:		1/27/37.
Body Style:		Sedanca de ville.
Registration:		Not listed.
First Owner:		Gordon L. Padley, UK.
Present Owner:		Prince Regent, Iraq (1949).

Pictures: CORR/86.
Comments:

3AZ204.   *(Photo: Mr. Holmes).*

Coachbuilder:	Kellow-Falkiner.	**3AZ204.**
Engine:		Y74B.
Delivered:		3/7/38.
Body Style:		(First) Limousine.
Registration:		Not listed.
First Owner:		J. L. Glick, Australia.
Present Owner:		A. Holmes, Australia.

Pictures: P/98, P/236, P/280, P/1341.
Comments: Rebodied with H. J. Mulliner saloon with division, 4472, ex wrecked 3CP146. Gearbox from 3CP146 also fitted.

3AZ206.

Coachbuilder:	Kellner.	**3AZ206.**
Engine:		Y54B.
Delivered:		12/14/36.
Body Style:		Sedanca de ville.
Registration:		Not listed.
First Owner:		Princesse J-L de Faucigny-Lucinge, France.
Present Owner:		L . Hardy, US.

Pictures: CORR/142 (Shown).
Comments: Paris Salon, 1936, Kellner stand. The Princesse later owned 3CM187.

3AZ208.
Coachbuilder: Kellner.
Engine: Y34B.
Delivered: 2/20/37.
Body Style: Sedanca de ville.
Registration: Not listed.
First Owner: Baroness Frieda Frasch von Seidlitz, France.
Present Owner: **M. Sauzeau, France.**

Pictures:
Comments: Paris Salon, 1936, FBA Ltd stand. Order placed by Contessa Constantini. Owned at one time by painter George Mathieu.

3AZ208. *(Photo: Mr. Sauzeau).*

3AZ210.
Coachbuilder: Barker.
Engine: (Original) B44Y.
Delivered: 1/29/37.
Body Style: Touring limousine.
Registration: Not listed.
First Owner: Commodore Louis D. Beaumont, France.
Present Owner: For sale by US dealer, 1994.

Pictures: Oldham/232d (Shown, misnumbered 3AZ120).
Comments: Originally with polished bonnet. Engine replaced with another Phantom III engine, 1993.

3AZ210.

3AZ212.
Coachbuilder: Kellner.
Engine: Y24B.
Delivered: 1/9/37.
Body Style: Limousine.
Registration: Not listed.
First Owner: Mme. Nora M. Fryer, France.
Present Owner: Dr. Garcia Orceyen, Spain (1954).

Pictures: Rolls-Royce Ltd. *Bulletin* 3.38/15 (Shown).
Comments: Steve Stuckey suggests this photo may be of a chassis other than 3AZ212.

3AZ212.

3AZ214.
Coachbuilder: Kellner.
Engine: N44M.
Delivered: 7/9/37.
Body Style: Landaulette.
Registration: Not listed.
First Owner: Princessa Ella Della Torre e Tasso, Italy.
Present Owner: W. J. Davidson, US.

Pictures: CORR/142.
Comments: Dr. Unger sold the car to someone in Hilton Head, SC., from whom Mr. Davidson acquired it.

3AZ214. When owned by Dr. Unger. *(Photo: Dr. Unger).*

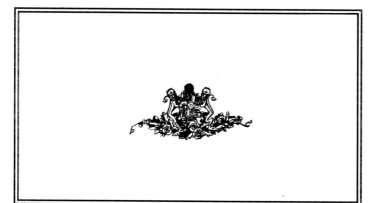

Coachbuilder: Vesters & Neirinck.   **3AZ216.**
Engine: (Original) H54S.
Delivered: 2/15/37.
Body Style: Saloon.
Registration: Not listed.
First Owner: Jean Washers, Belgium.
Present Owner: R. van Caneghem, Belgium.

Pictures:
Comments: Brussels Show, 1937, Vesters & Nierinck Stand. Fitted with non-standard engine, before 1992.

3AZ216.

Coachbuilder: Barker.   **3AZ218.**
Engine: N84M.
Delivered: 1/4/37.
Body Style: (First) Sedancalette.
Registration: DLF 728.
First Owner: Mrs. E. C. Snagge, UK.
Present Owner: **E. Gabiati, US.**

Pictures: Oldham/232e, B123/14.
Comments: Ordered without mascot. Later converted to limousine.

3AZ218. The limousine.   *(Photo: Mr. Gabiati).*

Coachbuilder: Thrupp & Maberly.   **3AZ220.**
Engine: N54M.
Delivered: 12/1/36.
Body Style: Limousine.
Design No: Drawing SLE.1072E.
Body No: 6414.
Registration: DLF 66.
First Owner: Douglas D. James, UK.
Present Owner: P. J. Fischer, UK.

Pictures:
Comments: James also owned 3CP2.

3AZ220.

Coachbuilder: Barker.   **3AZ222.**
Engine: J34Q.
Delivered: 11/6/36.
Body Style: Sports saloon.
Registration: DGW 555.
First Owner: E. B. Beck, UK.
Present Owner: **R. F. Lorkowski, US.**

Pictures:
Comments:

3AZ222   *(Photo: Mr. Lorkowski).*

3AZ224
Coachbuilder: Hooper.
Engine: T74G.
Delivered: 4/6/37.
Body Style: Sports limousine.
Design No: 6700.
Body No: 8703.
Registration: COV 999.
First Owner: Miss C. G. Tailby, UK.
Present Owner: B. Gillum, US.

Pictures: Phantoms/369 (Shown).
Comments:

3AZ224.

3AZ226.
Coachbuilder: Hooper.
Engine: N14M.
Delivered: 12/23/36.
Body Style: Limousine.
Design No: 6273.
Body No: 8667.
Registration: DGT 369.
First Owner: Sir (1937, Baron) Walter Russell Rea, Bart, UK.
Present Owner: M. E. Bacon, US.

Pictures:
Comments: Phantom II 195XJ used as trade-in. Baron Rea's brother owned 3AZ64.

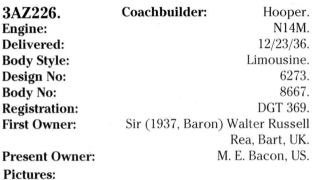

3AZ226. *(Photo: Mr. Bacon).*

3AZ228.
Coachbuilder: Gurney Nutting.
Engine: N64M.
Delivered: 2/24/37.
Body Style: Sports saloon.
Registration: DLY 858.
First Owner: Commander Sir Charles Worthington Craven, UK.
Present Owner: For sale US dealer, 1994.

Pictures:
Comments:

3AZ228. *(Photo: Stuckey Collection).*

3AZ230.
Coachbuilder: Park Ward.
Engine: N94M.
Delivered: 11/24/36.
Body Style: Touring limousine.
Body No: 4152.
Registration: DLR 369.
First Owner: Sir Walter Forrest, UK.
Present Owner: A. Bagdjian, France.

Pictures:
Comments: To France by 1966.
This picture was reproduced from an old faded newspaper clipping.

3AZ230. *(Photo: Mr. Andre Blaize).*

3AZ232. (Photo: Mr. DeRees).

Coachbuilder:	Hooper. **3AZ232.**
Engine:	G14T.
Delivered:	11/18/36.
Body Style:	Limousine.
Design	6396.
Number:	8628.
Body Number:	DGX 133.
Registration:	Victor Cavendish, 9th Duke of
First Owner:	Devonshire, UK.
	R. O. DeRees, US.

3AZ234. (Photo: Mr. Revere).

Coachbuilder:	Gurney Nutting. **3AZ234.**
Engine:	G24T.
Delivered:	2/22/37.
Body Style:	Sedanca de ville.
Registration:	DXU 657.
First Owner:	William Wentworth, Viscount Milton, UK.
Present Owner:	**P. Revere, US.**
Pictures:	
Comments:	

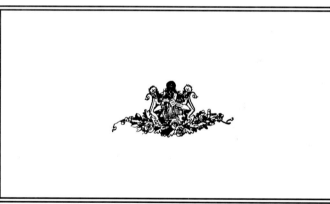

3AZ236.

Coachbuilder:	H. J. Mulliner. **3AZ236.**
Engine:	G34T.
Delivered:	12/15/36.
Body Style:	Sedanca de ville.
Design No:	Drawing 5804.
Body No:	4439.
Registration:	MF 3366.
First Owner:	Mrs. C. A. Bealey, UK.
Present Owner:	A. Thompson, US.
Pictures:	
Comments:	Originally ordered by J. C. Sword.

3AZ238.

Coachbuilder:	Park Ward. **3AZ238.**
Engine:	G44T.
Delivered:	11/19/36.
Body Style:	Touring saloon.
Body No:	4218.
Registration:	AJF 242.
First Owner:	A. F. P. Wheeler, UK.
Present Owner:	D. Z. de Ferranti, Ireland.
Pictures:	CORR/260 (Shown).
Comments:	

The AX Series
of
Phantom III Cars

The AX series was numbered odd,

3AX1 through

3AX203, minus 3AX13 and 3AX113.

3AX203 was built as 3CM92

for a total of 99 cars, delivered

in 1936 and early 1937.

The Phantom III Directory and Register, 1994

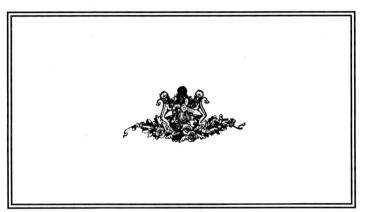

3AX1.

Coachbuilder:	H. J. Mulliner.	**3AX1.**
Engine:		G54T.
Delivered:		1/5/37.
Body Style:		Sedanca de ville.
Body No:		4400.
Registration:		AYR 111.
First Owner:		Captain Rt. Hon. (David) Euan Wallace M. C., UK.
Present Owner:		J. S. Nicol, South Africa, (1957).

Pictures:
Comments:

3AX3.

Coachbuilder:	Thrupp & Maberly.	**3AX3.**
Engine:		G64T.
Delivered:		12/10/36.
Body Style:		Limousine.
Design No:		Drawing SLE.1072F.
Body No:		6479.
Registration:		DLA 600.
First Owner:		William Henry Collins, UK.
Present Owner:		**R. Sullivan, US.**

Pictures:
Comments: Collins also owned 3CM112.

3AX5. *The Hooper estate car.*

Coachbuilder:	Hooper.	**3AX5.**
Engine:		G94T.
Delivered:		12/23/36.
Body Style:	(First)	Sports limousine.
Design No:		6348.
Body No:		8595.
Registration:		DUL 360.
First Owner:		Countess Beatrice Lindsay, UK.
Present Owner:		D. M. Harbottle, UK.

Pictures: PIIITS/42, B158/43 (Shown).
Comments Original order by S. H. White, then to Jack Barclay Ltd. as stock. Body converted to estate car by Hooper's of Edinburgh. Countess Lindsay also owned 3AX43, used, in 1938.

Coachbuilder:	H. J. Mulliner.	**3AX7.**
Engine:		H84S.
Delivered:		11/7/36.
Body Style:		Saloon with division.
Design No:		Drawing 5764.
Body No:		4462.
Registration:		HSS 632.
First Owner:		George Urie Scott, UK.
Present Owner:		B. Peters, Germany.

Pictures:
Comments: Scottish Show, 1936, Clyde Automobiles stand.

3AX7.   *(Photo: Mr. Peters).*

3AX9.
Coachbuilder:	H. J. Mulliner.
Engine:	H74S.
Delivered:	11/6/36.
Body Style:	Saloon with division.
Design No:	Drawing 5811.
Body No:	4415.
Registration:	ASC 345, PMN 495.
First Owner:	W. S. Murphy, UK.
Present Owner:	G. Peake, UK.

Pictures: BA91/40, BA92/23.
Comments: Scottish Show, 1936, John Croall stand.

3AX9. *(Photo: Mr. Peake).*

3AX11.
Coachbuilder:	Hooper.
Engine:	G74T.
Delivered:	12/15/36.
Body Style:	Sports limousine.
Design No:	6609.
Body No:	8663.
Registration:	DLK 607.
First Owner:	Maga Senta, Mrs. George Joseph, UK.
Present Owner:	R. Boydell, UK.

Pictures: BA111/41, TERR/120.
Comments:

3AX11. *(Photo: Mr. Boydell).*

3AX15.
Coachbuilder:	J. S. Woolley.
Engine:	T24G.
Delivered:	4/9/37.
Body Style:	(First) Saloon limousine.
Registration:	Not listed.
First Owner:	Sir Julien Cahn, Bart, UK.
Present Owner:	M. G. Deming, US.

Pictures: PIIITS/40 (Shown).
Comments: Sir Julien also owned 3AX37. Rebodied as hearse, and then with Hooper limousine 9031 ex 3DL66, March, 1973.

3AX15. *The Hooper limousine coachwork.*

3AX17.
Coachbuilder:	Freestone & Webb.
Engine:	(Original) T34G.
Delivered:	12/19/36.
Body Style:	Limousine de ville.
Design No:	1691.
Registration:	1201.
First Owner:	VG 9136.
Present Owner:	H. W. Sunderland, UK.

Pictures:
Comments: Ordered without mascot. Later fitted with Perkins diesel, then B80.

3AX17. *(Photo: Mr. Klaus–Josef Rossfeldt).*

3AX19.

Coachbuilder:	Arthur Mulliner.	**3AX19.**
Engine:	T14G.
Delivered:	12/15/36.
Body Style:	Landaulette.
Registration:	DLM 953.
First Owner:	A. C. Adams, UK.
Present Owner:	**Scrapped,** 1965.

Pictures:
Comments: Original order by Hugh Watkins. Last owner J. C. Denne.

Coachbuilder:	Hooper.	**3AX21.**
Engine:	T64G.
Delivered:	12/21/36.
Body Style:	Landaulette.
Design No:	6527.
Body No:	8644.
Registration:	Not listed.
First Owner:	John C. Rossage, UK.
Present Owner:	Perino, US.

Pictures: FL/1074.
Comments: Possibly converted to tourer.

3AX21.   (Photo: RROC Foundation).

Coachbuilder:	Hooper.	**3AX23.**
Engine:	N34M.
Delivered:	11/25/36.
Body Style:	Limousine de ville.
Design No:	6622.
Body No:	8676.
Registration:	DGT 364.
First Owner:	John Henly Batty, UK.
Present Owner:	R. Wilson, US.

Pictures: PIIITS/44, TERR/122 (Shown).
Comments: Phantom I 113SC used as trade-in.

3AX23.

3AX25.   (Photo: Mr. Trapp).

Coachbuilder:	Barker.	**3AX25.**
Engine:	T54G.
Delivered:	1/8/37.
Body Style:	Touring saloon.
Registration:	Not listed.
First Owner:	Frederick Brant Rentschler, US.
Present Owner:	**D. M. Trapp, US.**

Pictures: FL/175, FL/1943.
Comments: Rentschler also owned 3BT53.

3AX27.
Coachbuilder:	Barker.
Engine:	M14N.
Delivered:	1/4/37.
Body Style:	Sedanca de ville.
Registration:	Not listed.
First Owner:	Arthur G. Bendir, UK.
Present Owner:	T. Holtorf, US.

Pictures:
Comments:

3AX27. *(Photo: Mr. Holtorf via RROC Foundation).*

3AX29.
Coachbuilder:	Hooper.
Engine:	T44G.
Delivered:	1/18/37.
Body Style:	Limousine.
Design No:	6273.
Body No:	8680.
Registration:	FPA 1.
First Owner:	Leonard Bentall, UK.
Present Owner:	H. Green, UK (1957).

Pictures:
Comments: Ordered without mascot.

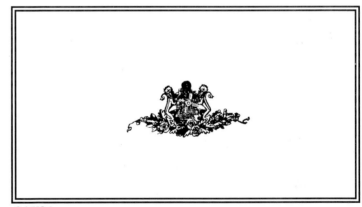

3AX29.

3AX31.
Coachbuilder:	Gurney Nutting.
Engine:	T84G.
Delivered:	4/15/37.
Body Style:	Sedanca coupé.
Registration:	Not listed.
First Owner:	(Cedric) Treherne Thomas, UK.
Present Owner:	Col. L. H. Armstrong, Kenya (1960).

Pictures:
Comments: Original order by E. Goldie Taubman.
Thomas also owned 3CP62.

3AX31.

3AX33.
Coachbuilder:	Barker.
Engine:	(Original) M64N.
Delivered:	10/11/37.
Body Style:	Sports saloon.
Registration:	ELR 519.
First Owner:	Albert A. Glickstein, UK.
Present Owner:	**N. R. Benham, US.**

Pictures: TERR/51 (Shown).
Comments: Original order by Robert Sabbaq,
Lebanon. Engine M64N for sale, UK, January 1991.

3AX33.

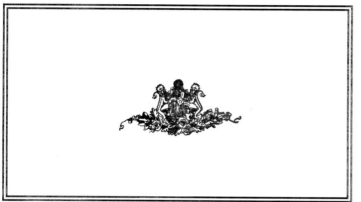

3AX35.

Coachbuilder:	Hooper. **3AX35.**
Engine:	T94G.
Delivered:	1/14/37.
Body Style:	Limousine.
Design No:	6273.
Body No:	8613.
Registration:	G 0.
First Owner:	Lord Mayor, Glasgow Corporation, UK (4/37).
Present Owner:	**D. A. Wetzel, US.**

Pictures: RRB9.37/28 (Shown).
Comments: "Showroom car", Rolls-Royce Ltd. stock, used by Inspection Department.

3AX37.

Coachbuilder:	J. S. Woolley. **3AX37.**
Engine:	M34N.
Delivered:	3/9/37.
Body Style:	Limousine.
Registration:	Not listed.
First Owner:	Sir Julien Cahn, Bart, UK.
Present Owner:	J. H. Shorten, UK (1953).

Pictures:
Comments: Sir Juilien also owned 3AX15. Owned by British Army, used by Lt. General Sir Gordon N. Macready, 1950.

3AX39.

Coachbuilder:	H. J. Mulliner. **3AX39.**
Engine:	M24N.
Delivered:	4/3/37.
Body Style:	Sedanca de ville.
Design No:	Drawing 5940.
Body No:	4515.
Registration:	Not listed.
First Owner:	Ian Anderson, UK.
Present Owner:	Unknown.

Pictures:
Comments: 'Showroom car". Chassis originally delivered to Barker & Co.

3AX41.   *(Photo: Mr. Laska).*

Coachbuilder:	H. J. Mulliner. **3AX41.**
Engine:	M44N.
Delivered:	12/24/36.
Body Style:	Saloon with division.
Design No:	Drawing 5860.
Body No:	4459.
Registration:	DUC 635.
First Owner:	Major Victor G. Walker, UK.
Present Owner:	**I. H. Laska, Austria.**

Pictures: Phantoms/370, PIIITS/44.
Comments: Mrs. Walker owned 3DL72.

3AX43.

Coachbuilder:	Park Ward.
Engine:	W14D.
Delivered:	11/27/36.
Body Style:	Sedanca de ville.
Body No:	4230.
Registration:	BFG 909.
First Owner:	Mrs. F. H. Montgomery, UK.
Present Owner:	To Japan, 1993.

Pictures: TERR/186.
Comments: Ordered without mascot. Owned 1938 by Countess Beatrice Lindsay, who had owned 3AX5. In Malaya 1957.

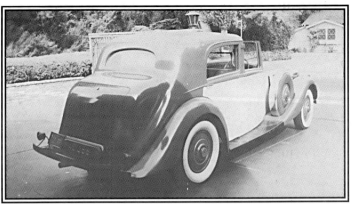

3AX43. *(Photo: Mr. Gary Wales).*

3AX45.

Coachbuilder:	Barker.
Engine:	(Original) M54N.
Delivered:	1/4/37.
Body Style:	Limousine.
Registration:	DLF 740.
First Owner:	Major Sidney Griffiths, UK.
Present Owner:	W. J. Harnett, US.

Pictures: Oldham/232e (Shown).
Comments: Later fitted with Ford V8 engine. For sale 1972 for £700.

3AX45.

3AX47.

Coachbuilder:	Hooper.
Engine:	M94N.
Delivered:	1/19/37.
Body Style:	Saloon limousine.
Design No:	6582.
Body No:	8688.
Registration:	Not listed.
First Owner:	J. E. Smallman, Canada.
Present Owner:	**J. O. Hemmingsen, Canada.**

Pictures: B146/26, B161/23.
Comments: For sale 1952 for $2,500, Canadian.

3AX47. *(Photo: Mr. Hemmingsen).*

3AX49.

Coachbuilder:	Hooper.
Engine:	M74N.
Delivered:	1/7/37.
Body Style:	Sedanca de ville.
Design No:	6702.
Body No:	8696.
Registration:	Not listed.
First Owner:	Alexandra Mary, Duchess of Marlborough, UK.
Present Owner:	J. G. Porter, UK.

Pictures: CORR/130.
Comments:

3AX49. *(Photo: RREC Photo Library).*

3AX51.

Coachbuilder:	Freestone & Webb.	**3AX51.**
Engine:		G84T.
Delivered:		1/27/37.
Body Style:		Limousine.
Design No:		1641.
Body No:		1223.
Registration:		FML 191.
First Owner:		Sidney Freeman, UK.
Present Owner:		P. Pym, UK.

Pictures: Robinson/'81, TERR/80 (Shown).
Comments: Original order by H. G. L. Garnett via Green Park Motors.

3AX53.   *(Photo: D. S. Archives).*

Coachbuilder:	Hooper.	**3AX53.**
Engine:		B24Y.
Delivered:		1/25/37.
Body Style:		Sports saloon.
Design No:		6461.
Body No:		8643.
Registration:		CYB 300.
First Owner:		Miss Helen Garnett, UK.
Present Owner:		G. R. Normand, US.

Pictures: TERR/122.
Comments: Phantom II 33JS used as trade-in.

3AX55.   *(Photo: Mr. Hay).*

Coachbuilder:	Gurney Nutting.	**3AX55.**
Engine:		M84N.
Delivered:		4/2/37.
Body Style:		Sedanca de ville.
Registration:		KLP 49.
First Owner:		Hon. Mrs. Aileen Sibell Mary Plunket, UK.
Present Owner:		K. J. Hay, Canada.

Pictures:
Comments: To Canada 1964.

3AX57.   *The Keswick Body.*

Coachbuilder:	Inskip.	**3AX57.**
Engine:		P18L.
Delivered:		(First) 3/20/37.
Body Style:		Keswick town car.
Registration:		Not listed.
First Owner:		Dr. Seth Gegory, US.
Present Owner:		C. F. Garbutt, UK(1963).

Pictures: DeCampi/160 Center (Shown, mislabled).
Comments: Rebodied with Hooper limousine ex 3DH7 Aug. 1949. Returned to UK and sold to George Newman Ltd., December 1949.

3AX59. Coachbuilder: Freestone & Webb.
Engine: B14Y.
Delivered: 1/18/37.
Body Style: (First) Sedanca de ville.
Design No: 1751.
Body No: 1213.
Registration: DVK 894, 188 BRX, OSU 966.
First Owner: John C. F. Simpson, UK.
Present Owner: N. R. F. Whitaker, UK.

Pictures: BA88/33, CORR/78 (Shown).
Comments: Converted to saloon by sealing up open-able front roof, by 1941.

3AX59.

3AX61. Coachbuilder: Barker.
Engine: P48L.
Delivered: 2/11/37.
Body Style: Sedanca de ville.
Registration: DLW 656, JJ 5614.
First Owner: J. H. Keeling, UK.
Present Owner: K. G. M. Kjellqvist, UK.

Pictures: TERR/51 (Shown).
Comments:

3AX61.

3AX63. Coachbuilder: Hooper.
Engine: Y18C.
Delivered: 1/7/37.
Body Style: Sports limousine.
Design No: 6665.
Body No: 8690.
Registration: DGX 136.
First Owner: Dr. R. Scott-Mason, UK.
Present Owner: J. Laurent, Belgium.

Pictures: Oliver/114.
Comments: Scott-Mason exchanged this car, with which he was not satisfied, for 3CM57.

3AX63. (Photo: Mr. Mason).

3AX65. Coachbuilder: Van Den Plas.
Engine: P38L.
Delivered: (Guarantee) 2/15/37.
Body Style: Sedanca de ville.
Registration: WKO 251.
First Owner: Mme. Fernard Pisart, Belgium.
Present Owner: **M. Coomber, UK.**

Pictures: Car/1668, B166/38, B126/33.
Comments: Brussels Show, 1937. Expropriated by German Army. Owned by UK Legation to Luxembourg, 1952.

3AX65. (Photo: Mr. Coomber).

3AX67.   *(Photo: Mr. Hindersson).*

Coachbuilder:	Barker.	**3AX67.**
Engine:		Y38C.
Delivered:		3/11/37.
Body Style:		Sedanca de ville.
Registration:		DUU 611.
First Owner:		Eric Vansittart Bowater, UK.
Present Owner:		K. M. Hindersson, Finland.

Pictures:
Comments: Car in the USA from 1960's to 1990.

3AX69.   *(Photo: Mr. Leverton).*

Coachbuilder:	Hooper.	**3AX69.**
Engine:	(Original) Y88C.	
Delivered:		2/8/37.
Body Style:		Limousine.
Design No:		6687.
Body No:		8697.
Registration:		BAC 821.
First Owner:		George Pearson, UK.
Present Owner:		B. L. Leverton, UK.

Pictures: P3TS/30.
Comments: Original order by W. L. Barber. Later fitted with Princess 4 litre engine.

3AX71.   *(Photo: Mr. Jordan).*

Coachbuilder:	Gurney Nutting.	**3AX71.**
Engine:	(Original) Y48C.	
Delivered:		7/16/37.
Body Style:		Sedanca de ville.
Registration:		DYM 789.
First Owner:		George Gee, UK.
Present Owner:		J. L. Jordan, US.

Pictures:
Comments: Latter fitted with B80 engine B1357WS.

3AX73.   *(Photo: Mr. Kennette).*

Coachbuilder:	H. J. Mulliner.	**3AX73.**
Engine:		B94Y.
Delivered:		1/14/37.
Body Style:		Saloon with division.
Design No:		Drawing 5798.
Body No:		4461.
Registration:		DLT 426.
First Owner:		E. Davenport, UK.
Present Owner:		H. P. Kennette, Canada.

Pictures: B104/30, FL/1415.
Comments: Original order by A. M. Mitchell and then N. Princep (via Barclays).

3AX75.   Coachbuilder: Hooper.
Engine: B64Y.
Delivered: 1/20/37.
Body Style: Limousine.
Design No: 6580.
Body No: 8689.
Registration: Not listed.
First Owner: Mrs. C. K. Morgan OBE, Canada.
Present Owner: **G. F. Beck, US.**

Pictures:
Comments: To Canada 1954.

3AX75.   *(Photo: Science Museum, London).*

3AX77.   Coachbuilder: Barker.
Engine: Y58C.
Delivered: 1/26/37.
Body Style: Limousine.
Registration: Not listed.
First Owner: Alphonse Brenninkmeyer, UK.
Present Owner: **F.P. Meserow, US.**

Pictures:
Comments: Chassis for sale, not running, 1975 for
$7,500.

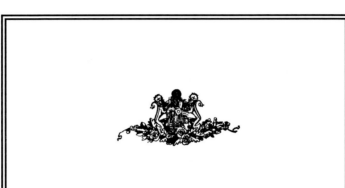

3AX77.

3AX79.   Coachbuilder: H. J. Mulliner.
Engine: E98W.
Delivered: 2/8/37.
Body Style: Saloon with division.
Body No: 4345.
Registration: DUV 553.
First Owner: Alan S. Butler, UK.
Present Owner: **H. C. Dorner, US.**

Pictures: Oldham/232e, Auto Quarterly/160,
B126/40. Ullyett/54 (Shown).
Comments: Ordered without mascot. Owned by
Lord Gort, and then Field-Marshal Viscount
Montgomery (until 1963).

3AX79.

3AX81.   Coachbuilder: Thrupp & Maberly.
Engine: Y68C.
Delivered: 12/12/36.
Body Style: 4-Light limousine.
Design No: Drawing SLE.1108E.
Body No: 6376.
Registration: DLF 77.
First Owner: Mrs. F. E. Stephens, UK.
Present Owner: D. L. Amason, US.

Pictures:
Comments:

3AX81.   *(Photo: Frank Dale & Stepsons).*

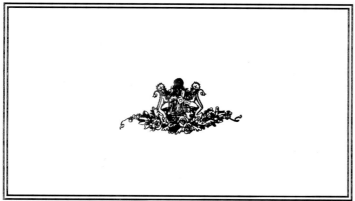

3AX83.

Coachbuilder:	Park Ward.	**3AX83.**
Engine:		W38E.
Delivered:		1/6/37.
Body Style:		Limousine.
Body No:		4231.
Registration:		BTE 1.
First Owner:		Sir George Mellor, UK.
Present Owner:		J. C. Denne, UK.

Pictures:
Comments: Original order by H. C. Sutton.

3AX85.

Coachbuilder:	Inskip.	**3AX85.**
Engine:		B74Y.
Delivered:		6/10/37.
Body Style:		5-Passenger limousine.
Body No:		5006.
Registration:		Not listed.
First Owner:		Mrs. Florence A. V. Twombly, US.
Present Owner:		**Scrapped**, 1965.

Pictures:
Comments: Engine and coachwork to 3BU100, August, 1953.

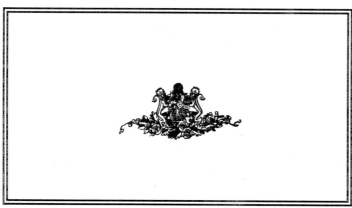

3AX87.

Coachbuilder:	Barker.	**3AX87.**
Engine:		B84Y.
Delivered:		5/5/37.
Body Style:		Saloon limousine.
Registration:		Not listed.
First Owner:		HRH Sir Sadiq, Nawab of Bahawalpur, India.
Present Owner:		Unknown.

Pictures: Oldham/232f (Shown).
Comments: Car reported to be armored, with Lewis guns front and rear.

3AX89.

Coachbuilder:	Hooper.	**3AX89.**
Engine:		P88L.
Delivered:		3/18/37.
Body Style:		Sports limousine.
Design No:		6542.
Body No:		8752.
Registration:		Not listed.
First Owner:		S. B. Peek, UK.
Present Owner:		Unknown.

Pictures:
Comments: Original order by K. Redgrave via Barclays. To Singapore, 1939.

3AX91.
Coachbuilder:	Thrupp & Maberly.
Engine:	W28E.
Delivered:	1/14/37.
Body Style:	Saloon.
Design No:	Drawing SLF.1133A.
Body No:	6467.
Registration:	BAC 44.
First Owner:	J. A. Jefferson, UK.
Present Owner:	Rev. R. J. Luker, UK.

Pictures: Robinson/'83.
Comments:

3AX91. *Photo: Country Life).*

3AX93.
Coachbuilder:	Hooper.
Engine:	P58L.
Delivered:	1/30/37.
Body Style:	(First) Limousine.
Design No:	6549.
Body No:	8693.
Registration:	UD 8343.
First Owner:	Vivian Hugh Smith (later Lord Bicester), UK.
Present Owner:	**S. A. Morris, US.**

Pictures:
Comments: Rebodied as Bamber boat-tail tourer, by 1990.

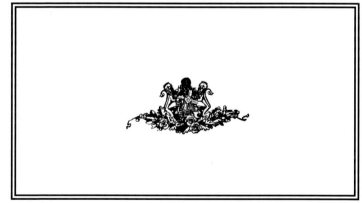
3AX93. The Bamber boat-tail. *(Photo: Mr. Morris).*

3AX95.
Coachbuilder:	H. J. Mulliner.
Engine:	P68L.
Delivered:	2/13/37.
Body Style:	Pullman limousine.
Design No:	Drawing 5863.
Body No:	4443.
Registration:	DAU 600.
First Owner:	John D. Player, UK.
Present Owner:	W. Travis, UK (1946).

Pictures:
Comments: Originally built for Ian Hamilton via L. C. Rawlence, with E type steering. Returned for modification and despatched 8/1/37.

3AX95.

3AX97.
Coachbuilder:	Barker.
Engine:	B54Y.
Delivered:	2/23/37.
Body Style:	Landaulette.
Registration:	Not listed.
First Owner:	Sir John Latta, Bart, UK.
Present Owner:	D. M. Stanley, US.

Pictures: Oldham/232f.
Comments: Latta also owned 3CP110, with a duplicate body. Owned by the actor, (and later Lord), Laurence Olivier, 1947.

3AX97. *(Photo: Mr. Wilkenson via RROC Foundation).*

3AX99.   *(Photo: Mr. Boyd Rasmussen).*

Coachbuilder:	Park Ward.	**3AX99.**
Engine:		E18W.
Delivered:		1/25/37.
Body Style:		Limousine.
Body No:		4244.
Registration:		DUL 353.
First Owner:	Lt. Colonel Sir John Humphrey, UK.	
Present Owner:	R. A. McDermott, Australia.	

Pictures: P/116.
Comments: Original order by J. C. Sword. To Australia 1938. Owned by Russian Legation, Canberra, 1940's. Syncromesh fitted to 3rd and 4th, 1939. Road tested in *The Sydney Morning Herald*, 27 June 1939. Now chassis only.

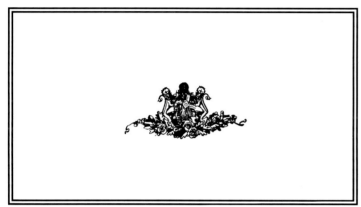

3AX101.

Coachbuilder:	Gurney Nutting.	**3AX101.**
Engine:		Y78C.
Delivered:		3/6/37.
Body Style:		Sedanca de ville.
Registration:		DKR 316.
First Owner:	H. J. Yates, UK.	
Present Owner:	Estate of J. C. Bidwell-Topham, UK.	

Pictures:
Comments: Original order by F. Kerr.

3AX103.

Coachbuilder:	Vesters & Neirinck.	**3AX103.**
Engine:		P98L.
Delivered:		2/15/37.
Body Style:		Saloon.
Registration:		Not listed.
First Owner:	Baron Robert Hankar, Belgium.	
Present Owner:	Baron R. Hankar, Belgium (1954).	

Pictures:
Comments: Brussels Show, 1937, Rolls-Royce stand.

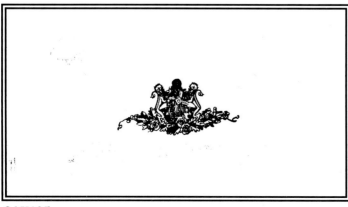

3AX105.

Coachbuilder:	H. J. Mulliner.	**3AX105.**
Engine:		E48W.
Delivered:		1/1/37.
Body Style:		Sedanca de ville.
Design No:		Drawing 5804.
Body No:		4460.
Registration:		DUV 5.
First Owner:	Harold Lotery, UK.	
Present Owner:	K. R. Yeeles, UK.	

Pictures:
Comments: Three orders cancelled for this chassis.

3AX107.
Coachbuilder: Park Ward.
Engine: P78L.
Delivered: 12/21/36.
Body Style: Limousine.
Body No: 4204.
Registration: BDP 980, YBL 999, 832 HRY.
First Owner: Hugo, 1st Baron Hirst of Witton, UK.
Present Owner: For sale US dealer, 1994.
Pictures:
Comments: Original order by A. F. Black. For sale Sept. 1968 for £650.

3AX107. (Photo: Mr. Glyn Morris).

3AX109.
Coachbuilder: Gurney Nutting.
Engine: E38W.
Delivered: 11/23/36.
Body Style: Sedanca de ville.
Registration: DXE 782.
First Owner: Francis Douglas, 10th Marquess of Queensberry, UK.
Present Owner: W. J. Forrest, UK.

Pictures: Auto Quarterly/153, Phantoms/371.
Comments: Original order by Nawab of Rampur.

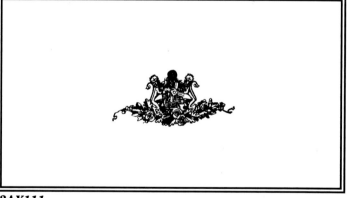
3AX109. (Photo: RROC Foundation).

3AX111.
Coachbuilder: Lancefield.
Engine: E28W.
Delivered: 12/31/36.
Body Style: Limousine.
Registration: DLL 155.
First Owner: Walter Guinness, 1st Baron Moyne, UK.
Present Owner: J. W. Evans, UK.

Pictures:
Comments:

3AX111.

3AX115.
Coachbuilder: Park Ward.
Engine: E58W.
Delivered: 2/2/37.
Body Style: Touring limousine.
Body No: 4154.
Registration: DKX 410.
First Owner: Dorothy, Mrs. James A. de Rothschild, UK.
Present Owner: Unknown.
Pictures:
Comments: Ordered without mascot.

3AX115. (Photo: Mr. Wallace Donoghue).

3AX117.   *(Photo: Mr. Reeves).*

Coachbuilder:	Thrupp & Maberly. **3AX117.**
Engine:	E68W.
Delivered:	12/21/36.
Body Style:	Sports saloon.
Design No:	Drawing SLF.1067F.
Body No:	6202.
Registration:	DLL 777.
First Owner:	H. J. Lane, UK.
Present Owner:	T. J. Reeves, US.

Pictures:
Comments: To USA 1960.

3AX119.

Coachbuilder:	Inskip. **3AX119.**
Engine:	Y28C.
Delivered:	4/13/37.
Body Style:	5-passenger limousine.
Registration:	Not listed.
First Owner:	Mrs. Anne Taylor Thomas, US.
Present Owner:	S. Buka, US.

Pictures: deCampi/162, CORR/430 (Shown).
Comments: Car forfeited for repair bill, 1956.

3AX121.

Coachbuilder:	Barker **3AX121.**
Engine:	N58N.
Delivered:	4/15/37.
Body Style:	Limousine.
Registration:	Not listed.
First Owner:	A. G. Clark, UK.
Present Owner:	**C. Butterworth, Australia.**

Pictures: P/103, Oldham/232f (Shown).
Comments:

3AX123.   *(Photo: Mr. Millett via RROC Foundation).*

Coachbuilder:	Cooper. **3AX123.**
Engine:	W78E.
Delivered:	5/15/37.
Body Style:	Phaeton.
Registration:	DUV 817.
First Owner:	Henry McLaren, 2nd Baron Aberconway, UK.
Present Owner:	V. Millet, US.

Pictures: B72/36, FL/856, FL/1415.
Comments:

3AX125.

Coachbuilder:	Barker.
Engine:	W88E.
Delivered:	2/8/37.
Body Style:	Limousine.
Registration:	Not listed.
First Owner:	E. A. Wigam, UK.
Present Owner:	N. Birkett, UK (1946).

Pictures:
Comments:

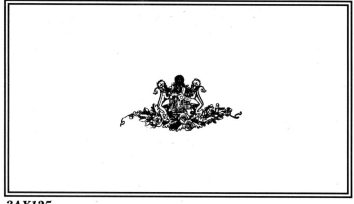
3AX125.

3AX127.

Coachbuilder:	Thrupp & Maberly.
Engine:	W18E.
Delivered:	12/15/36.
Body Style:	Sports saloon.
Design No:	Drawing SLF.1067G.
Body No:	6203.
Registration:	DUL 444.
First Owner:	Frank Parkinson, UK.
Present Owner:	J. Huni, Switzerland.

Pictures: Auto Quarterly/152, BA116/8.
Comments: Reportedly later owned by Aristotle Onassis.

3AX127.   *(Photo: Mr. Huni).*

3AX129.

Coachbuilder:	Hooper.
Engine:	Y98C.
Delivered:	2/26/37.
Body Style:	Sports limousine.
Design No:	6713.
Body No:	8713.
Registration:	CVP 50, USU 890.
First Owner:	T. Barclay, UK.
Present Owner:	I. A. F. Bleaney, UK.

Pictures: Sotheby/'90, BA106/8 (Shown).
Comments: Car in the USA for some years.

3AX129.   *(Photo: Mr. Bleaney).*

3AX131.

Coachbuilder:	Freestone & Webb.
Engine:	(Original) L38P.
Delivered:	2/8/37.
Body Style:	Saloon limousine.
Design No:	1763.
Body No:	1200.
Registration:	Not listed.
First Owner:	Thomas F. Nash, UK.
Present Owner:	**A. Boode, US.**

Pictures:
Comments: Fitted with Ford Thunderbird engine by 1973.

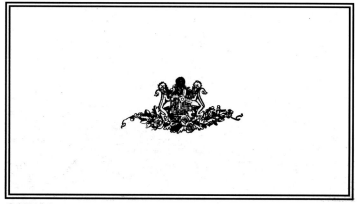
3AX131.

3AX133.   *(Photo: Mr. Davison).*

Coachbuilder:	Park Ward.	**3AX133.**
Engine:		W48E.
Delivered:		1/21/37.
Body Style:		Touring saloon.
Body No:		4155.
Registration:		DUC 532.
First Owner:		Miss Lena Cooper, UK.
Present Owner:		J. O. Davison, US.

Pictures:
Comments:

3AX135.

Coachbuilder:	James Young.	**3AX135.**
Engine:		N18N.
Delivered:		6/1/37.
Body Style:		Saloon.
Registration:		UOC 1.
First Owner:		A. Kohn, UK.
Present Owner:		C. E. A. Brownlow, UK.

Pictures: Jubilee/19, Phantoms/372 (Shown).
Comments:

3AX137.   *(Photo: RROC Foundation).*

Coachbuilder:	Rippon.	**3AX137.**
Engine:		W68E.
Delivered:		3/5/37.
Body Style:		Limousine.
Registration:		Not listed.
First Owner:		John O. Anderson, UK.
Present Owner:		Mokaytzky, US.

Pictures:
Comments:

3AX139.   *(Photo: Stuckey Collection).*

Coachbuilder:	Park Ward.	**3AX139.**
Engine:		W58E.
Delivered:		2/5/37.
Body Style:		Limousine.
Body No:		4248.
Registration:		Not listed.
First Owner:		John E. Fattorini, UK.
Present Owner:		J. Hay & Sons, UK (1948).

Pictures: Bird/262.
Comments: Original order by Miss Effie Hancock. Ordered without mascot. Engine later fitted in 3BU114.

3AX141.
Coachbuilder:	Inskip.
Engine:	N48N.
Delivered:	3/27/37.
Body Style:	Convertible coupé.
Body No:	211.
Registration:	Not listed.
First Owner:	Anne Burnett, Mrs. J. Goodwin Hall, US.
Present Owner:	C. I. Schwartz, US.

Pictures: deCampi/157, FL/211 (Shown).
Comments: Cost of car was $9,500 plus Phantom II 290AJS as trade-in. For sale by Inskip 1948 for $12,500.

3AX141. *(Photo: D. S. Archives).*

3AX143.
Coachbuilder:	Arthur Mulliner.
Engine:	W98E.
Delivered:	1/28/37.
Body Style:	Sports saloon.
Registration:	DUV 166.
First Owner:	Dr. Rowland J. Perkins, UK.
Present Owner:	J. Durham, UK.

Pictures: B188/52, CORR/162 (Shown).
Comments: To USA, then returned to UK.

3AX143.

3AX145.
Coachbuilder:	Park Ward.
Engine:	N28N.
Delivered:	1/15/37.
Body Style:	Limousine.
Body No:	4241.
Registration:	YJ 4455.
First Owner:	P. S. Brown, UK.
Present Owner:	Unknown.

Pictures:
Comments:

3AX145.

3AX147.
Coachbuilder:	Gurney Nutting.
Engine:	N38N.
Delivered:	2/6/37.
Body Style:	Limousine.
Registration:	Not listed.
First Owner:	HRH Maharajah Rao Holkar of Indore, India.
Present Owner:	Unknown.

Pictures:
Comments: Ordered without mascot. Packard used as trade-in.

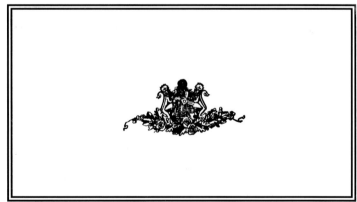

3AX147. *(Photo: RROC Foundation).*

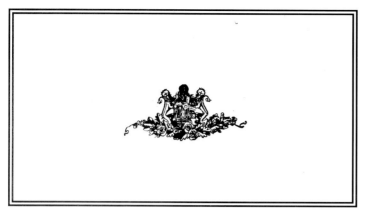

3AX149.

Coachbuilder: Thrupp & Maberly.   **3AX149.**
Engine: E78W.
Delivered: 12/21/36.
Body Style: Limousine.
Design No: Drawing SLE.1162D.
Body No: 6480.
Registration: DLU 1.
First Owner: Sir David Milne-Watson, Bart, UK.
Present Owner: C. F. Pope, UK (1957).

Pictures:
Comments: Ordered without mascot. In Malaya 1951-1956.

3AX151.   *(Photo: Mr. Bill Dobson).*

Coachbuilder: H. J. Mulliner.   **3AX151.**
Engine: N78N.
Delivered: 1/30/37.
Body Style: Limousine.
Body No: 4369.
Registration: ASF 707.
First Owner: Thomas Strang, UK.
Present Owner: R. M. Crawford, US.

Pictures:
Comments: Division is fitted with full china and silver picnic service.

3AX153.

Coachbuilder: Abbott.   **3AX153.**
Engine: P28L.
Delivered: 6/5/37.
Body Style: Sports saloon.
Registration: Not listed.
First Owner: Mary Elsie, Countess Cowley, UK.
Present Owner: Perozini, Canada.

Pictures: TERR/266 (Shown).
Comments: Original order by Mrs. Edward Duffus.

3AX155.

Coachbuilder: Erdmann & Rossi.   **3AX155.**
Engine: B34Y.
Delivered: 2/20/37.
Body Style: Cabriolet.
Body No: 2871.
Registration: Not listed.
First Owner: Geheimrat Kurt Elschner, Germany.
Present Owner: Unknown.

Pictures: FL/751,Stuhlemmer/92, CORR/421 (Shown).
Comments: Elschner also owned 3CM43.

3AX157.
Coachbuilder: H. J. Mulliner.
Engine: (Original) C18Y.
Delivered: 3/8/37.
Body Style: Sedanca de ville.
Body No: 4469.
Registration: DUL 366.
First Owner: Jack Buchanan, UK.
Present Owner: L. Scull, UK (1966).

Pictures: Phantoms/373 (Shown).
Comments: Original order by Lloyd S. Gilmour. Ordered without mascot. Replacement engine, 1966.

3AX157.

3AX159.
Coachbuilder: Park Ward.
Engine: N98N.
Delivered: 2/11/37.
Body Style: Sedanca de ville.
Body No: 4156.
Registration: DUV 26.
First Owner: R. C. Leaman, UK.
Present Owner: Unknown, Spain.

Pictures: P3TS/40 (Shown).
Comments: Car in USA for some years.

3AX159.

3AX161.
Coachbuilder: Barker.
Engine: C38Y.
Delivered: 4/9/37.
Body Style: Limousine.
Design No: Drawing E11400.
Registration: ANJ 496.
First Owner: Rt. Hon Sir Eric Campbell Geddes, UK.
Present Owner: H. W. Fraser, UK (1945).

Pictures: Phantoms/373 (Shown).
Comments: Phantom II 143TA used as trade-in.

3AX161.

3AX163.
Coachbuilder: Windovers.
Engine: N88N.
Delivered: 1/9/37.
Body Style: (First) Limousine.
Body No: 6368.
Registration: DLF 344.
First Owner: Cyril O. Smith, UK.
Present Owner: **R. D. Shaffner, US.**

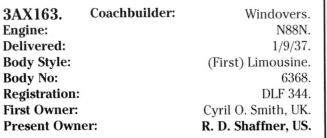

Pictures:
Comments: Body for sale Feb., 1975. Rebodied with Inskip limousine, 1977.

3AX163. The Inskip body.   (Photo: Mr. Shaffner).

3AX165.

Coachbuilder:	Hooper.	**3AX165.**
Engine:		C48Y.
Delivered:		2/24/37.
Body Style:		Limousine.
Design No:		6764.
Body No:		8744.
Registration:		Not listed.
First Owner:		W. J. Sawyer, UK.
Present Owner:		A. H. Goddard, UK.

Pictures:

Comments: Mr. Goddard writes that nothing remains of the Hooper body. He plans to lengthen the chassis and install a V-12 R-R Meteor tank engine.

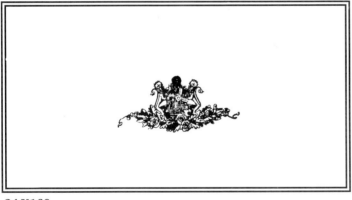

3AX167.   *(Photo: National Motor Museum, England).*

Coachbuilder:	Barker.	**3AX167.**
Engine:		E88W.
Delivered:		1/11/37.
Body Style:		Limousine.
Registration:		Not listed.
First Owner:		Major Montague J. Gluckstein, UK.
Present Owner:		International Car Hire Ltd, UK (1949).

Pictures:

Comments:

3AX169.

Coachbuilder:	Barker.	**3AX169.**
Engine:		C28Y.
Delivered:		2/19/37.
Body Style:		Limousine.
Design No:		Drawing E11195.
Registration:		DMY 996.
First Owner:		H. C. Slingsby, UK.
Present Owner:		L. M. Austin, UK (1958).

Pictures:

Comments:

3AX171.   *(Photo: Mr. Johnson).*

Coachbuilder:	Park Ward.	**3AX171.**
Engine:		C68Y.
Delivered:		3/2/37.
Body Style:		Limousine.
Body No:		4205.
Registration:		DXE 274.
First Owner:		Mrs. Daniel W. Macmillan, UK.
Present Owner:		K. B. Johnson, US.

Pictures:

Comments:

3AX173.

Coachbuilder:	Windovers.
Engine:	C58Y.
Delivered:	3/1/37.
Body Style:	Limousine.
Body No:	6397.
Registration:	DLW 642.
First Owner:	Wyndham Portal, 1st Baron Portal, UK.
Present Owner:	**R. L. Hawk, US.**

Pictures:
Comments:

3AX173.   *(Photo: Mr. Hawk).*

3AX175.

Coachbuilder:	Windovers.
Engine:	C78Y.
Delivered:	1/20/37.
Body Style:	Sedanca de ville.
Body No:	6394.
Registration:	DLP 320.
First Owner:	Julius Salmon, UK.
Present Owner:	R. J. Williams, US.

Pictures: FL/4239, FL/4294 (Shown).
Comments:

3AX175.

3AX177.

Coachbuilder:	Barker.
Engine:	L18P.
Delivered:	7/19/37.
Body Style:	Drophead coupe.
Body No:	7312.
Registration:	DKB 830.
First Owner:	John Moores, UK.
Present Owner:	**W. J. Harwood, US.**

Pictures: Bolster/154, FL/1893 (Shown).
Comments: Original order by A. A. Packer, for sports saloon.

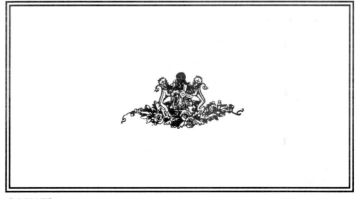
3AX177.

3AX179.

Coachbuilder:	Barker.
Engine:	L28PX.
Delivered:	1/18/37.
Body Style:	Limousine.
Design No:	Drawing F11090.
Registration:	DLX 330.
First Owner:	Antonio Aranguren, Venezuela.
Present Owner:	V. C. Braun, US.

Pictures:
Comments: Phantom I 80KR used as trade-in.
Engine later fitted to 3CM92.

3AX179.

3AX181.   *(Photo: Frank Dale & Stepsons).*

Coachbuilder:	Windovers.
Engine:	V18F.
Delivered:	3/12/37.
Body Style:	Saloon.
Body No:	6431.
Registration:	DLW 644.
First Owner:	Sir Edmund Frank Crane, UK.
Present Owner:	J. W. Rowland-Hobson, UK.

3AX181.

Pictures:
Comments: Crane also owned 3DL130.

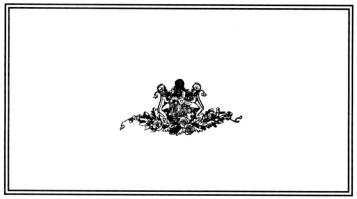

3AX183.

Coachbuilder:	Park Ward.
Engine:	N68N.
Delivered:	2/16/37.
Body Style:	Limousine.
Body No:	4157.
Registration:	ERF 35.
First Owner:	G. H. Downing, UK.
Present Owner:	Unknown.

3AX183.

Pictures:
Comments:

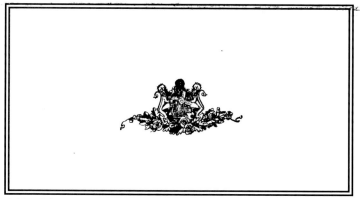

3AX185.

Coachbuilder:	Barker.
Engine:	V78F.
Delivered:	2/8/37.
Body Style:	Touring limousine.
Registration:	Not listed.
First Owner:	E. G. Sparrow, France.
Present Owner:	Pulsifer, US.

3AX185.

Pictures:
Comments: Geneva Show, 1937. Also originally intended for Amsterdam Show.

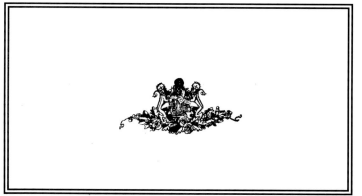

3AX187.

Coachbuilder:	Barker.
Engine:	V28F.
Delivered:	3/2/37.
Body Style:	Limousine.
Registration:	Not listed.
First Owner:	F. Milburn, UK.
Present Owner:	Major W. N. Hillias, UK (1944).

3AX187.

Pictures:
Comments:

3AX189.   **Coachbuilder:**   Rippon.
Engine: C98Y.
Delivered: 3/4/37.
Body Style: Limousine.
Registration: DMB 473.
First Owner: Samuel Robert Wainwright, UK.
Present Owner: J. E. Fattorini, UK (1940).

Pictures:
Comments:

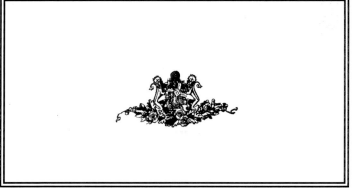
3AX189.

3AX191.   **Coachbuilder:**   Park Ward.
Engine: V48F.
Delivered: 4/26/37.
Body Style: Limousine de ville.
Body No: 4280.
Registration: US 65.
First Owner: John A. MacTaggart, UK.
Present Owner: S. A. MacTaggart, Canada.

Pictures:
Comments:

3AX191.

3AX193.   **Coachbuilder:**   James Young.
Engine: (Original) V58F.
Delivered: 4/20/37.
Body Style: Drophead sedanca coupé.
Registration: FSV 146.
First Owner: S. Harris, UK.
Present Owner: W. Leuthausel, Germany.

Pictures: Phantoms/374, B139/20.
Comments: Ordered without mascot. Engine replaced by 1983. Car in France for some years.

3AX193.   *(Photo: Dr. Leuthausel).*

3AX195.   **Coachbuilder:**   Barker.
Engine: V88F.
Delivered: 4/28/37.
Body Style: Limousine.
Design No: Drawing SF11432.
Registration: XH 8888, CLL 789, LGY 408.
First Owner: HRH Prince Henry, Duke of Gloucester, UK.
Present Owner: R. A. Benge, UK.

Pictures: P/103, B82/13 (Shown).
Comments: Used by Duke as Governor-General of Australia, 1945-1947.

3AX195.

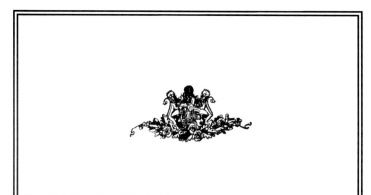

3AX197.

Coachbuilder: Gurney Nutting   **3AX197.**
Engine: GV68F.
Delivered: 4/29/37.
Body Style: Sedanca de ville.
Registration: Not listed.
First Owner: Henry Walter, US.
Present Owner: **F. Gabrielli/A. Mitchell, US.**

Pictures:
Comments: Chassis only by 1989.

3AX199.   *(Photo: Frank Dale & Stepsons).*

Coachbuilder: Hooper.   **3AX199.**
Engine: V38F.
Delivered: 1/26/37.
Body Style: Sports saloon.
Design No: 6682.
Body No: 8711.
Registration: DLK 610, T 5400, HPP 10 G.
First Owner: Major James Onslow Kingsmill Delap, UK.
Present Owner: C. O'Connor, US..

Pictures: Oldham/232f, 53/49, CORR/132 (Shown).
Comments: Delivered with special engine equipment and sealed boot for use in Africa. Engine recently overhauled for actor Carol O'Connor.

3AX201.

Coachbuilder: Hooper.   **3AX201.**
Engine: L48P.
Delivered: 3/6/37.
Body Style: Limousine.
Design No: 6746.
Body No: 8747.
Registration: DLN 470.
First Owner: HRH Maharajah Gaekwar Sir Sayaji of Baroda, India.
Present Owner: Unknown.
Pictures: Oldham/232g (Shown).
Comments: The Maharanee owned 3BU106; The Crown Prince owned 3CP112.

3AX203 built as 3CM92.

The BU Series
of
Phantom III Cars.

The BU series consists of

100 cars, numbered even,

3BU2 through 3BU200.

All BU series cars were delivered in 1937.

3BU2.   *(Photo: Mr. K-J. Rossfeldt).*

Coachbuilder:	Barker. **3BU2.**
Engine:	V98F.
Delivered:	3/18/37.
Body Style:	Coupé limousine.
Registration:	Not listed.
First Owner:	Mrs. Dennistoun M. Bell, US.
Present Owner:	M. Dewar, Australia.

Pictures: Car/1674, Phantoms/375.
Comments: Dr. Bell also owned 3DL190.

3BU4.   *(Photo: Mr. Gehring).*

Coachbuilder:	Thrupp & Maberly. **3BU4.**
Engine:	L88P.
Delivered:	4/15/37.
Body Style:	Fixed-head cabriolet.
Design No:	Drawing SLE.1203A.
Body No:	6595.
Registration:	Not listed.
First Owner:	Benjamin Rosenthal, US.
Present Owner:	**W. M. Gehring, US.**

Pictures: TERR/222, FL/344.
Comments: Later fitted with overdrive.

3BU6.

Coachbuilder:	Park Ward. **3BU6.**
Engine:	L58P.
Delivered:	3/24/37.
Body Style:	Touring limousine.
Body No:	4234.
Registration:	WG 6000, MN 6000.
First Owner:	F. S. Muirhead, UK.
Present Owner:	Unknown, UK.

Pictures: B115/28, Phantoms/375 (Shown).
Comments: Ordered without mascot.

3BU8.   *(Photo: PIIITS Archives).*

Coachbuilder:	Arthur Mulliner. **3BU8.**
Engine:	(Original) L78P.
Delivered:	5/8/37.
Body Style:	Limousine.
Registration:	GMT 1.
First Owner:	S. B. Plummer, UK.
Present Owner:	G. E. Colgett, US.

Pictures: TERR/138.
Comments: Later fitted with engine W48P.

3BU10.
Coachbuilder: Barker.
Engine: L68P.
Delivered: 3/17/37.
Body Style: Limousine.
Registration: CBJ 717.
First Owner: Captain John Murray Cobbold, UK.
Present Owner: K. Kleve, US.

Pictures: FL/791 (Not reproducible).
Comments:

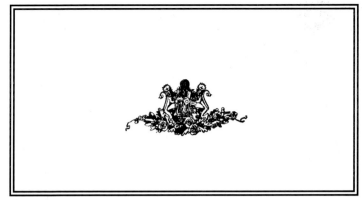
3BU10.

3BU12.
Coachbuilder: Windovers.
Engine: K48Q.
Delivered: 6/9/37.
Body Style: Sedanca de ville.
Body No: 6444.
Registration: DYR 67.
First Owner: Dr. D. Henegan, UK.
Present Owner: P. C. Compton, US.

Pictures: CORR/359.
Comments:

3BU12. *(Photo: Mr. Compton).*

3BU14.
Coachbuilder: Hooper.
Engine: B18Z.
Delivered: 3/6/37.
Body Style: Limousine.
Design No: 6642.
Body No: 8756.
Registration: DUL 362.
First Owner: Sir Ralph Millbourn, UK.
Present Owner: **W. J. Harwood, US.**

Pictures: Phantoms/376 (Shown).
Comments: Not delivered until October 1938.
Chassis only, 1979.

3BU14.

3BU16.
Coachbuilder: Park Ward.
Engine: L98P.
Delivered: 4/21/37.
Body Style: Sedanca de ville.
Body No: 4288.
Registration: UA 1, KUM 1.
First Owner: Sir George William Martin, UK.
Present Owner: A. Cameron, US.

Pictures:
Comments: Used in film "Doctor at Leisure".

3BU16. *(Photo: Frank Dale & Stepsons).*

3BU18.

Coachbuilder:	Hooper.	**3BU18.**
Engine:		B58Z.
Delivered:		4/10/37.
Body Style:		Sports limousine.
Design No:		6828.
Body No:		8754.
Registration:		DLU 998.
First Owner:		(James) Craig Harvey, UK.
Present Owner:		B. Crooker, US.

Pictures: CORR/130, Oldham/232g, FL/3174 (Shown).
Comments:

3BU20.   *(Photo: National Motor Museum. England).*

Coachbuilder:	Barker.	**3BU20.**
Engine:		T68H.
Delivered:		5/4/37.
Body Style:		Limousine.
Registration:		DYE 810.
First Owner:		B. S. Gluckstein, UK.
Present Owner:		C. M. Schonherr, Germany.

Pictures:
Comments: Owned by Decca Records Co., 1954.

3BU22.   *(Photo: Mr. Heathcote).*

Coachbuilder:	Windovers.	**3BU22.**
Engine:		B68Z.
Delivered:		4/29/37.
Body Style:		Limousine.
Body No:		6433.
Registration:		RRP 111.
First Owner:		E. E de Winton Wills, UK.
Present Owner:		D. M. Heathcote, UK.

Pictures:
Comments: Fitted with Grebel headlamps.

3BU24.   *(Photo: Mr. Howard via RROC Foundation).*

Coachbuilder:	Hooper.	**3BU24.**
Engine:		B98Z.
Delivered:		3/1/37.
Body Style:		Limousine.
Design No:		6273.
Body No:		8790.
Registration:		DLU 999.
First Owner:		F. Baer, UK.
Present Owner:		W. D. Howard, US.

Pictures: FL/1714.
Comments:

3BU26.
Coachbuilder:	Barker.
Engine:	K18Q.
Delivered:	3/19/37.
Body Style:	Limousine.
Registration:	PF 749.
First Owner:	G. H. Cook, UK.
Present Owner:	C. E. Lindros, US.

Pictures:
Comments: In Malaysia in the 1960's, Thailand in 1965.

3BU26. *(Photo: Mr. Lindros).*

3BU28.
Coachbuilder:	Barker.
Engine:	B78A.
Delivered:	4/1/37.
Body Style:	Sports saloon.
Body No:	7188.
Registration:	FPB 221.
First Owner:	E. R. Grote, UK.
Present Owner:	**G. B. Pollard, US.**

Pictures: Eves/107, FL/3069, FL/3245.
Comments:

3BU28. *(Photo: Mr. Pollard).*

3BU30.
Coachbuilder:	Barker.
Engine:	B88Z.
Delivered:	4/8/37.
Body Style:	Sports saloon.
Design No:	Drawing E11235.
Registration:	DKT 2.
First Owner:	Arthur Gibbs, UK.
Present Owner:	**C. K. Beers, US.**

Pictures: Bird/264, TERR/52, FL/894.
Comments: Ordered without mascot.

3BU30. *(Photo: RROC Foundation).*

3BU32.
Coachbuilder:	Barker.
Engine:	T78H.
Delivered:	6/17/37.
Body Style:	Sedanca de ville.
Registration:	Not listed.
First Owner:	Captain T. Ansell Fairhurst, UK.
Present Owner:	Unknown.

Pictures:
Comments:

3BU32. *(Photo: National Motor Museum, England).*

3BU34.   *(Photo: Mr. Krueger).*

Coachbuilder:	Hooper. **3BU34.**
Engine:	B28A.
Delivered:	4/2/37.
Body Style:	Sports saloon.
Design No:	6852.
Body No:	8764.
Registration:	KSU 953.
First Owner:	Col. Sir Albert (Edward) Bingham, Bart., UK.
Present Owner:	D. A. Krueger, US.

Pictures: CORR/132.

Comments: Ordered without mascot, and with black-finish lamps. Sold in UK 1989.

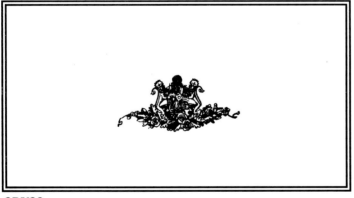

3BU36.   *(Photo: Mr. Johnson).*

Coachbuilder:	H. J. Mulliner. **3BU36.**
Engine:	T88H.
Delivered:	3/8/37.
Body Style:	Allweather.
Design No:	Drawing 5791.
Body No:	4370.
Registration:	Not listed.
First Owner:	I. M. Sieff, UK.
Present Owner:	J. D. H. Johnson, US.

Pictures: FL/1893.

Comments: Ordered without mascot. Car in Portugal for some years.

3BU38.

Coachbuilder:	William Arnold. **3BU38.**
Engine:	K58Q.
Delivered:	4/12/37.
Body Style:	Limousine.
Registration:	Not listed.
First Owner:	S. H. Davies, UK.
Present Owner:	W. Reed, UK (1947).

Pictures:

Comments:

3BU40.   *(Photo: Country Life).*

Coachbuilder:	H. J. Mulliner. **3BU40.**
Engine:	T98H.
Delivered:	2/22/37.
Body Style:	Saloon with division.
Body No:	4466.
Registration:	DUL 359.
First Owner:	Mrs. Leslie Hamilton Gault, UK.
Present Owner:	Government of Sudan (1946).

Pictures:

Comments:

3BU42.

Coachbuilder:	H. J. Mulliner.
Engine:	T28H.
Delivered:	4/1/37.
Body Style:	Saloon with division.
Design No:	Drawing 5912.
Body No:	4465.
Registration:	DXM 476, MAN 50 A.
First Owner:	R. A. Hornby, UK.
Present Owner:	S. Barraclough, UK.

Pictures: Phantoms/377, B164/45.
Comments:

3BU42.   *(Photo: Mr. Tom Clarke).*

3BU44.

Coachbuilder:	Hooper.
Engine:	K78Q.
Delivered:	3/17/37.
Body Style:	Limousine.
Design No:	6642.
Body No:	8755.
Registration:	Not listed.
First Owner:	W. T. Proctor, UK.
Present Owner:	John Bardgett & Son Ltd., UK. (1945).

Pictures:
Comments:

3BU44.

3BU46.

Coachbuilder:	Hooper.
Engine:	(Original) K38Q.
Delivered:	3/23/37.
Body Style:	Limousine.
Design No:	6273.
Body No:	8770.
Registration:	DUL 370.
First Owner:	Sir Alfred Butt, Bart, UK.
Present Owner:	P. Reeves, UK.

Pictures: Phantoms/377, PIIITS/30.
Comments: Later fitted with Bentley 4 1/4 engine.

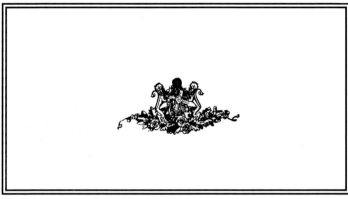

3BU46.   *(Photo: RREC Photo Library).*

3BU48.

Coachbuilder:	Park Ward.
Engine:	K68Q.
Delivered:	5/5/37.
Body Style:	Sedanca de ville.
Design No:	12556.
Body No:	4286.
Registration:	DUL 600.
First Owner:	W. S. Verrells, UK.
Present Owner:	P. M. Lind, US.

Pictures: CORR/261, Woudenberg/49, FL/3068.
Comments: Phantom II 163TA used as trade-in.

3BU48.   *(Photo: Mr. Lind).*

3BU50.   *(Photo: D. S. Archives).*

Coachbuilder:	Thrupp & Maberly.	**3BU50.**
Engine:		T48H.
Delivered:		3/18/37.
Body Style:		Landualet.
Registration:		DXR 555.
First Owner	Sir Kameshar Singh, Maharajah of	
	Darbhanga, India.	
Present Owner:	Maharajah of Darbhanga, India.	

Pictures:
Comments: The Maharajah also owned, used, 3AZ178.

3BU52.   *(Photo: National Motor Museum, England).*

Coachbuilder:	Barker.	**3BU52.**
Engine:		B18A.
Delivered:		4/20/37.
Body Style:		Limousine.
Registration:		Not listed.
First Owner:	Lady Geraldine Adelaide King, UK.	
Present Owner:		Unknown.

Pictures:
Comments: Ordered without mascot.

3BU54.

Coachbuilder:	Windovers.	**3BU54.**
Engine:		K98Q.
Delivered:		4/12/37.
Body Style:		Limousine.
Body No:		6437.
Registration:		Not listed.
First Owner:	Simon Marks, UK.	
Present Owner:	John M. Newton & Sons Ltd., UK	
	(1954).	

Pictures:
Comments:

3BU56.   *(Photo: Ted Reich Archives).*

Coachbuilder:	Park Ward.	**3BU56.**
Engine:		T58H.
Delivered:		3/19/37.
Body Style:		Touring saloon.
Body No:		4271.
Registration:		DXM 471.
First Owner:	Frederick H. Reeves, UK.	
Present Owner:		White, UK.

Pictures: TERR/187.
Comments:

3BU58.
Coachbuilder:	Freestone & Webb.
Engine:	C88Y.
Delivered:	4/5/37.
Body Style:	Saloon with division.
Design No:	1760.
Body No:	1240.
Registration:	FV 8910.
First Owner:	William Spencer, UK.
Present Owner:	R. C. Gartner, US.

Pictures: PIIITS/10, PIIITS/40, TERR/83 (Shown).
Comments:

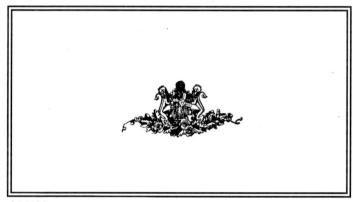

3BU58.

3BU60.
Coachbuilder:	Hooper.
Engine:	R68J.
Delivered:	3/24/37.
Body Style:	Limousine.
Design No:	6273.
Body No:	8608.
Registration:	CAA 566.
First Owner:	Colonel A. E. Jenkins, UK.
Present Owner:	**B. H. Birkbeck, US.**

Pictures:
Comments: Phantom I 2AL used as trade-in.

3BU60.

3BU62.
Coachbuilder:	Thrupp & Maberly.
Engine:	B38Z.
Delivered:	5/1/37.
Body Style:	Saloon.
Design No:	Drawing SLE.1243/C.
Body No:	6629.
Registration:	CCG 200.
First Owner:	Captain G. J. R. Cooper, UK.
Present Owner:	Unknown, Saudi Arabia.

Pictures:
Comments: Originally allocated to Mme. Ossorio, who took 3BT77. To Canada, 1951. Car in the Netherlands for some years.

3BU62. *(Photo: Frank Dale & Stepsons).*

3BU64.
Coachbuilder:	Inskip.
Engine:	B48Z.
Delivered:	3/16/37.
Body Style:	(First) Limousine.
Registration:	Not listed.
First Owner:	Mrs. Phoebe K. Higgins, US.
Present Owner:	R. A. Hinshaw, US.

Pictures: deCampi/161, Auto Quarterly/159.
Comments: Converted to sedanca de ville.

3BU64. *(Photo: Mr. Hinshaw).*

3BU66.   *(Photo: National Motor Museum, England).*

Coachbuilder:	Barker.	**3BU66.**
Engine:		B48A.
Delivered:		5/5/37.
Body Style:		Sedanca de ville.
Registration:		Not listed.
First Owner:		Joseph E. Widener, US.
Present Owner:	Nahum Fabrice Ltd., UK (1951).	

Pictures:
Comments: Car returned to UK by 1947.

3BU68.

Coachbuilder:	Hooper.	**3BU68.**
Engine:		B78Z.
Delivered:		4/22/37.
Body Style:		Sedanca de ville.
Design No:		6803.
Body No:		8763.
Registration:		Not listed.
First Owner:	HRH Sultan Sir Mohamed Shah Aga Khan, France.	
Present Owner:		Unknown.

Pictures: Oldham/232g (Shown).
Comments: Seized by the German Army in France in 1940. Returned to the Agha Kahn in 1946. Renovated by Hoooper 1946-1948.

3BU70.   *(Photo: RREC Photo Library).*

Coachbuilder:	Park Ward.	**3BU70.**
Engine:		R58J.
Delivered:		5/3/37.
Body Style:		4-Light limousine.
Body No:		4290.
Registration:		DYO 953.
First Owner:	Captain A. M. Talbot-Fletcher, UK.	
Present Owner:		O. Fowler, Canada.

Pictures: Phantoms/377, FL/1215.
Comments: Car rejected by A. Colin Kingham, who later owned 3CP98.

3BU72.

Coachbuilder:	Schutter & van Bakel.	**3BU72.**
Engine:		B58A.
Delivered:		1/30/37.
Body Style:		Saloon.
Registration:		Not listed.
First Owner:	B. J. V van Hees, Netherlands.	
Present Owner:		Unknown, US.

Pictures: Automobile Quarterly 19/3/268 (Shown).
Comments: Car imported to UK 1954.

3BU74. **Coachbuilder:** Windovers.
Engine: R18J.
Delivered: 4/2/37.
Body Style: (First) Saloon with division.
Body No: 6402.
Registration: Not listed.
First Owner: Orlando Bridgeman, 5th Earl of Bradford, UK.
Present Owner: Mistele, US.

Pictures:
Comments: Rebodied with D. Woods roadster.

3BU74. The roadster. *(Photo: Mr. Alton Walker).*

3BU76. **Coachbuilder:** Barker.
Engine: T18H.
Delivered: 6/24/37.
Body Style: Sedanca de ville.
Registration: DYK 487.
First Owner: Sir Sawai Mansingh, Maharajah of Jaipur, India.
Present Owner: Hon. A. MacKenzie-Clark, UK.

Pictures: Hugo/43, B75/12, B77/39.
Comments:

3BU76. *(Photo: RROC Foundation).*

3BU78. **Coachbuilder:** Barker.
Engine: J78R.
Delivered: 6/18/37.
Body Style: Sports saloon.
Registration: AYE 1, OYE 3.
First Owner: John Gibson-Jarvie, UK.
Present Owner: H. Eymann, Switzerland.

Pictures: Bird, TERR/52.
Comments: Original order by A. Webber.

3BU78. *(Photo: Mr. Hans Enzler).*

3BU80. **Coachbuilder:** Park Ward.
Engine: K28Q.
Delivered: 3/22/37.
Body Style: Touring saloon.
Body No: 4281.
Registration: DUL 363.
First Owner: Walter Dunkels, UK.
Present Owner: R. S. Bach, Canada.

Pictures:
Comments: Ordered without mascot.

3BU80. *(Photo: Mr. Bach).*

3BU82.   *(Photo: Mr. Dongre).*

Coachbuilder:	Hooper.	**3BU82.**
Engine:		R38J.
Delivered:		6/6/37.
Body Style:		Sedanca de ville.
Design No:		6928.
Body No:		8789.
Registration:		UF 1.
First Owner:		Maharanee of Nabha, India.
Present Owner:		P. Bhogalai, India.

Pictures: FL/838.
Comments:

3BU84.   *(Photo: Mr. David Kelley).*

Coachbuilder:	H. J. Mulliner.	**3BU84.**
Engine:		(Original) T38H.
Delivered:		5/6/37.
Body Style:		Saloon with division.
Design No:		Drawing 648.
Body No:		4467.
Registration:		DWX 648.
First Owner:		C. J. Carney, UK.
Present Owner:		J. R. Spina, UK.

Pictures: FL/151.
Comments: To USA by 1952. Engine B74Y from 3AX85 fitted August 1953.

3BU86.   *(Photo: Mr. Sherper).*

Coachbuilder:	Thrupp & Maberly.	**3BU86.**
Engine:		B38A.
Delivered:		4/16/37.
Body Style:		Allweather.
Design No:		Drawing SLE 1188/A.
Body No:		6561.
Registration:		DXH 4.
First Owner:		Nawab Hamidullah Khan, Ruler of Bhopal.
Present Owner:		**K. H. Sherper, US.**

Pictures:
Comments: Owned by Maharajah of Patiala, 1940.

Coachbuilder:	Park Ward.	**3BU88.**
Engine:		B28Z.
Delivered:		4/1/37.
Body Style:		Limousine.
Body No:		4279.
Registration:		DXN 909.
First Owner:		L. N. Mills, UK.
Present Owner:		**D. F. Pickett, US.**

Pictures:
Comments:

3BU88.   *(Photo: Mr. Pickett).*

3BU90.
Coachbuilder: H. J. Mulliner.
Engine: R88J.
Delivered: 3/19/37.
Body Style: Limousine.
Design No: Drawing 5928.
Body No: 4477.
Registration: Not listed.
First Owner: Miss Stewart Clark, UK.
Present Owner: H. Cairns & Son Garage, UK.

Pictures:
Comments: Original order by C. A. Gibbs via J. Cróall.

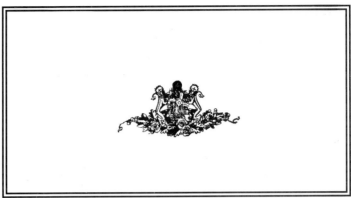
3BU90.

3BU92.
Coachbuilder: Hooper.
Engine: B68A.
Delivered: 4/15/37.
Body Style: Limousine.
Design No: 6242.
Body No: 8749.
Registration: DXW 662.
First Owner: Lady Maud Irene Buckland, UK.
Present Owner: **M. Tuttle, US.**

Pictures: FL/2250.
Comments: Original order from P. Squire via Jack Olding, Ltd. Lady Buckland also owned 3AZ176. Now chassis only.

3BU92. *(Photo: Mr. Sam Girdler).*

3BU94.
Coachbuilder: Binder.
Engine: B88A.
Delivered: 5/22/37.
Body Style: Sedanca de ville.
Registration: Not listed.
First Owner: Marquis de Villeroy, France.
Present Owner: J. W. Nevers, Netherlands.

Pictures:
Comments: Marquis Marie de Villeroy owned 3DH1, in USA.

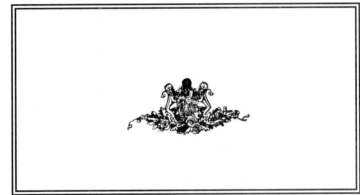
3BU94.

3BU96.
Coachbuilder: Cockshoot.
Engine: Q48K.
Delivered: 2/8/37.
Body Style: Limousine.
Body No: 1140.
Registration: DND 116.
First Owner: Albert Hartley, UK.
Present Owner: J. H. Wells, UK.

Pictures: TERR/72 (Shown).
Comments:

3BU96.

3BU98.   *(Photo: Stuckey Collection).*

Coachbuilder:	Windovers.	**3BU98.**
Engine:		R48J.
Delivered:		3/12/37.
Body Style:		Sedanca de ville.
Body No:		6422.
Registration:		Not listed.
First Owner:		Laurence T. Locan, UK.
Present Owner:		S. Hansen, Denmark.

Pictures: Jubilee/58, B151/11, TERR/247.
Comments: *undergoing Restoration Pictures later —*

3BU100.   *(Photo: Mr. Westlund).*

Coachbuilder:	Inskip.	**3BU100.**
Engine:		K88Q.
Delivered:		8/30/37.
Body Style:		Limousine.
Registration:		Not listed.
First Owner:		Alice H., Mrs. Arthur C. Burrage, US.
Present Owner:		**B. Westlund, US.**

Pictures: FL/4592.
Comments: Mrs. Burrage also owned 3DL184.
Bodied with Inskip limousine ex 3CP124, Feb. 1940.

3BU102.   *(Photo: Mr. R.M. Bowers).*

Coachbuilder:	Hooper.	**3BU102.**
Engine:		B98A.
Delivered:		4/12/37.
Body Style:		Limousine.
Design No:		6790.
Body No:		8762.
Registration:		Not listed.
First Owner:		Colonel Sir Umaid Singh, Raj of Jodhpur, India.
Present Owner:		K. Higgins, US.

Pictures: CORR/131.

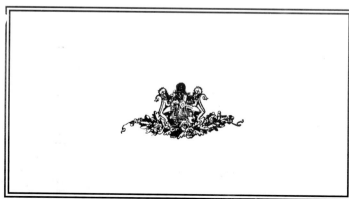

3BU104.

Coachbuilder:	Hooper.	**3BU104.**
Engine:		J88R.
Delivered:		5/3/37.
Body Style:		Limousine.
Design No:		6755.
Body No:		8794.
Registration:		Not listed.
First Owner:		T. von Riedemann, Switzerland.
Present Owner:		S. M. Steiner, US.

Pictures:
Comments: Phantom II 201XJ used as trade-in. Car in UK by 1948.

3BU106. Coachbuilder: Kellner.
Engine: Q88K.
Delivered: 5/8/37.
Body Style: Limousine.
Registration: Not listed.
First Owner: Maharanee Chimna Bai of Baroda, India.
Present Owner: R. Chander, India.

Pictures:
Comments: Maharajah Bai owned 3AX201. The Crown Prince owned 3CP112.

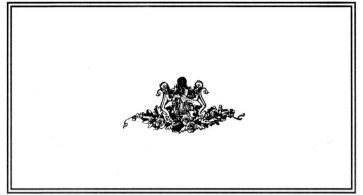
3BU106.

3BU108. Coachbuilder: H. J. Mulliner.
Engine: Q28K.
Delivered: 5/11/37.
Body Style: Sedanca de ville.
Body No: 4510.
Registration: CFC 174.
First Owner: C. F. Clark, UK.
Present Owner: **H. C. Friedman, US.**

Pictures: PIIITS/5 (Shown).
Comments:

3BU108.

3BU110. Coachbuilder: Barker.
Engine: J18R.
Delivered: 5/14/37.
Body Style: Limousine.
Registration: DUU 628.
First Owner: Norman MacCullum, UK.
Present Owner: A. Griffiths, UK.

Pictures:
Comments:

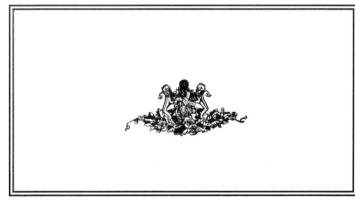
3BU110.

3BU112. Coachbuilder: Barker.
Engine: R98J.
Delivered: 5/31/37.
Body Style: Limousine.
Registration: DYK 474.
First Owner: Captian Neil MacEacharn, UK.
Present Owner: **W. H. W. Doyle, US.**

Pictures: FL/3299.
Comments: To Canada by 1963.

3BU112. (Photo: Mr Doyle).

3BU114.

Coachbuilder:	Arthur Mulliner. **3BU114.**
Engine:	(Original) J48R.
Delivered:	2/18/37.
Body Style:	Touring limousine.
Registration:	FML 7.
First Owner:	Mrs. E. M. Grimes, UK.
Present Owner:	**J. E. Little, UK.**

Pictures: TERR/138 (Shown).
Comments: Arthur Mulliner Ltd. Trials. Later fitted with engine W58E ex 3AX139.

3BU116.   *(Photo: Mr. Hans Enzler).*

Coachbuilder:	Hooper. **3BU116.**
Engine:	J58R.
Delivered:	5/4/37.
Body Style:	Sports limousine.
Design No:	Design 6542.
Body No:	8765.
Registration:	BTJ 918, LU 500 066 (Swiss).
First Owner:	John Hamer, UK.
Present Owner:	O. Eigensatz, Switzerland.

Pictures: Schrader/168.
Comments: Sold January 1969 for £1,775.

3BU118.

Coachbuilder:	Arthur Mulliner. **3BU118.**
Engine:	Y28D.
Delivered:	6/7/37.
Body Style:	4-Light limousine.
Registration:	UJ 9669.
First Owner:	Lt.Colonel John N. Price-Wood, UK.
Present Owner:	W. B. Hartman, US.

Pictures:
Comments: Owned by Stanley E. Sears from 1948-1950.

3BU120.   *(Photo: Mr. Jaiswal).*

Coachbuilder:	Windovers. **3BU120.**
Engine:	Z68C.
Delivered:	5/10/37.
Body Style:	Limousine.
Body No:	6443.
Registration:	Not listed.
First Owner:	Max V. Linde, UK.
Present Owner:	J. Jaiswal, India.

Pictures: B190/16.
Comments:

3BU122.
Coachbuilder:	Barker.
Engine:	Q68K.
Delivered:	2/15/37.
Body Style:	Touring limousine.
Registration:	Not listed.
First Owner:	Lord Herbert (Andrew) Scott, UK.
Present Owner:	R. Mascort, Spain.

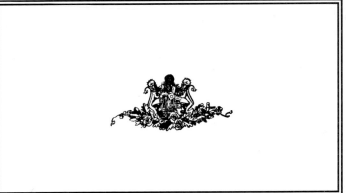

Pictures:
Comments: Lord Scott Trials (Chairman of Rolls-Royce). Owned by Rt. Hon. Sir Samuel John Gurney Hoare, UK Ambassador to Spain, 1943.

3BU122.

3BU124.
Coachbuilder:	Barker.
Engine:	Z28C.
Delivered:	5/5/37.
Body Style:	Landaulet.
Registration:	Not listed.
First Owner:	E. R. Makower, UK.
Present Owner:	Newbit, UK.

Pictures: Oldham/232h (Shown).
Comments:

3BU124.

3BU126.
Coachbuilder:	Hooper.
Engine:	(Original) Z18C.
Delivered:	6/30/37.
Body Style:	Sports limousine.
Design No:	Design 6945.
Body N\o:	8837.
Registration:	DBP 500, FYT 1.
First Owner:	Miss Annie Jeffery, UK.
Present Owner:	C. E. Green, UK.

Pictures:
Comments: Miss Jefferey also owned 3CP130. Owned by Brazilian Ambassador to UK, 1946. Later fitted with engine J48R ex 3BU114.

3BU126.   *(Photo: Mr. Klaus-Josef Rossfeldt).*

3BU128.
Coachbuilder:	H. J. Mulliner.
Engine:	J38R.
Delivered:	3/17/37.
Body Style:	Sedanca de ville.
Body No:	4401.
Registration:	DXB 496.
First Owner:	Sir (William) Edgar Horne, Bart, UK.
Present Owner:	Jack Barclay Ltd., UK (1994).

Pictures:
Comments: Ordered without mascot. Stolen in the **UK,** September 1987.

3BU128.

3BU130.   *(Photo: Mr. Strother MacMinn).*

Coachbuilder:	H. J. Mulliner.	**3BU130.**
Engine:		J28R.
Delivered:		4/20/37.
Body Style:		Saloon with division.
Design No:		Drawing 5937.
Body No:		4473.
Registration:		DXA 9.
First Owner:		Colonel W. A. Bristow, UK.
Present Owner:		V. Millet, US.

Pictures: Bishop/45.
Comments: Owned by Stanley Sedgwick, 1952.
Interior modified by H.J. Mulliner to a non-division
sports saloon when owned by Briggs Cunningham..

3BU132.   *(Photo: Mr. Tindall).*

Coachbuilder:	Hooper.	**3BU132.**
Engine:		J98R.
Delivered:		4/15/37.
Body Style:		Limousine.
Design No:		6744.
Body No:		8783.
Registration:		GV 5351.
First Owner:		William Tatem, 1st Baron Glanely, UK.
Present Owner:		E. Tindall, UK.

Pictures: B162/56.
Comments: Lord Glanely also owned 3DL148.
Owned by Prince Regent of Iraq, 1947-1955. Back in
UK 1955-1983. In Nigeria 1983-1986.

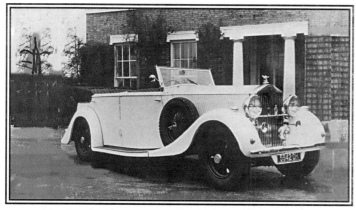

3BU134.   *(Photo: National Motor Museum, England).*

Coachbuilder:	Barker.	**3BU134.**
Engine:		R78J.
Delivered:		7/5/37.
Body Style:		Tourer.
Design No:		Drawing E7618.
Registration:		5942 DH.
First Owner:		HRH Shri Rajaram, Maharajah of Kolhapur
Present Owner:		For sale by US dealer, 1993.

Pictures: Bird/262, Oldham/232h, Hugo/189.
Comments:

3BU136.   *(Photo: Mr. Thompson).*

Coachbuilder:	Freestone & Webb.	**3BU136.**
Engine:		Z98C.
Delivered:		5/3/37.
Body Style:		Sedanca Cabriolet.
Design No:		1787.
Body No:		1238.
Registration:		DXT 7.
First Owner:		Sir John Leigh, Bart, UK.
Present Owner:		M. H. Thompson, UK.

Pictures: Phantoms/379, B164/9.
Comments: Sir John also owned 3AZ68, 3BT99, and
3DL134.

3BU138.
Coachbuilder:	Barker.
Engine No:	(Original) Q78K.
Delivered:	7/27/37.
Body Style:	Saloon with division.
Design No:	Drawing E11946.
Registration:	DYX 864.
First Owner:	H. O. Short, UK.
Present Owner:	S. C. Forrest, US.

Pictures: TERR/56 (Shown).
Comments: Short also owned 3AZ124, which was a trade-in car in Gold Coast, West Africa, 1953. Later engine J94Q, ex 3AZ124, then to 3AZ180.

3BU138.

3BU140.
Coachbuilder:	Vanvooren.
Engine No:	Z48C.
Delivered:	10/15/37.
Body Style:	Saloon.
Registration:	Not listed.
First Owner:	A. Allizon, France.
Present Owner:	Musée de l'Automobile, France.

Pictures: Drehsen/168.
Comments: Original order by N. Mermillon, France.

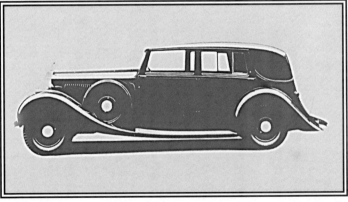

3BU140. (Photo: Mr. Hans Enzler).

3BU142.
Coachbuilder:	Barker.
Engine No:	Q18K.
Delivered:	4/23/37.
Body Style:	Sedanca de ville.
Registration:	Not listed.
First Owner:	Mrs. Seton Porter, France.
Present Owner:	M. O. Johnson, US.

Pictures: P3TS/15 (Engine only).
Comments: To US by 1962.

3BU142. (Photo: National Motor Museum, England).

3BU144.
Coachbuilder:	Barker.
Engine No:	Z58C.
Delivered:	4/23/37.
Body Style:	Limousine.
Registration:	DBB 623.
First Owner:	Arthur Cocks, 6th Baron Somers, UK.
Present Owner:	A. B. Culver, US.

Pictures: FL486, Phantoms/379.
Comments:

3BU144. (Photo: Mr. Culver).

3BU146.   *(Photo: Mr. MacDonald).*

Coachbuilder:	Thrupp & Maberly.	**3BU146.**
Engine:		Z38C.
Delivered:		3/10/37.
Body Style:		Sports saloon.
Design No:		Drawing SLF.1067.
Body No:		6594.
Registration:		DXF 777.
First Owner:		C. J. Dawson, UK.
Present Owner:		J. S. MacDonald, Canada.

Pictures:

Comments:

3BU148.

Coachbuilder:	Hooper.	**3BU148.**
Engine:		Q38K.
Delivered:		4/30/37.
Body Style:		Limousine.
Design No:		6705.
Body No:		8766.
Registration:		Not listed.
First Owner:		G. H. Whigham, UK.
Present Owner:		Trans-Travel Car Hire Ltd., UK (1956).

Pictures: Coachwork drawings, National Science Museum, London.

Comments:

3BU150.

Coachbuilder:	Barker.	**3BU150.**
Engine:		Z78C.
Delivered:		7/15/37.
Body Style:		Limousine.
Registration:		CYL 327.
First Owner:		W. Whitworth, UK.
Present Owner:		F. de Wachter, Belgium.

Pictures: B89/30, Phantoms/379 (Shown).

Comments:

3BU152.   *(Photo: Mr. Crabtree).*

Coachbuilder:	Windovers.	**3BU152.**
Engine:		Q58K.
Delivered:		10/11/37.
Body Style:		Saloon.
Body No:		6479.
Registration:		ECW 654.
First Owner:		Major George Wills, UK.
Present Owner:		G. J. Crabtree, UK.

Pictures: FL/1928, BA99/8.

Comments: Original order by Colonel Harry Day. Car in USA and Canada for some years.

3BU154.
Coachbuilder: Erdmann & Rossi.
Engine: J68R.
Delivered: 12/1/37.
Body Style: (First) Cabriolet.
Registration: Not listed.
First Owner: Firma Johann A. Wulfing, Germany.
Present Owner: Unknown, Switzerland.

Pictures:
Comments: Rebodied with cabriolet by Dutch coachbuilder Nessemann.

3BU154. The second body. (Photo: Mr. Matti

3BU156.
Coachbuilder: Rippon.
Engine: Z88C.
Delivered: 5/10/37.
Body Style: Limousine.
Registration: BWX 890.
First Owner: Major Harry Smith, UK.
Present Owner: Major H. Smith, UK (1951).

Pictures:
Comments:

3BU156.

3BU158.
Coachbuilder: Windovers.
Engine: Q98K.
Delivered: 5/10/37.
Body Style: Sedanca de ville.
Body No: 6435.
Registration: DFL 346.
First Owner: T. A. Macauley, UK.
Present Owner: C. J. Sellner, US.

Pictures: BA114/23 (Shown).
Comments:

3BU158   *(Photo: Mr. Ivor Bleaney).*

3BU160.
Coachbuilder: Arthur Mulliner.
Engine: F38V.
Delivered: 4/12/37.
Body Style: Sedanca de ville.
Registration: DXM 473.
First Owner: Myron C. Taylor, US.
Present Owner: **J. G. Patten, US.**

Pictures: CORR/162, FL/598.
Comments:

3BU160.   *(Photo: Mr. Patten).*

3BU162.

Coachbuilder: Gurney Nutting.   **3BU162.**
Engine: F58V.
Delivered: 6/9/37.
Body Style: Sports sedanca de ville.
Registration: DYR 6.
First Owner: Mrs. E. Hesketh-Wright, UK.
Present Owner: Pagoda (Asia) Ltd., HK.

Pictures: TS/16, Phantoms/380 (Shown).
Comments:

3BU164.   (Photo: Mr. Heathcote).

Coachbuilder: Hooper.   **3BU164.**
Engine: F28V.
Delivered: 5/13/37.
Body Style: Limousine.
Design No: 6273.
Body No: 8668.
Registration: DXV 604.
First Owner: F. R. Chitham, UK.
Present Owner: D. M. Heathcote, UK.

Pictures: Phantoms/380.
Comments:

3BU166.   (Photo: Mr. Shiel).

Coachbuilder: Barker.   **3BU166.**
Engine: (Original) F18V.
Delivered: 6/10/37.
Body Style: Limousine.
Registration: DYK 481.
First Owner: L. H. Lebus, UK.
Present Owner: N. Shiel, UK.

Pictures:
Comments: Latter fitted with B80 engine #4818 at
124,594 miles.

3BU168.   (Photo: PIIITS Archives).

Coachbuilder: Barker.   **3BU168.**
Engine: F48V.
Delivered: 6/25/37.
Body Style: Sedanca de ville.
Registration: Not listed.
First Owner: Urban Broughton, 1st Baron
                                   Fairhaven, UK.
Present Owner: Unknown, US.

Pictures: Oldham/232h, FL/1605
Comments: Phantom II 183RY used as trade-in.
Lady Fairhaven, Urban's mother, owned 3CM55.
Used in film "Goldfinger".

3BU170.
Coachbuilder: Hooper.
Engine: F88V.
Delivered: 5/19/37.
Body Style: Saloon limousine.
Design No: 6597.
Body No: 8784.
Registration: Not listed.
First Owner: W. W. Gallaher, UK.
Present Owner: E. B. Burch, US.

Pictures:
Comments:

3BU170. *(Photo: Mr. Burch).*

3BU172.
Coachbuilder: Hooper.
Engine: F68V.
Delivered: 4/29/37.
Body Style: Limousine.
Design No: 6273.
Body No: 8612.
Registration: Not listed.
First Owner: Sir Abe Bailey, Bart, UK.
Present Owner: LeMay, US.

Pictures:
Comments: Car in South Africa, 1948. Mr. LeMay bought the car from the late Mr. Ben Robertson and stored it in a warehouse where it is inaccessible for pictures.

3BU172. *(Photo: Mr. LeMay).*

3BU174.
Coachbuilder: Barker.
Engine: F98V.
Delivered: 7/28/37.
Body Style: Landaulet.
Registration: DYK 490.
First Owner: Sir Montagu Maurice Burton, UK.
Present Owner: A. J. Wheeler, UK.

Pictures: CORR/34.
Comments:

3BU174. *(Photo: Mr. Wheeler).*

3BU176.
Coachbuilder: Barker.
Engine: Y48D.
Delivered: 6/12/37.
Body Style: Sedanca de ville.
Registration: DYK 488.
First Owner: Minoru, Baroness Foley, UK.
Present Owner: **T. R. Campi, US.**

Pictures: FL/3799, FL/4090
See Page 279 for another photograph of this car during restoration.

3BU176. *(Photo: Dr. Campi).*

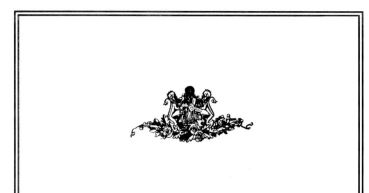

Coachbuilder:	Park Ward. **3BU178.**
Engine:	Y18D.
Delivered:	6/1/37.
Body Style:	Touring limousine.
Body No:	4278.
Registration:	DYF 860.
First Owner:	Mrs. Walter Palmer, UK.
Present Owner:	**Scrapped.**

Pictures:
Comments: Last owner F. Wilcock, UK. Engine and gearbox for sale for £575, February 1978.

3BU178.

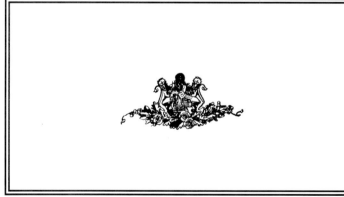

Coachbuilder:	Windovers. **3BU180.**
Engine:	Y68D.
Delivered:	4/2/37.
Body Style:	Limousine de ville.
Body No:	6436.
Registration:	DXO 771.
First Owner:	Mrs. W. S. Cottingham, UK.
Present Owner:	C. Schneider, US.

Pictures:
Comments:

3BU180.

Coachbuilder:	H. J. Mulliner. **3BU182.**
Engine:	Y58D.
Delivered:	4/14/37.
Body Style:	Pullman limousine.
Body No:	4493.
Registration:	DXT 100.
First Owner:	Arthur Henry Wrey, UK.
Present Owner:	A. W. Wood, UK (1953).

Pictures:
Comments: Engine later fitted to 3CM101.

3BU182.

Coachbuilder:	Rippon. **3BU184.**
Engine:	W68F.
Delivered:	5/14/37.
Body Style:	(First) Limousine.
Registration:	DYH 500, XOB 460.
First Owner:	E. W. Smith, UK.
Present Owner:	**R. F. Lorkowski, US.**

Pictures: B195/14.
Comments: Used by Lord Mayor of Birmingham, 1946. Rebodied with replica coupé by Mr. Lorkowski.

3BU184.   *(Photo: Mr. Lorkowski).*

3BU186. Coachbuilder: Park Ward.
Engine: Q28L.
Delivered: 7/19/37.
Body Style: Touring limousine.
Body No: 4308.
Registration: DYR 688.
First Owner: Sir Bracewell Smith, UK (9/37).
Present Owner: R. E. Harvie, US.

Pictures: FL/1303.
Comments: Jack Barclay Ltd. Trials.

3BU186.   *(Photo: Mr. Harvie).*

3BU188. Coachbuilder: Park Ward.
Engine: R28J.
Delivered: 4/6/37.
Body Style: Touring saloon.
Body No: 4289.
Registration: DXP 115.
First Owner: R. E. Brandt, UK.
Present Owner: R. J. Simpson, US.

Pictures:
Comments: Ordered without mascot.

3BU188.

3BU190. Coachbuilder: Barker.
Engine: Y88D.
Delivered: 7/9/37.
Body Style: Touring limousine.
Body No: 7245.
Registration: DXX 128.
First Owner: W. G. Weston, UK (4/38).
Present Owner: **F. Gabrielli, US.**

Pictures: RRB12.37/9, FL/3942 (Shown).
Comments: Rolls-Royce Ltd. Trials, Major Len Cox
(CX).

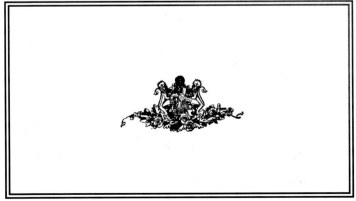

3BU190.   *(Photo: Mr. Gabrielli).*

3BU192. Coachbuilder: Arthur Mulliner.
Engine: Y38D.
Delivered: 5/7/37.
Body Style: Limousine.
Registration: Not listed.
First Owner: Mrs. D. K. Hawkins, UK.
Present Owner: Fletcher & Sons, UK (1952).

Pictures:
Comments: Ordered without mascot.

3BU192.

3BU194. The Barker body.

Coachbuilder:	Vesters & Neirinck. **3BU194.**
Engine:	X48E.
Delivered:	2/18/37.
Body Style:	(First) Saloon.
Registration:	JBY 20, XX 3883.
First Owner:	Paul Vuylsteke, Belgium.
Present Owner:	N. E. Herstein, US.

Pictures: FL/1502 (Shown).
Comments: Original owner was Mayor of Brussels. Rebodied with Barker saloon.

3BU196. With tourer body.

Coachbuilder:	Gurney Nutting. **3BU196.**
Engine:	X38E.
Delivered:	8/20/37.
Body Style:	(First) Sedanca de ville.
Registration:	EGH 513.
First Owner:	Terence Conyngham, 6th Baron Plunket, UK.
Present Owner:	**S. Fortenbach, US.**

Pictures: FL/1564, FL/2114 (Shown).
Comments: Converted to tourer.

3BU198.   *(Photo: Frank Dale & Stepsons).*

Coachbuilder:	Windovers. **3BU198.**
Engine:	X18E.
Delivered:	4/29/37.
Body Style:	Sedanca de ville.
Body No:	6456.
Registration:	Not listed.
First Owner:	Sir Vijayasinghi, Maharajah of Rajpipla, India.
Present Owner:	A. J. H. King, UK (1962).

Pictures:
Comments:

3BU200.   *(Photo: Briggs Cunningham Museum).*

Coachbuilder:	Thrupp & Maberly. **3BU200.**
Engine:	Y98D.
Delivered:	5/7/37.
Body Style:	Saloon with division.
Design No:	Drawing SLF.1242.
Body No:	6620.
Registration:	Not listed.
First Owner:	Countess Curt Haugwitz-Reventlow, UK.
Present Owner:	C. Reventlow Post, US.

Pictures: Eves/105, Bishop/40, Wood/40.
Comments: The Count owned similar 3AZ96. In the Briggs Cunningham Museum for some years.

The BT Series
of
Phantom III Cars

The BT series consists of 100 cars,

numbered odd, 3BT1

thorough 3BT203, minus, of course, 3BT13

and 3BT113. All BT series cars were delivered in 1937,

3BT1. *(Photo: Musée de Mougins, France).*

Coachbuilder:	Barker.	**3BT1.**
Engine:		X98E.
Delivered:		8/19/37.
Body Style:		Sedanca de ville.
Registration:		Not listed.
First Owner:	Don Antenor Patino, France.	
Present Owner:	Musée de Mougins, France.	

Pictures:
Comments: Original order by Alberto R. Ovendo, who died.

3BT3. *(Photo: Mr. Ritter via RROC Foundation).*

Coachbuilder:	Binder.	**3BT3.**
Engine:		Q18L.
Delivered:		7/23/37.
Body Style:		Saloon with division.
Body No:		5917.
Registration:		Not listed.
First Owner:	Jean A. Seligman, France.	
Present Owner:	**P. Whyte, Australia.**	

Pictures: FL/223, FL/3809.
Comments: In USA from 1950's to 1989.

3BT5. *(Photo: Mr. Posedly).*

Coachbuilder:	Hooper.	**3BT5.**
Engine:		Q48L.
Delivered:		5/28/37.
Body Style:		Sports limousine.
Design No:		6910.
Body No:		8809.
Registration:		DYH 140.
First Owner:	Fitz-James, 17th Duque de Alba, Spain.	
Present Owner:	B. Posedly, US.	

Pictures: CORR/132, FL/816, FL/928, FL/1097.
Comments: Duque de Alba was also 10th Duke of Berwick. To USA 1964. (This was the Editor's car).

3BT7. The sedanca body. *(Photo: Mr. McWilliams).*

Coachbuilder:	Park Ward.	**3BT7.**
Engine:		X58E.
Delivered:		6/7/37.
Body Style:		(First) Sedanca de ville.
Body No:		4306.
Registration:		Not listed.
First Owner:	Mrs. Walter Howard, US.	
Present Owner:	D. J. McWilliams, US.	

Pictures: FL/509, FL/767.
Comments: Shipped to USA 18 June 1937. Converted to tourer.

3BT9.
Coachbuilder:	Kellner.
Engine:	(Original) X98E.
Delivered:	6/9/37.
Body Style:	Limousine.
Registration:	Not listed.
First Owner:	D. Schnur, France.
Present Owner:	P. E. Kelley, US.

Pictures: CORR/142.
Comments: To USA 1952. Engine fitted to 3CP50, and engine J28S from 3CP50 fitted to this chassis, 1950's. For sale 1957 for $1,000.

3BT9. *(Photo: Mr. Ken Karger)*

3BT11.
Coachbuilder:	Windovers.
Engine:	X88E.
Delivered:	5/3/37.
Body Style:	Limousine.
Body No:	6441.
Registration:	DXO 776.
First Owner:	Sir George Harvey MP, UK (12/38).
Present Owner:	Hartman, US.

Pictures: CORR/356 (Shown).
Comments: Windovers Ltd. Trials (Lord Portarlington).

3BT11.

3BT15.
Coachbuilder:	Windovers.
Engine:	(Original) X28E.
Delivered:	7/12/37.
Body Style:	(First) Limousine.
Body No:	6460
Registration:	DYX 643, ESV 464.
First Owner:	Hon. Lady Jean Ward, UK.
Present Owner:	For sale US dealer, 1994.

Pictures: Christie Frey/45.
Comments: Ordered without mascot. Engine later to 3BT93; fitted with B80 engine 1962. Rebodied with H. J. Mulliner 2-door cabriolet 5077 ex 4AF6, (Phantom IV), 1956.

3BT15. *(Photo: Mr. Bill Dobson).*

3BT17.
Coachbuilder:	Barker.
Engine:	Q78L.
Delivered:	8/30/37.
Body Style:	Sedanca de ville.
Registration:	EJJ 777.
First Owner:	C. Frederick Bernhard, UK.
Present Owner:	R. A. McDermott, Australia.

Pictures: Christie/60.
Comments: To Australia 1989, from the USA.

3BT17. *(Photo: Mr. H. W. Aungst via RROC Foundation).*

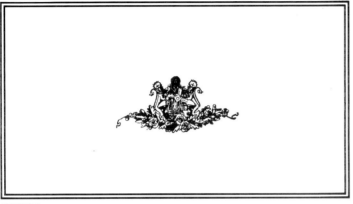

3BT19.   *(Photo: Mr. R. M. Bowers).*

Coachbuilder:	Hooper.	**3BT19.**
Engine:		X68E.
Delivered:		5/6/37.
Body Style:		Landaulette.
Design No:		6926.
Body No:		8817.
Registration:		AMO 249.
First Owner:		Edaward Mauger, 1st Baron Iliffe, UK.
Present Owner:		R. P. R. Iliffe, UK.

Pictures: BA88/20-21, CORR/131.
Comments: Car owned by members of the Iliffe family from new.

3BT21.

Coachbuilder:	Barker.	**3BT21.**
Engine:		Q38L.
Delivered:		6/4/37.
Body Style:		Touring limousine.
Design No:		Drawing E11519.
Registration:		Not listed.
First Owner:		Mrs. A. G. May, South Africa.
Present Owner:		A. F. Wallace, UK (1948).

Pictures:
Comments:

3BT23.   *(Photo: Mr. Tuttle).*

Coachbuilder:	H. J. Mulliner.	**3BT23.**
Engine:		(Original) Q58L.
Delivered:		5/21/37.
Body Style:		Saloon with division.
Design No:		Drawing 5937.
Body No:		4468.
Registration:		DXW 647.
First Owner:		P. Dubonnet, France.
Present Owner:		**M. Tuttle, US.**

Pictures: Kobayashi/108, Kobayashi/110, FL/390, FL/466.
Comments: Original order by C. Hillard of Somerset. Ordered withut mascot. Car in Japan, 1958. Later engine A94A ex 3AZ36.

3BT25.   *(Photo: Mr. André Blaize).*

Coachbuilder:	Hooper.	**3BT25.**
Engine:		F78V.
Delivered:		4/7/37.
Body Style:		Landaulette.
Design No:		6927.
Body No:		8801.
Registration:		Not listed.
First Owner:		Governor-General Sir Patrick Duncan, South Africa.
Present Owner:		Unknown, Germany.

Pictures:
Comments: Car altered from limousine before delivery.

3BT27. Coachbuilder: Mann Egerton.
Engine: Q68L.
Delivered: 6/5/37.
Body Style: Limousine.
Registration: Not listed.
First Owner: Mrs. Henrietta S. Fisher, UK.
Present Owner: W. H. Blake, UK (1946).

Pictures:
Comments:

3BT27.

3BT29. Coachbuilder: H. J. Mulliner.
Engine: (Original) G78V.
Delivered: 5/22/37.
Body Style: (First) Limousine.
Design No: Drawing 5887.
Body No: 4474.
Registration: GS 7196, AEG 755 A.
First Owner: Miss. M. C. Todd, UK.
Present Owner: P. Shellcock, UK.

Pictures: CORR/196.
Comments: Later hearse, then Robinson replica roadster. Later B80 engine.

3BT29. The Robinson body. (Photo: Mr. Ken Batchelor).

3BT31. Coachbuilder: Hooper.
Engine: (Original) G88V.
Delivered: 5/11/37.
Body Style: Limousine.
Design No: 6782.
Body No: 8791.
Registration: CNX 596.
First Owner: Miss M. Payne, UK.
Present Owner: G. van Bree, Netherlands.

Pictures: B113/19.
Comments: Engine G88V later fitted to 3CP182. This chassis later fitted with B80 engine.

3BT31. (Photo: Science Museum, London).

3BT33. Coachbuilder: Park Ward.
Engine: G48V.
Delivered: 5/27/37.
Body Style: Sedanca de ville.
Body No: 4304.
Registration: DYE 22.
First Owner: Duncan McMartin, Canada.
Present Owner: **J. G. Patten, US.**

Pictures: TS/33, FL/3712, FL/3802, CORR/261 (Shown).
Comments: Car in France, 1949.

3BT33.

3BT35.

Coachbuilder:	Gurney Nutting.	**3BT35.**
Engine:	(Original) Q88L.	
Delivered:	4/27/37.	
Body Style:	Sports saloon.	
Registration:	Not listed.	
First Owner:	J. C. Stein, US.	
Present Owner:	J. C. Denne, UK.	

Pictures:
Comments: Car to UK by 1954. Later fitted with B80 engine.

3BT37.   *(Photo: Mr. Neale).*

Coachbuilder:	Abbott.	**3BT37.**
Engine:	G28V.	
Delivered:	6/23/37.	
Body Style:	Saloon limousine.	
Design No:	3625.	
Registration:	DXX 130.	
First Owner:	Miss M. E. H. Lloyd, UK.	
Present Owner:	T. R. Neale, UK.	

Pictures: BA100/4.
Comments: Phantom I 46KR used as trade-in.

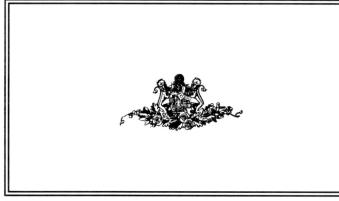

3BT39.

Coachbuilder:	Hooper.	**3BT39.**
Engine:	G18V.	
Delivered:	5/21/37.	
Body Style:	Limousine.	
Design No:	6856.	
Body No:	8795.	
Registration:	Not listed.	
First Owner:	James D. Paterson, UK.	
Present Owner:	William McPhail & Sons Ltd., UK (1951).	

Pictures:
Comments:

3BT41.

Coachbuilder:	Hooper.	**3BT41.**
Engine:	(Original) Q98L.	
Delivered:	6/10/37.	
Body Style:	Limousine.	
Design No:	6273.	
Body No:	8665.	
Registration:	EGH 514.	
First Owner:	William Ewert Berry, 1st Baron Camrose, UK.	
Present Owner:	C. P. Pensavalle, US.	

Pictures:
Comments: Original order by J. A. Whitehead. H. R. Owen Ltd. stock. Baron Camrose's son owned 3AZ62. Fitted with non-standard engine by 1971, when car was for sale for £725.

3BT43.

Coachbuilder:	Windovers.
Engine:	G38V.
Delivered:	6/1/37.
Body Style:	Limousine.
Body No:	6442.
Registration:	Not listed.
First Owner:	Lady Grace Dance, UK.
Present Owner:	J. Walker, UK (1954).

Pictures:
Comments: Engine G38V later fitted to 3CP194.

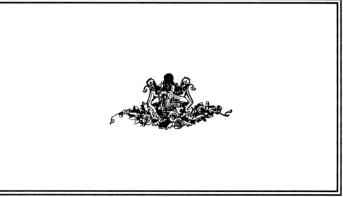
3BT43.

3BT45.

Coachbuilder:	Windovers.
Engine:	G68V.
Delivered:	8/10/37.
Body Style:	Limousine.
Body No:	6439.
Registration:	DLA 777, EKL 596.
First Owner:	N. S. Holland, UK.
Present Owner:	D. Parker, UK.

Pictures: Phantoms/381, CORR/356 (Shown).
Comments: Original order by C. Mitchell. Owned by Mme. Chiang Kai-shek, China, 1946. In UK by 1963.

3BT45. *(Photo: Mr. R. M. Bowers).*

3BT47.

Coachbuilder:	Hooper.
Engine:	G98V.
Delivered:	6/3/37.
Body Style:	Sedanca de ville.
Design No:	6881.
Body No:	8819.
Registration:	SUL 739.
First Owner:	(Joseph) Stanley Holmes, UK.
Present Owner:	Unknown, US.

Pictures: FL/290 (Shown).
Comments: Holmes created Lord Dovercourt, 1939. For sale 1957 for £1,250.

3BT47.

3BT49.

Coachbuilder:	Barker.
Engine:	W38F.
Delivered:	9/1/37.
Body Style:	Sedanca de ville.
Design No:	Drawing E11488.
Registration:	Not listed.
First Owner:	SIgma, Mrs. Alfred Bushiel, US.
Present Owner:	H. M. McDougald, Canada.

Pictures:
Comments:

3BT49. *(Photo: National Motor Museum, England).*

3BT51. *The first body.*

Coachbuilder: Barker.   **3BT51.**
Engine: (Original) W18F.
Delivered: 7/16/37.
Body Style: (First) Limousine de ville.
Registration: MMD 116C.
First Owner: Madeline, Mrs. S. W. Tanfield, UK.
Present Owner: T. Mason, UK.

Pictures: TERR/56 (Shown).
Comments: Mrs. Tanfield also owned 3CM67. Austin engine fitted and rebodied as hearse. Engine W18F fitted to 3BT135.

3BT53. *With the Barker body.*   *(Photo: Mr. Haimowitz).*

Coachbuilder: Inskip.   **3BT53.**
Engine: W28F.
Delivered: 8/25/37.
Body Style: (First) 5-Passenger limousine.
Registration: Not listed.
First Owner: Frederich Brant Rentchhler, US.
Present Owner: **E. Haimowitz, US.**

Pictures: FL/56, FL/209, FL1097, FL2979.
Comments: Rentschler also owned 3AX25. Body to 3DH7, July 1941. Rebodied with Park Ward limousine 4482 ex Wraith WHC24, July 1947, then Barker limousine ex 151GN June 1947.

3BT55.   *(Photo: Mr. Buzzi).*

Coachbuilder: Hooper.   **3BT55.**
Engine: W58F.
Delivered: 5/22/37.
Body Style: Sports limousine.
Design No: 6877.
Body No: 8790.
Registration: AMO 434.
First Owner: Madame R. Albertini, UK.
Present Owner: **P. V. Buzzi, US.**

Pictures: CORR/134, P3TS/16.
Comments:

3BT57.   *(Photo: Mr. R. M. Bowers).*

Coachbuilder: Windovers.   **3BT57.**
Engine: (Original) Y78D.
Delivered: 8/5/37.
Body Style: Limousine.
Body No: 6472.
Registration: Not listed.
First Owner: Sir (Alexander) Kay Muir, Bart, UK.
Present Owner: *(Member)* M. Evans, US.

Pictures: Phantoms/381 (Shown).
Comments: Engine for sale, UK. for £800, Nov. 1975. Later fitted with Wraith engine.

3BT59.
Coachbuilder:	Windovers.
Engine:	W48F.
Delivered:	6/14/37.
Body Style:	Sedanca de ville.
Body No:	6386.
Registration:	DYR 65.
First Owner:	R. H. Haslam, UK.
Present Owner:	Estate of the late R. C. Mertz.

Pictures: FL/473, FL/542.
Comments: To USA December 1958.

3BT59. *(Photo: RROC Foundation).*

3BT61.
Coachbuilder:	Windovers.
Engine:	M58P.
Delivered:	5/21/37.
Body Style:	Sports saloon.
Body No:	6415.
Registration:	ELF 319.
First Owner:	Captain J. Farr, UK.
Present Owner:	D. W. Harris, US.

Pictures: TERR/267.
Comments: Original order by Sir William Jaffray, Bart. Held as Windovers Ltd. stock. To Bermuda, 1954.

3BT61. *(Photo: Mr. Harris).*

3BT63.
Coachbuilder:	Windovers.
Engine:	(Original) M28P.
Delivered:	7/31/37.
Body Style:	(First) Landaulette.
Body No:	6438
Registration:	RRR 939.
First Owner:	Sir Robert Abbott Hadfield, Bart, UK.
Present Owner:	P. G. Payne, UK.

Pictures: CORR/357 (Shown).
Comments: Rebodied as drophead by owner Attenborough. Later B80 engine B80654 fitted.

3BT63. *As rebodied.* *(Photo: Mr. Payne).*

3BT65.
Coachbuilder:	H. J. Mulliner.
Engine:	(Original) W88F.
Delivered:	6/15/37.
Body Style:	Saloon with division.
Design No:	Drawing 5899.
Body No:	4528.
Registration:	EGF 1.
First Owner:	H. J. Caro, UK.
Present Owner:	von Bentheim, Germany.

Pictures: TERR/15 (Shown).
Comments: Original order from Windovers by Irene Dunn. Jack Barclay Ltd stock. Ordered without mascot. Engine replaced 1980s with engine Z78D from 3CM39.

3BT65.

3BT67.   *(Photo: Mr. Parkinson).*

Coachbuilder:	Hooper.	**3BT67.**
Engine:		M48P.
Delivered:		6/16/37.
Body Style:		Allweather.
Design No:		6918.
Body No:		8812.
Registration:		ACE 1, 345 GOT, GRG 400.
First Owner:		R. A. Camenisch, UK.
Present Owner:		P. F. Parkinson, UK.

Pictures: Oldham/256a, Robinson/'83, B152/48, FL/3184.
Comments: Allweather body fitted with "Kellner head". Ordered without mascot.

3BT69.   *(Photo: Mr. Fane).*

Coachbuilder:	James Young.	**3BT69.**
Engine:		G58V.
Delivered:		5/20/37.
Body Style:		Saloon with division.
Registration:		DYL 200.
First Owner:		Sir (Edward) Hugh Bray, UK.
Present Owner:		**H. M. Fane, Canada.**

Pictures: B164/30, FL/3295.
Comments:

3BT71.   *(Photo: Mr. Matti Schumacher).*

Coachbuilder:	Rippon.	**3BT71.**
Engine:		W78F.
Delivered:		7/6/37.
Body Style:		Limousine.
Registration:		BWY 934, 6309 KH.
First Owner:		John Thomas Field, UK.
Present Owner:		J. Hug, Switzerland.

Pictures:
Comments: Original order by Ernest Waddilove. Used by Mayor of Kingston-upon-Hull, 1952. Car in the USA for some years, including the Crawford Museum.

Coachbuilder:	Barker.	**3BT73.**
Engine:		W98F.
Delivered:		7/26/37.
Body Style:		Touring limousine.
Design No:		Drawing E11468.
Body No:		7244.
Registration:		BPW 1, 122 CBP.
First Owner:		John Musker, UK.
Present Owner:		T. Kirkman, US.

Pictures: Phantoms/382, FL/3387, FL/3174 (Shown).
Comments:

3BT73.

3BT75.

Coachbuilder:	Windover
Engine:	M38P.
Delivered:	7/7/37.
Body Style:	7-Passenger saloon.
Design No:	5744.
Body No:	Not listed.
Registration:	
First Owner:	Sir Bhupal Singh, Maharajah of Udaipur, India.
Present Owner:	**P. Bhogilal, India.**

Pictures: CORR/357 (Shown).
Comments: Originally ordered by Hon. Charles Fitzroy, son of Lord Southampton.

3BT75. *(Photo: Mr. R.M. Bowers).*

3BT77.

Coachbuilder:	Park Ward.
Engine:	M18P.
Delivered:	6/4/37.
Body Style:	Touring limousine.
Design No:	4303.
Body No:	DYR 671.
Registration:	
First Owner:	Major Lionel Beaumont-Thomas, UK.
Present Owner:	Milosevich, US.

Pictures:
Comments: Rootes Ltd. Trials.

3BT77. *(Photo: Mr. Milosevich).*

3BT79.

Coachbuilder:	Thrupp & Maberly
Engine:	V58G.
Delivered:	7/20/37.
Body Style:	Sports limousine.
Body No:	Drawing SLE.1245/C.
Registration:	6631.
First Owner:	DYY 37.
	Mme P. Y. de Ossorio, UK.
Present Owner:	**P. L. Jacobs, US.**

Pictures: Phantoms/382. (Shown)
Comments: Original order by N. Princep via Jack Barclay.

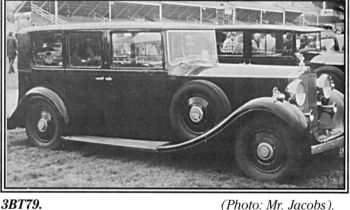

3BT79. *(Photo: Mr. Jacobs).*

3BT81.

Coachbuilder:	Gurney Nutting.
Engine:	F48W.
Delivered:	10/6/37.
Body Style:	Drophead sedanca coupé
Registration:	EXP 110.
First Owner:	Sir Herbert Smith, Bart, UK (8/38).
Present Owner:	M. F. C. Schicht, UK.

Pictures:
Comments: H. R. Owen Ltd. stock. Sir Herbert also owned 3AZ168, 3CM31, and 3DL104.

3BT81. *(Photo: Mr. Schicht).*

3BT83.

Coachbuilder:	Windovers.	**3BT83.**
Engine:		M98P.
Delivered:		7/9/37.
Body Style:		Limousine.
Body No:		6462.
Registration:		EKE 316.
First Owner:		Ronald Gale, UK.
Present Owner:		T. J. Elzinga, Netherlands.

Pictures: Phantoms/383 (Shown).
Comments: Ordered without mascot.

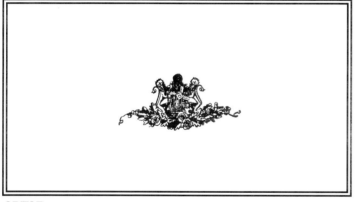

3BT85.   *(Photo: Mr. Martin).*

Coachbuilder:	Hooper.	**3BT85.**
Engine:		V88G.
Delivered:		7/9/37.
Body Style:		Sports limousine.
Design No:		6898.
Body No:		8821.
Registration:		DYV 100.
First Owner:		Colin Gilbert, UK.
Present Owner:		R. Martin, US.

Pictures: Tubbs/43, CORR/133.
Comments:

3BT87.

Coachbuilder:	Hooper.	**3BT87.**
Engine:		(Original) M78P.
Delivered:		6/18/37.
Body Style:		Limousine.
Design No:		6806.
Body No:		8822.
Registration:		Not listed.
First Owner:		William, 1st Baron Vestey, UK.
Present Owner:		Hole, US.

Pictures:
Comments: Baron Vestey's son owned 3CP12. Engine removed, 1952. Fitted with Canadian Chrysler engine.

Coachbuilder:	Hooper.	**3BT89.**
Engine:		F18W.
Delivered:		5/19/37.
Body Style:		Sedanca de ville.
Design No:		6437.
Body No:		8797.
Registration:		DYR 672.
First Owner:		Sir Keith Charles Adolphus Fraser, Bart, UK.
Present Owner:		B. May, UK.

Pictures: TERR/124 (Shown).
Comments: Jack Barclay Ltd. stock.

3BT91.
Coachbuilder:	Hooper.
Engine:	(Original) M68P.
Delivered:	6/1/37.
Body Style:	Limousine.
Design No:	6273.
Body No:	8511.
Registration:	DXF 505.
First Owner:	A. Nettlefold, UK.
Present Owner:	Unknown, UK.

Pictures: Oldham/208g (Shown).
Comments: Body at Olympia Show, 1935, Rolls-Royce stand, on dummy chassis. Showroom stock. Later fitted with B80 engine.

3BT91.

3BT93.
Coachbuilder:	Freestone & Webb.
Engine:	(Original) F38W.
Delivered:	6/16/37.
Body Style:	4-Light saloon.
Design No:	1782.
Body No:	1244.
Registration:	Not listed.
First Owner:	G. H. Spencer, UK.
Present Owner:	F. W. Buess, US.

Pictures: CORR/78.
Comments: Ordered without mascot. Later fitted with engine X28E ex 3BT15.

3BT93. *(Photo: Mr. Buess).*

3BT95.
Coachbuilder:	Barker.
Engine:	F68W.
Delivered:	7/21/37.
Body Style:	Limousine.
Registration:	Not listed.
First Owner:	(George) Rowland Blades, 1st Baron Ebbisham, UK
Present Owner:	de Lamatre, US.

Pictures:
Comments:

3BT95.

3BT97
Coachbuilder:	Hooper.
Engine:	M88P.
Delivered:	6/10/37.
Body Style:	Limousine.
Design No:	6443.
Body No:	8810.
Registration:	Not listed.
First Owner:	Arthur Francis Bassett, UK.
Present Owner:	**J. H. Vallis, US.**

Pictures:
Comments: First chassis with standard Hooper limousine body. Ordered without mascot. Vice-Regal car, Straits Settlements, Singapore, 1946.

3BT97. *(Photo: Mr. Vallis).*

3BT99.   (Photo: Mr. Provencher).

Coachbuilder:	Freestone & Webb,	**3BT99.**
Engine:		F58W.
Delivered:		7/12/37.
Body Style:		Sports saloon.
Design No:		Design 1700.
Body No:		1253.
Registration:		Not listed.
First Owner:		Sir John Leigh, Bart, UK.
Present Owner:		G. Provencher, US.

Pictures: Phantoms/383.
Comments: Leigh also owned 3AZ68, 3BU136, and 3DL154.

3BT101.   (Photo: Mr. Smith).

Coachbuilder:	Arthur Mulliner.	**3BT101.**
Engine:		F28W.
Delivered:		7/21/37.
Body Style:		Sedanca de ville.
Registration:		DYV 8.
First Owner:		F. L. Bishop, UK.
Present Owner:		B. P. Smith, South Africa.

Pictures:
Comments: Original order by W. Butlin via A. Mulliner Ltd.

3BT103.   (Photo: RREC Photo Library).

Coachbuilder:	H. J. Mulliner.	**3BT103**
Engine:		F88W.
Delivered:		6/11/37.
Body Style:		Fixed-head sedanca coupé.
Design No:		Drawing 5904B.
Body No:		4488.
Registration:		DXX 125.
First Owner:		Apsley George Benet Cherry-Garrad, UK.
Present Owner:		**W. J. Harwood, US.**

Pictures: TERR/153.
Comments: Owned by actor (later Sir) Ralph Richardson, 1946.

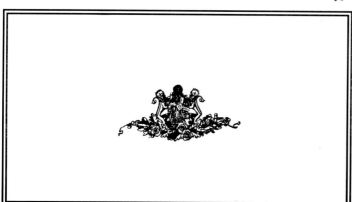

3BT105.

Coachbuilder:	Hooper.	**3BT105.**
Engine:		F78W.
Delivered:		6/22/37.
Body Style:		Limousine.
Design No:		6901.
Body No:		8796.
Registration:		MMD 114 C.
First Owner:		H. S. Frost, UK.
Present Owner:		G. D. Hussey, UK.

Pictures:
Comments:

3BT107.

Coachbuilder:	Hooper.
Engine:	F98W.
Delivered:	6/16/37.
Body Style:	Limousine.
Design No:	6748.
Body No:	8811.
Registration:	DXT 224, ONE 1.
First Owner:	Mrs. David Dows, UK.
Present Owner:	J. Knock, UK.

Pictures:
Comments: Official car for Manchester University, 1952-1964.

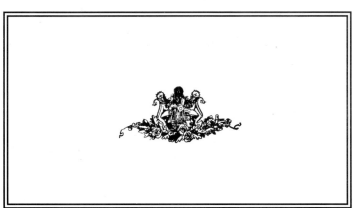
3BT107.

3BT109.

Coachbuilder:	James Young.
Engine:	E98X.
Delivered:	7/14/37.
Body Style:	Saloon with division.
Registration:	Not listed.
First Owner:	Mrs. F. M. Kelly, Ireland.
Present Owner:	Dr. A. Tindal, UK (1956).

Pictures:
Comments: Pass & Joyce Ltd. Trials.

3BT109.

3BT111.

Coachbuilder:	Barker.
Engine:	V38G.
Delivered:	6/30/37.
Body Style:	Touring limousine.
Design No:	Drawing E11468.
Body No:	7243.
Registration:	BUE 165.
First Owner:	R. J. Wormell, UK.
Present Owner:	R. M. Ryan, US.

Pictures: TERR/52 (Shown).
Comments:

3BT111.

3BT115.

Coachbuilder:	Hooper.
Engine:	L18Q.
Delivered:	6/21/37.
Body Style:	Limousine.
Design No:	Design 6885.
Body No:	8827.
Registration:	DXX 126.
First Owner:	Captain Cecil William Paulet Slade, UK.
Present Owner:	K. W. Fozard, UK.

Pictures: Bird, TERR/124 (Shown).
Comments: Phantom II 70PY used as trade-in.

3BT115.

3BT117.

Coachbuilder: Binder.   **3BT117.**
Engine: V28G.
Delivered: 9/4/37.
Body Style: Saloon.
Registration: 7291 AS 75 (French)..
First Owner: Francis Langstaff, France.
Present Owner: M. Rousseau, France.

Pictures: B91/28, Phantoms/383 (Shown).
Comments: Fitted with Marchal headlamps.

3BT119.   *(Photo: Mr. Tucker).*

Coachbuilder: Barker.   **3BT119.**
Engine: V48G.
Delivered: 8/23/37.
Body Style: Sedanca de ville.
Registration: ALF 677.
First Owner: Mrs. Robert Tritton, UK.
Present Owner: R. D. Tucker, US.

Pictures: Oldham/256a.
Comments:

3BT121.

Coachbuilder: Mayfair.   **3BT121.**
Engine: V68G.
Delivered: 6/11/37.
Body Style: Drophead sedanca coupé.
Registration: DYR 232, EWY 585.
First Owner: Richard Banmeyer, UK.
Present Owner: D. P. McClelland, UK.

Pictures: P/1215, Harvey-Bailey/73, B158/55(Shown).
Comments: Ordered without mascot. Winner of
Coupé de l'Exposition, France, 1937.

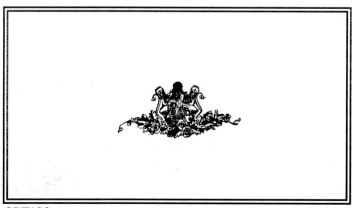

3BT123.

Coachbuilder: Park Ward.   **3BT123.**
Engine: L38Q.
Delivered: 7/13/37.
Body Style: Limousine.
Body No: 4311.
Registration: Not listed.
First Owner: Mrs. Cora E. de Witt, US (6/40).
Present Owner: **C. W. Curtin, US.**
Dismant led.

Pictures:
Comments: Original order by Frank Shaw. Jack
Barclay Ltd. stock. Car not paid for until October
1946. Mr. Curtin says the car has been dismantled
as a parts car. No photographs are available.

3BT125.   **Coachbuilder:**   Park Ward.
Engine: V98G.
Delivered: 6/30/37.
Body Style: Brougham de ville.
Body No: 4256.
Registration: DYM 4, DUV 717.
First Owner: Mrs. V. I. Hamilton, UK.
Present Owner: J. Hibbert, Australia.

Pictures: CORR/261.
Comments: Car in Rhodesia for some years.
Shipped to Australia 1978.

3BT125.   *(Photo: Mr. Hibbert).*

3BT127.   **Coachbuilder**:   Hooper.
Engine: V78G.
Delivered: 6/14/37.
Body Style: (First) Limousine.
Design No: 6443.
Body No: 8826.
Registration: CS 6128.
First Owner: A. C. Robertson, UK.
Present Owner: Aenis, US.

Pictures:
Comments: Body converted to tourer.

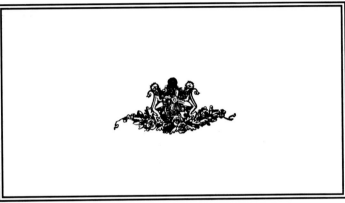

3BT127.

3BT129.   **Coachbuilder:**   Inskip.
Engine: E18X.
Delivered: (Guarantee) 9/16/37.
Body Style: (First) Sedanca coupé
Registration: Not listed.
First Owner: Thomas F. Manville Jnr., US.
Present Owner: C. C. Curtiss, US.

Pictures: deCampi/162.
Comments: Sedanca coupé body exchanged with
3BT165's Brewster Newmarket Sedan 4037, ex 216
AMS (PII) three times before 3BT129 ends up with
Newmarket shown. See 3BT165 for more.

3BT129. The Newmarket body.   *(Photo: Mr. Curtiss).*

3BT131.   **Coachbuilder:**   Vesters & Neirinck.
Engine: L48Q.
Delivered: 10/11/37.
Body Style: Saloon.
Registration: Not listed.
First Owner: Mme Jacqmotte, Belgium.
Present Owner: Prince Regent Charles, Belgium
    (1945).

Pictures:
Comments: Brussels Show, 1937.

3BT131.   *(Photo: National Motor Museum, England).*

3BT133.   *(Photo: Mr. Scoggins).*

Coachbuilder:	Hooper.	**3BT133.**
Engine:		L58Q.
Delivered:		7/7/37.
Body Style:		Sedanca de ville.
Design No:		Design 6816.
Body No:		8816.
Registration:		G 541.
First Owner:		H. H. Leven, UK.
Present Owner:		I. M. Scoggins, UK.

Pictures: Woudenberg/50, B162/9, B164/45.
Comments: Shipped to USA 1962, after major rebuild; back to UK.

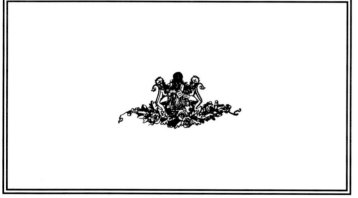

3BT135.

Coachbuilder:	Thrupp & Maberly.	**3BT135.**
Engine:		(Original) L88Q.
Delivered:		7/7/37.
Body Style:		Landaulette.
Design No:		Drawing SLE.1255/B.
Body No:		6657.
Registration:		CFG 8, 2 TKM.
First Owner:		R. Wemyss Honeyman, UK.
Present Owner:		T. Mason, UK.

Pictures: Oldham/256a (Shown).
Comments: Later fitted with Austin engine, then W18F ex 3BT51. Used as taxi on Jersey, 1960's.

3BT137.

Coachbuilder:	Park Ward.	**3BT137.**
Engine:		L68Q.
Delivered:		7/1/37.
Body Style:		Limousine.
Body No:		4277.
Registration:		ACE 2.
First Owner:		John Arthur Dewar, UK.
Present Owner:		R. B. Montgomery, UK.

Pictures:
Comments: Later fitted with a two-seater racer body, 1950's.

3BT139.   *(Photo: Ted Reich Archives).*

Coachbuilder:	Arthur Mulliner.	**3BT139.**
Engine:		E78X.
Delivered:		7/27/37.
Body Style:		Saloon with division.
Registration:		EGF 541, SY 9115.
First Owner:		R. E. Weber, UK.
Present Owner:		P. R. Blond, UK.

Pictures:
Comments: Original order by C. Gordon Thompson.

3BT141.

Coachbuilder:	Hooper.
Engine:	L98Q.
Delivered:	6/18/37.
Body Style:	Sports limousine.
Design No:	6713.
Body No:	8787.
Registration:	EXV 707, SN 8162.
First Owner:	Major J. R. Harrison, UK.
Present Owner:	**W. Leuthausel, Germany.**

Pictures: Robinson/'81, Christie Frey/43, B56/1, B89/26.
Comments: Hooper & Co. Trials (G. L. Sclater-Booth).

3BT141. *(Photo: Dr. Leuthausel).*

3BT143.

Coachbuilder:	Barker.
Engine:	E38X.
Delivered:	11/3/37.
Body Style:	Touring limousine.
Registration:	ELF 351.
First Owner:	Frederick William Wignall, UK.
Present Owner:	J. H. Broadbent, UK.

Pictures:
Comments: 20/25 GBJ65 used as trade-in. Car in the USA from 1966 to 1989.

3BT143. *(Photo: Mr. Broadbent).*

3BT145.

Coachbuilder:	Hooper.
Engine:	E28X.
Delivered:	7/7/37.
Body Style:	Limousine.
Design No:	6831.
Body No:	8815.
Registration:	TL 6730.
First Owner:	F. W. Dennis, UK.
Present Owner:	**D. Newton, UK.**

Pictures:
Comments:

3BT145 *(Photo: Mr. Newton).*

3BT147.

Coachbuilder:	Park Ward.
Engine:	E48X.
Delivered:	7/29/37.
Body Style:	Touring saloon.
Body No:	4257.
Registration:	RH 1, LKH 869.
First Owner:	F. Bilton, UK.
Present Owner:	Sir James Cayzer, Bart., UK.

Pictures:
Comments: Ordered without mascot.

3BT147. *(Photo: RREC Photo Library).*

3BT149. *(Photo: Mr. Mills B. Lane).*

Coachbuilder:	Barker.	**3BT149.**
Engine:		E58X.
Delivered:		9/8/37.
Body Style:		Fixed-head sedanca coupé.
Registration:		WYF 111.
First Owner:		T. J. Hughes, UK.
Present Owner:		**W. M. Davis, US.**

Pictures: Oldham/256b, FL/413, FL/731.
Comments: Car renovated by Caffyns, and second spare fitted, 1960. To USA 1961.

3BT151. *(Photo: Mr. Richard Kughn).*

Coachbuilder:	Hooper.	**3BT151.**
Engine:		E88X.
Delivered:		7/12/37.
Body Style:		Sedanca de ville.
Design No:		6778.
Body No:		8808.
Registration:		DYO 333, RJ 500.
First Owner:		H. Wormlieghton, UK.
Present Owner:		For sale, US dealer, 1994.

Pictures: TS/10, FL/298, FL/631, FL/1377.
Comments:

3BT153.

Coachbuilder:	Arthur Mulliner.	**3BT153.**
Engine:		U18H.
Delivered:		4/30/37.
Body Style:		(First) Limousine.
Registration:		Not listed.
First Owner:		Mrs. Ida Szlumper, UK.
Present Owner:		O. K. Nilsson, Sweden.

Pictures:
Comments: Two original sales orders cancelled. Body converted to tourer.

3BT155. *(Photo: Mr. Barrett).*

Coachbuilder:	H. J. Mulliner.	**3BT155.**
Engine:		E68X.
Delivered:		6/30/37.
Body Style:		Saloon with division.
Design No:		Drawing 5899.
Body No:		4518.
Registration:		DYR 699.
First Owner:		D. S. Momand, UK.
Present Owner:		**T. W. Barrett, US.**

Pictures: Phantoms/385, FL/1848, FL/1925.
Comments: Original order by F. Sidney Cotton via Jack Barclay. To USA 1953.

3BT157.   **Coachbuilder:**   Arthur Mulliner.
Engine: V18G.
Delivered: 10/14/37.
Body Style: (First) Limousine.
Registration: CDR 501, 399 GJB.
First Owner: Hans Schowanek, Czechoslovakia.
Present Owner: **T. J. Morey, US.**

Pictures: FL/2743 (Shown).
Comments: Body 2 is Park Ward touring saloon 4196
ex 3AZ52, fitted July, 1946.

3BT157.   *The Park Ward touring saloon.*

3BT159.   **Coachbuilder:**   Barker.
Engine: U28H.
Delivered: 8/21/37.
Body Style: Limousine de ville.
Registration: Not listed.
First Owner: Herman Andrew Harris Lebus, UK.
Present Owner: C. Cussler, US.

Pictures: Phantoms/385, FL/1824.
Comments:

3BT159.   *(Photo: Mr. Cussler).*

3BT161.   **Coachbuilder:**   Inskip.
Engine: U48H.
Delivered: 6/15/37.
Body Style: (First) 5-Passenger limousine.
Registration: Not listed.
First Owner: John T. Paine, US.
Present Owner: C. Bronson, US.

Pictures: deCampi/162.
Comments: Rebodied with Inskip-inspired sedanca
de ville, 1993.

3BT161.   *(Photo: Mr. Mark Tuttle).*

3BT163.   **Coachbuilder:**   Inskip.
Engine: U58H.
Delivered: 6/29/37.
Body Style: Town car.
Body No: 7010.
Registration: Not listed.
First Owner: Walter C. Baker, US.
Present Owner: **A. B. Mitchell, US.**

Pictures: FL/1618, FL183/16.
Comments:

3BT163.   *(Photo: Mr. Mitchell).*

3BT165.

Coachbuilder:	Brewster.	**3BT165.**
Engine:		U58H.
Delivered:		8/4/37.
Body Style:		(First) Newmarket sedan.
Body No:		4037.
Registration:		Not listed.
First Owner:		Federick F. Brewster, US.
Present Owner:		Unknown.

Pictures: deCampi/159 (Shown).
Comments: Newmarket sedan (ex PII 216AMS) exchanged with Inskip sedanca coupé from 3BT129 (Shown) three times. 3BT165 ends up with sedanca coupé, believed to have been destroyed by fire.

3BT167.   *(Photo: Mr. Vonbank).*

Coachbuilder:	Barker:	**3BT167.**
Engine:		U68H.
Delivered:		9/13/37.
Body Style:		Limousine.
Body No:		CPT 251.
Registration:		Charles, 7th Marquess of
First Owner:		Londonderry, UK.
Present Owner:		F. Vonbank, Switzerland.

Pictures: B139/11.
Comments: Ordered without mascot.

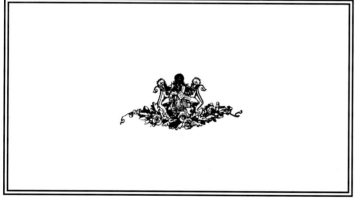

3BT169.

Coachbuilder:	Barker.	**3BT169.**
Engine:		U88H.
Delivered:		9/29/37.
Body Style:		(First) Touring limousine.
Design No:		Drawing E11510.
Registration:		TH 9299, DS 180.
First Owner:		R. D. Elliott, UK.
Present Owner:		M. A. Forte, UK.

Pictures:
Comments: Rebodied with K. W. Bodies tourer.

3BT171. With utility body.   *(Photo: Mr. Bill Dobson).*

Coachbuilder:	Barker.	**3BT171.**
Engine:		(Original) U78H.
Delivered:		9/20/37.
Body Style:		(First) Limousine.
Registration:		EGJ 40.
First Owner:		Colonel Sir Harold Augustus
		Wernher, UK.
Present Owner:		G. Hudson, Australia.

Pictures: P3TS/11.
Comments: Ordered without mascot. Body later converted to utility to accomodate a caliope. Fitted with a B80 engine; now converted to drophead coupé with dickey.

3BT173.

Coachbuilder:	Hooper.
Engine:	U98H.
Delivered:	7/6/37.
Body Style:	Sedanca de ville.
Design No:	6904.
Body No:	8841.
Registration:	AMO 820, BWP 1.
First Owner:	Lt-Colonel Harold Philip Green, UK.
Present Owner:	F. W. Hardach, Germany.

Pictures: FL/777 (Shown).
Comments: Phantom II 84GY and 20/25 GSR30 used as trades-in. New engine and clutch fitted, March 1953.

3BT173.

3BT175.

Coachbuilder:	Hooper.
Engine:	L28Q.
Delivered:	6/24/37.
Body Style:	Cabriolet.
Design No:	6960.
Body No:	8842.
Registration:	*FP F6* Not listed.
First Owner:	R. H. Wagner, UK.
Present Owner:	W. E. Cunny, US.

Pictures: CORR/133 (Shown).
Comments:

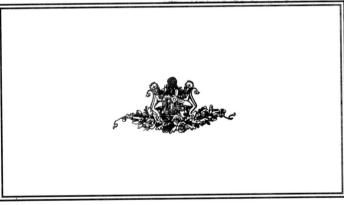
3BT175.

3BT177.

Coachbuilder:	Hooper.
Engine:	K28R.
Delivered:	7/14/37.
Body Style:	Sedanca de ville.
Design No:	6860.
Body No:	8824.
Registration:	Not listed.
First Owner:	Mildred Cecilia, Hon. Lady Charles Montagu, UK.
Present Owner:	G. A. Vaughn, US.

Pictures:
Comments:

3BT177.

BT179.

Coachbuilder:	H. J. Mulliner.
Engine:	K18R.
Delivered:	7/14/37.
Body Style:	Sedanca de ville.
Body No:	4470.
Registration:	DYR 689, CTJ 42, LRU 583.
First Owner:	Hon. Wiliam Gladstone Bethell, UK.
Present Owner:	J. B. Nethercutt, US.

Pictures: FL/272, FL/352.
Comments: J. Barclay Ltd. stock.

3BT179.   *(Photo: Mr. Nethercutt).*

3BT181.   *(Photo: Mr. Brauer).*

Coachbuilder:	Barker	**3BT181.**
Engine:		K38R.
Delivered:		9/6/37.
Body Style:		Sports cabriolet.
Design No:		Drawing F9392.
Body No:		Not listed.
Registration:		Ruling Chief of Keonjhar State,
First Owner:		India.
Present Owner:		**S. F. Brauer, US.**

Pictures: CORR/34, FL/1287.
Comments: Fitted with folding seat on luggage rack for servant.

3BT183.   *(Photo: Mr. Hans Enzler).*

Coachbuilder:	Barker.	**3BT183.**
Engine:		K48R.
Delivered:		7/26/37.
Body Style:		Limousine.
Registration:		Not listed.
First Owner:		Miss Mary E. McOnie, UK.
Present Owner:		T. Ganter, Germany.

Pictures:
Comments: Ordered without mascot.

3BT185.   *(Photo: PIIITS Archives).*

Coachbuilder:	Vanden Plas.	**3BT185.**
Engine:		K68R.
Delivered:		7/9/37.
Body Style:		Cabriolet.
Design No:		1456.
Body No:		3581.
Registration:		Not listed.
First Owner:		Gerneraldirektor Fritz Mandl,
		Austria.
Present Owner:		**T. M. Long, US.**

Pictures: Smith/211, TERR/233.
Comments: Featured in *The Motor*, 3 August 1937.

3BT187.   *(Photo: Mr. Collins).*

Coachbuilder:	Voll & Ruhrbeck.	**3BT187.**
Engine:		D18Y.
Delivered:		5/31/37.
Body Style:		Cabriolet.
Registration:		NOW 149, HZ36100.
First Owner:		Johnkheer J. A. G. Sandberg,
		Netherlands.
Present Owner:		E. B. Collins, US.

Pictures: B144/59, B146/69, FL/436, FL/778.
Comments: Used by British Army on the Rhine, 1946-1953. Imported to US, 1958.

3BT189.

Coachbuilder:	Hooper.
Engine:	K98R.
Delivered:	6/29/37.
Body Style:	Limousine.
Design No:	Design 6273.
Body No:	8800.
Registration:	Not listed.
First Owner:	A. C. Ernst, US.
Present Owner:	K. R. Herlin, US.

Pictures:

Comments: Returned to the UK and sold, Oct. 1948.

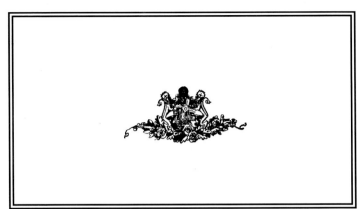

3BT189.

3BT191.

Coachbuilder:	Thrupp & Maberly.
Engine:	L78Q.
Delivered:	8/10/37.
Body Style:	Sedanca de ville.
Design No:	Drawing SLF.1238/A.
Body No:	6653.
Registration:	EUC 7.
First Owner:	D. Stewart Fraser, UK.
Present Owner:	H. N. Cooke, UK (1959).

Pictures: TERR/221 (Shown).

Comments: Original order by Colonel Jacob Schicht, Canada.

3BT191.

3BT193.

Coachbuilder:	Hooper.
Engine:	K78R.
Delivered:	6/30/37.
Body Style:	Limousine.
Design No:	Design 6273.
Body No:	8823.
Registration:	Not listed.
First Owner:	Sir (Joseph) John Jarvis, Bart.MP, UK.
Present Owner:	H. W. Simpson, UK (1955).

Pictures:

Comments: Vice-Regal car in Malaya, 1946-1952. Returned to UK 1954.

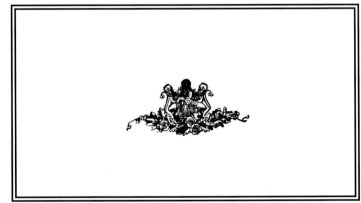

3BT193.

3BT195.

Coachbuilder:	Park Ward.
Engine:	K88R.
Delivered:	6/16/37.
Body Style:	Limousine.
Body No:	4334.
Registration:	DTT 656.
First Owner:	A. C. Ballard, UK.
Present Owner:	J. Poupart, UK (1945).

Pictures: Phantoms/387 (Shown).

Comments: Original order by H. L. Urling Clark via Jack Barclay.

3BT195.

3BT197.   *(Photo: Mr. D. P. McLaren).*

Coachbuilder:	James Young.	**3BT197.**
Engine:		K58R.
Delivered:		7/30/37.
Body Style:		Limousine.
Registration:		BNM 600.
First Owner:		George H. C. Ratcliffe, UK.
Present Owner:		D.E. Coleman, UK.

Pictures:
Comments:

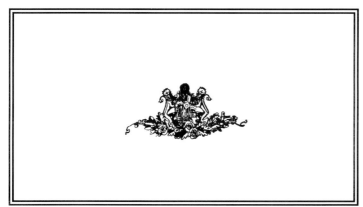

3BT199.

Coachbuilder:	Windovers.	**3BT199.**
Engine:		D38Y.
Delivered:		9/1/37.
Body Style:		6434.
Body No:		Limousine.
Registration:		Not listed.
First Owner:		H. G. Latilla, UK.
Present Owner:		F. Painter & Sons, UK (1961).

Pictures:
Comments:

3BT201.   *(Photo: Mr. Bannister).*

Coachbuilder:	Hooper.	**3BT201.**
Engine:		8/10/37.
Delivered:		Sports saloon.
Body Style:		7002.
Design No:		8859.
Body No:		AHS 79.
Registration:		Thomas Heywood Coats, UK.
First Owner:		H. E. Bannister, UK.
Present Owner:		

Pictures: CORR/133, Oldham/256b, B86/33.
Comments: Ordered without mascot.

3BT203.   *(Photo: Frank Dale and Stepsons).*

Coachbuilder:	H. J. Mulliner.	**3BT203.**
Engine:		D48Y.
Delivered:		7/6/37.
Body Style:		Limousine.
Design No:		Drawing 5941.
Body No:		4512.
Registration:		DTV 700.
First Owner:		A. O. T. Lemon, UK.
Present Owner:		Phillips, UK.

Pictures:
Comments: In Canada, 1959. Returned to UK 1960.

Page 134

The CP Series
of
Phantom III Cars

The CP series consists of
97 cars, numbered even, 3CP2
through 3CP200. Missing are 3CP90, built as
3CM114; 3CP152, built as 3CM104 and 3CP156, built as
3CM106. All CP series cars were delivered in 1937.

3CP2.

Coachbuilder:	Freestone & Webb.	**3CP2.**
Engine:		S38J.
Delivered:		8/23/37.
Body Style:		Saloon with division.
Design No:		1760.
Body No:		1257.
Registration:		Not listed.
First Owner:		Douglas D. James, UK.
Present Owner:		C. L. Kennedy, US.

Pictures: Phantoms/387 (Shown).
Comments: Ordered without mascot. Car sold on behalf of Baroness von Einem. James also owned 3AZ220.

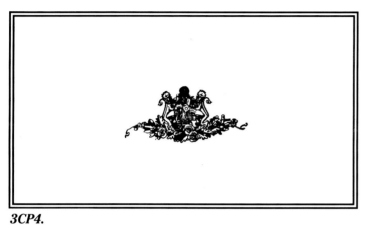

3CP4.

Coachbuilder:	Hooper.	**3CP4.**
Engine:		D78Y.
Delivered:		7/12/37.
Body Style:		Limousine.
Design No:		6443.
Body No:		8836.
Registration:		DLJ 11.
First Owner:		T. Fooks, UK.
Present Owner:		Prince Kretzulesco, Germany.

Pictures:
Comments: Hooper & Co. stock.

3CP6.

Coachbuilder:	Hooper.	**3CP6.**
Engine:		D88Y.
Delivered:		6/26/37.
Body Style:		Limousine.
Design No:		6277.
Body No:		8476.
Registration:		EGC 665.
First Owner:		Sir Cecil Ernest Rolls, Bart, UK.
Present Owner:		**Burned.**

Pictures: Oldham/208g (Shown).
Comments: Body at Olympia Show, 1935, Hooper stand, on a dummy chassis. Hooper Trials. The car eventually burned.

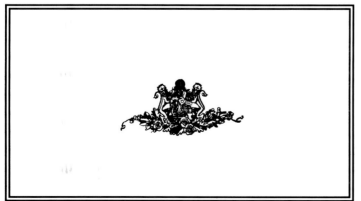

3CP8.

Coachbuilder:	James Young.	**3CP8.**
Engine:		S18J.
Delivered:		7/27/37.
Body Style:		Limousine.
Registration:		BGA 119.
First Owner:		R. L. Douglas, UK.
Present Owner:		Unknown, US.

Pictures:
Comments:

3CP10.
Coachbuilder:	Barker.
Engine:	(Original) S28J.
Delivered:	9/2/37.
Body Style:	Touring limousine.
Registration:	DYX 870.
First Owner:	Colonel Colman, UK (5/38).
Present Owner:	W. Persson, Sweden.

Pictures: Ullyett/53, Garnier/112, Phantoms/387 (Shown).
Comments: Rolls-Royce Ltd. Trials. Road Tested in The Autocar, 15 April 1938. Later fitted with Perkins engine.

3CP10.

3CP12.
Coachbuilder:	Hooper.
Engine:	D58Y.
Delivered:	7/19/37.
Body Style:	Landaulette.
Design No:	Design 6968.
Body No:	8851.
Registration:	EGC 666.
First Owner:	Hon. Samuel Vestey, UK.
Present Owner:	**M. Tuttle, US.**

Pictures: B100/3, B109/6.
Comments: Vestey's father owned 3BT87.

3CP12. *(Photo: Mr. Don Gray).*

3CP14.
Coachbuilder:	Rippon.
Engine:	S48J.
Delivered:	10/29/37.
Body Style:	Limousine.
Registration:	CWT 902.
First Owner:	Mrs. Edith S. Weatherhead, UK (3/38).
Present Owner:	**D. W. G. Richey, US.**

Pictures:
Comments: Rippon Bros. Trials (Major A. Seymour Mead). Woody Richie took over the car after his father's death.

3CP14 *(Photo: Mr. Ritchie).*

3CP16.
Coachbuilder:	Thrupp & Maberly.
Engine:	D68Y.
Delivered:	6/19/37.
Body Style:	Limousine.
Design No:	Drawing SLE.1162/K.
Body No:	6658.
Registration:	Not listed.
First Owner:	Brigadier-General Sir Alfred Cecil Critchley, UK.
Present Owner:	J. H. Nickels, US.

Pictures: P3TS/4 (Shown)
Comments:

3CP16. In 1972.

3CP18.   *(Photo: Mr. Darling).*

Coachbuilder:	Inskip.	**3CP18.**
Engine:		S98J.
Delivered:		7/31/37.
Body Style:		Coupé limousine.
Registration:		Not listed.
First Owner:		Colonel Joseph Samuels, US.
Present Owner:		A. D. Darling, US.

Pictures: TERR/64, DeCampi/158, Auto Quarterly/158, FL/142.
Comments: Body in style of Brewster Henley Roadster. Owned 1940-1953 by Dr. A. H. Rice, who owned 3DL62, new, and 3CM161, used.

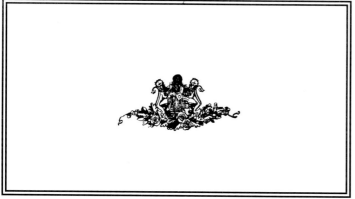

3CP20.   *(Photo: Mr. Mark Tuttle).*

Coachbuilder:	Inskip.	**3CP20.**
Engine:		(Original) C48Z.
Delivered:		9/18/37.
Body Style:		Fixed head coupé.
Registration:		Not listed.
First Owner:		Mrs. Tracy M. Flanagan, US.
Present Owner:		**M. Tuttle, US.**

Pictures: CORR/431, deCampi/159.
Comments: Features sunroof and boot access from passenger compartment. Cadillac engine installed 1955. To be restored with Phantom III V-12 W88F ex 3BT65.

3CP22.

Coachbuilder:	H. J. Mulliner.	**3CP22.**
Engine:		J58S.
Delivered:		8/24/37.
Body Style:		(First) Limousine de ville.
Design No:		5977.
Body No:		4514.
Registration:		EGH 723.
First Owner:		Sir Emsley Carr, UK.
Present Owner:		D. L. Amason, US.

Pictures:
Comments:

3CP24.   *(Photo: Mr. Matthews).*

Coachbuilder:	Hooper.	**3CP24.**
Engine:		S68J.
Delivered:		7/23/37.
Body Style:		Sports limousine.
Design No:		6883.
Body No:		8848.
Registration:		EGC 667.
First Owner:		R. Stevenson Middlemas, UK.
Present Owner:		J. F. Matthews, US.

Pictures: FL/3342, Schrader/152.
Comments:

3CP26.

Coachbuilder:	Barker.
Engine:	J98S.
Delivered:	8/16/37.
Body Style:	Touring limousine.
Design No:	Drawing E11468A.
Body No:	7247.
Registration:	Not listed.
First Owner:	Duchess de Talleyrand, France.
Present Owner:	Unknown.

Pictures:
Comments:

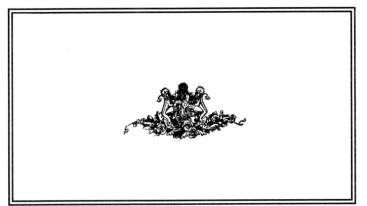
3CP26.

3CP28.

Coachbuilder:	Thrupp & Maberly.
Engine:	S 78J.
Delivered:	6/12/37.
Body Style:	Limousine.
Design No:	Drawing SLE1162.
Body No:	6483.
Registration:	Not listed.
First Owner:	J. Howard Wilson, UK.
Present Owner:	Lord Mayor of Sheffield, UK (1951).

Pictures:
Comments: George Heath Ltd. stock..

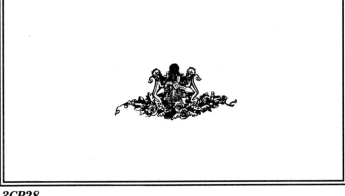
3CP28.

3CP30.

Coachbuilder:	Hooper.
Engine:	S88J.
Delivered:	7/21/37.
Body Style:	(First) Limousine.
Design No:	6443.
Body No:	8834.
Registration:	DYX 861.
First Owner:	Roe Wells, US (4/40).
Present Owner:	A. Monty, UK(1951).

Pictures: RRB 3/38.19 (Shown).
Comments: Rolls~Royce Ltd. trials. Body converted
to sedanca de ville by Inskip. Back to UK, 1949.

3CP30.

3CP32.

Coachbuilder:	Hooper.
Engine:	D98Y.
Delivered:	7/30/37.
Body Style:	Limousine.
Design No:	6642.
Body No:	8849.
Registration:	BGA 111.
First Owner:	D. C. Sloan, UK.
Present Owner:	E. Hind, UK.

Pictures:
Comments:

3CP32. (Photo: Mr. Hind).

3CP34.

Coachbuilder:	Park Ward.	**3CP34.**
Engine:		J68S.
Delivered:		6/21/37.
Body Style:		Touring limousine.
Body No:		4292.
Registration:		JB 1.
First Owner:		King Carol II, Romania.
Present Owner:		V. Prassa, Romania (1948).

Pictures: Oliver/116, Phantoms/388 (Shown).
Comments: Jack Barclay Ltd. Trials. King Carol also owned 3AZ50.

3CP36.   *(Photo: RROC Foundation).*

Coachbuilder:	Inskip.	**3CP36.**
Engine:		S58J.
Delivered:		11/4/37.
Body Style:		5-Passenger sedan.
Registration:		Not listed.
First Owner:		Mrs. George W. Robertson, US.
Present Owner:		**R. T. Parker, US.**

Pictures: deCampi/163, FL/382, FL/1097.
Comments:

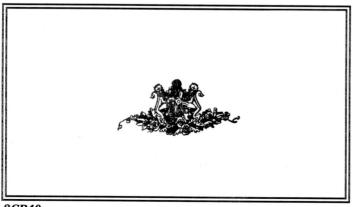

3CP38. The Freestone & Webb body.

Coachbuilder:	W. S. Atcherley.	**3CP38.**
Engine:		J18S.
Delivered:		9/6/37.
Body Style:		(First) Limousine.
Registration:		FOY 1.
First Owner:		J. M. Nicholson, UK.
Present Owner:		**R. Sinicki, US.**

Pictures: Brookland/52, FL/1724, TERR/83 (Shown)
Comments: Rebodied with Freestone & Webb sedanca de ville 1353, 1946. Car in South Africa, 1957. Sedanca coachwork features extensive use of copper.

3CP40.

Coachbuilder:	Barker.	**3CP40.**
Engine:		J48S.
Delivered:		9/24/37.
Body Style:		Touring limousine.
Registration:		Not listed.
First Owner:		Dr. James Craig Joyner, US.
Present Owner:		R. Hawkins, US.

Pictures:
Comments: J. S. Inskip Inc. stock. Returned to UK and for sale via George Newman Ltd. 1948.

3CP42.

Coachbuilder:	Hooper.
Engine:	J38S.
Delivered:	8/5/37.
Body Style:	Limousine.
Design No:	Design 6273.
Body No:	8798.
Registration:	Not listed.
First Owner:	Leonard Thompson, UK.
Present Owner:	C. L. Puckett, US.

Pictures:
Comments:

3CP42.

3CP44.

Coachbuilder:	Windovers.
Engine:	J78S.
Delivered:	7/15/37.
Body Style:	Limousine.
Body No:	6461.
Registration:	DYN 424.
First Owner:	J. J. Barrie, UK.
Present Owner:	D. G. Heyn, US.

Pictures:
Comments: 3BT11 bears a similar body.

3CP44.

3CP46.

Coachbuilder:	Hooper.
Engine:	(Original) T58J.
Delivered:	8/30/37.
Body Style:	Limousine.
Design No:	6443.
Body No:	8870.
Registration:	EGO 128.
First Owner:	Mrs. F. M. Floyd, UK.
Present Owner:	D. R. Goodwin, UK.

Pictures: P3TS/30 (Not reproducible).
Comments: Hooper & Co. stock. Phantom II 15JS used as trade-in. Later fitted with Bentley 4 1/4-litre engine.

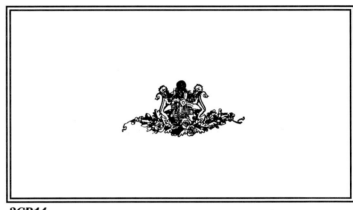

3CP46. *(Photo: Mr. Leverton).*

3CP48.

Coachbuilder:	Barker.
Engine:	R98K.
Delivered:	10/22/37.
Body Style:	Sedanca de ville.
Design No:	Drawing C11551.
Registration:	EXE 243.
First Owner:	Mrs. Sally L. Bondy, France (3/38).
Present Owner:	Atwell family, US.

Pictures: Phantoms/388, FL/925.
Comments: Barker & Co. stock.

3CP48. When owned by Dr. Sher. (Photo: RROC Foundation).

3CP50. *When owned by Dr. Shoup. (Photo: RROC Foundation).*

Coachbuilder:	Inskip.	**3CP50.**
Engine:		(Original) J28S.
Delivered:		7/15/37.
Body Style:		Touring limousine.
Registration:		Not listed.
First Owner:		Jeff J. Grey Jr., US.
Present Owner:		E. Webster, Canada.

Pictures: deCampi/163, P/1256, FL/51, FL/1287.
Comments: Body copy of Barker. Engine exchanged with X98E from 3BT9.

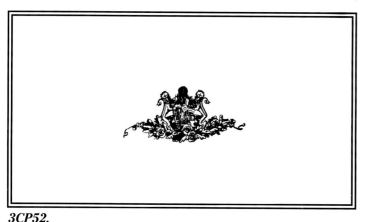

3CP52.

Coachbuilder:	Park Ward.	**3CP52.**
Engine:		(Original) C38Z.
Delivered:		7/22/37.
Body Style:		Limousine.
Design No:		Drawing 12616.
Body No:		4302.
Registration:		DYX 867.
First Owner:		Harold C. Drayton, UK.
Present Owner:		Heck, US.

Pictures:
Comments: Sunbeam 20HP used as trade-in. Engine removed and replaced with non-R-R engine by 1988.

3CP54.   *(Photo: Mr. Mark Tuttle).*

Coachbuilder:	Gurney Nutting.	**3CP54.**
Engine:		C28Z.
Delivered:		4/4/37.
Body Style:		Sedanca de ville.
Registration:		Not listed.
First Owner:		A. C. Morgan, UK.
Present Owner:		D. Theil, US.

Pictures:
Comments: HR Owen Ltd. stock. Car in Malaya, 1950's.

3CP56.   *(Photo: Mr. Bourchier).*

Coachbuilder:	Gurney Nutting.	**3CP56.**
Engine:		(Original) C18Z.
Delivered:		9/10/37.
Body Style:		Sports saloon with division.
Registration:		ASR 902.
First Owner:		R. G. Sharp, UK.
Present Owner:		C. D. Bourchier, UK.

Pictures: B73/36, FL/4127.
Comments: Originally ordered by F. Kerr. H. R. Owen Ltd. stock. Later fitted with B80 engine 667MK1.

3CP58. Coachbuilder: Park Ward.
Engine: C58Z.
Delivered: 7/14/37.
Body Style: Limousine.
Design No: Drawing 12804.
Body No: 4360.
Registration: DYH 1.
First Owner: Isaac Wannop Lamonby, UK.
Present Owner: C. Wells, US.

Pictures: FL/2839 (Shown).
Comments: 20/25 GTZ25 used as trade-in.

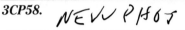

3CP58.

3CP60. Coachbuilder: Barker.
Engine: J88S.
Delivered: 10/7/37.
Body Style: Touring limousine.
Registration: UD 9009, LEL 159.
First Owner: Oliver Vernon Watney, UK.
Present Owner: Group Capt. J. S. Laird, UK (1967).

Pictures: TERR/56 (Shown).
Comments:

3BT60.

3CP62. Coachbuilder: Gurney Nutting.
Engine: C68Z.
Delivered: 2/8/38.
Body Style: Sports sedanca de ville.
Registration: ELL 584, ROH 1.
First Owner: (Cedric) Treherne Thomas, UK.
Present Owner: Matsuda Collection, Japan.

Pictures: TERR/94, TS/15.
Comments: Thomas also owned 3AX31.

3CP62. (Photo: D. S. Archives).

3CP64. Coachbuilder: Park Ward.
Engine: C98Z.
Delivered: 7/17/37.
Body Style: (First) Limousine.
Body No: 4320.
Registration: Not listed.
First Owner: F. C. Burgess, UK.
Present Owner: J. D. M. Pridmore, UK.

Pictures:
Comments: Park Ward stock. Rebodied with coupé.

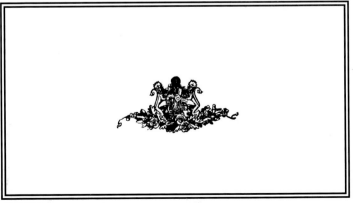

3CP64.

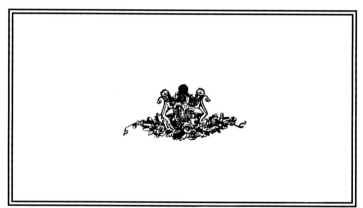
3CP66.

Coachbuilder:	Mann Egerton.	**3CP66.**
Engine:		C88Z.
Delivered:		8/30/37.
Body Style:		Limousine.
Registration:		Not listed.
First Owner:		B. H. Binder, UK.
Present Owner:	State Hire Service, UK (1947).	

Pictures:
Comments: Mann Egerton Ltd. stock.

3CP68.

Coachbuilder:	Park Ward.	**3CP68.**
Engine:		R28K.
Delivered:		8/11/37.
Body Style:		Limousine.
Body No:		4321.
Registration:		EYP 488.
First Owner:	Miss Mary Van Fleck Lidgerwood, UK (6/38).	
Present Owner:		Unknown.

Pictures:
Comments: Jack Barclay Ltd. stock. For sale in US, 1991; believed sold to UK.

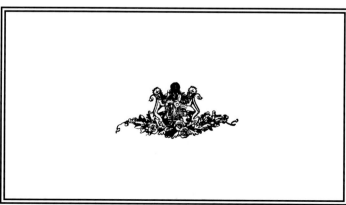
3CP70.

Coachbuilder:	Barker.	**3CP70.**
Engine:		B18B.
Delivered:		10/15/37.
Body Style:		Limousine.
Design No:		Drawing E11576A.
Registration:		EGO 126.
First Owner:		H. K. M. Kindersley, UK.
Present Owner:		G. W. Cadman, Canada.

Pictures: Phantoms/389 (Shown).
Comments:

3CP72.

Coachbuilder:	Arthur Mulliner.	**3CP72.**
Engine:		R58K.
Delivered:		10/26/37.
Body Style:		Limousine.
Registration:		ELF 357, DAK 820.
First Owner:		Arthur Waddilove, UK.
Present Owner:		R. A. Harvey, UK.

Pictures:
Comments: Earl's Court Show, 1937, Arthur Mulliner stand. 25/30 GWN81 used as trade-in.

3CP74.
Coachbuilder: H. J. Mulliner.
Engine: R88K.
Delivered: 8/27/37.
Body Style: Limousine.
Design No: Drawing 5978.
Body No: 4519.
Registration: S 3088.
First Owner: Mrs. Norah Kathleen Clark, UK.
Present Owner: K. R. Smith, US.

Pictures:
Comments: John Croall Ltd. stock.

3CP74. *(Photo: RROC Foundation).*

3CP76.
Coachbuilder: Thrupp & Maberly.
Engine: C78Z.
Delivered: 7/13/37.
Body Style: Limousine.
Design No: Drawing SLE.1162.
Body No: 6654.
Registration: ELD 678.
First Owner: W. Wilhelmsen, UK.
Present Owner: R. Mookerjee, India.
Pictures: B168/64, TERR/221 (Shown).
Comments: Rootes Ltd. stock. To India, 1938.

3CP76.

3CP78.
Coachbuilder: Hooper.
Engine: R38K.
Delivered: 8/9/37.
Body Style: Limousine.
Design No: 6850.
Body No: 8850.
Registration: Not listed.
First Owner: Dr. J. W. French, UK.
Present Owner: Unknown.

Pictures:
Comments:

3CP78. *(Photo: Science Museum, London).*

3CP80.
Coachbuilder: Rippon.
Engine: R48K.
Delivered: 9/13/37.
Body Style: Limousine.
Registration: CWX 65, 844 HWR.
First Owner: Mary, Mrs. Edward L. Field, UK.
Present Owner: Estate of the late E. C. Lindsey, US.

Pictures: Schrader/130.
Comments: Rippon Bros. stock.

3CP80. *(Photo: Mrs. Lindsey).*

3CP82.   *(Photo: Lawrence Dalton Collection).*

Coachbuilder:	H. J. Mulliner.	**3CP82.**
Engine:		R68K..
Delivered:		7/26/37.
Body Style:		Saloon with division.
Body No:		4434.
Registration:		BUU 700.
First Owner:		G. J. Dawson, UK.
Present Owner:		J. E. Matches, Australia.

Pictures: Bennett/35, P/103.
Comments: Car Mart Ltd. stock. Shipped to Australia 1958.

3CP84.

Coachbuilder:	Barker.	**3CP84.**
Engine:		H28U.
Delivered:		11/26/37.
Body Style:		Limousine.
Registration:		873 HPX.
First Owner:		Mrs. E. M. deV Harvey, UK.
Present Owner:		R. F. Lorkowski, US.

Pictures: Auto Quarterly/256, Oldham/256b (Shown).
Comments: To USA, 1966. Car severely damaged by fire, 1962. Chassis only.

3CP86. The Franay saloon.

Coachbuilder:	Barker.	**3CP86.**
Engine:		R78K.
Delivered:		10/4/37.
Body Style:		(First) Cabriolet de ville.
Registration:		EGJ 44.
First Owner:		Rt. Hon. Sir Philip Albert Sassoon, Bart, MP, UK.
Present Owner:		Polk, US.

Pictures: TERR/54, Oldham/156b, FL/330, FL/1335 (Shown).
Comments: Rebodied with Franay saloon.

3CP88.   *(Photo: Mr. Gorjat).*

Coachbuilder:	Binder.	**3CP88.**
Engine:		H38U.
Delivered:		10/12/37.
Body Style:		Saloon with division.
Registration:		570 EGX.
First Owner:		Herman Cron, Germany.
Present Owner:		J. M. Gorjat, US.

Pictures: TS/17, FL/400, FL/3468.
Comments: In Switzerland during World War II. To UK, 1948.

3CP90 built as 3CM114.

3CP92.   **Coachbuilder:**   Hooper.
Engine: H58U.
Delivered: 8/30/97.
Body Style: Limousine.
Design No: 6273.
Body No: 8799.
Registration: Not listed.
First Owner: Mrs. H. G. Travers, US.
Present Owner: F. Payne, US.
Pictures: FL/255 (Not reproducible).
Comments: Hooper & Co. stock.

3CP92.

3CP94.   **Coachbuilder:**   Barker.
Engine: H68U.
Delivered: 11/4/37.
Body Style: Touring limousine.
Registration: ELF 352.
First Owner: Sir Frederick Albert Minter, UK.
Present Owner: J. H. Bright, UK.

Pictures:
Comments: 25/30 GUL22 used as trade-in.

3CP94.   *(Photo: Coys of Kensington).*

3CP96.   **Coachbuilder:**   Gurney Nutting.
Engine: H48U.
Delivered: 8/27/37.
Body Style: Limousine de ville.
Registration: ELK 131.
First Owner: Arthur Sainsbury, UK.
Present Owner: E. G. Mausolf, US.

Pictures: CORR/87, FL/721.
Comments: Jack Barclay Ltd. stock. Sainsbury also owned 3AZ48. To USA 1960.

3CP96.   *(Photo: Ted Reich Archives).*

3CP98.

Coachbuilder:	Park Ward.	**3CP98.**
Engine:		(Original) H78U.
Delivered:		9/27/37.
Body Style:		4-Light limousine.
Body No:		4366.
Registration:		Not listed.
First Owner:		A. Colin Kingham, UK.
Present Owner:		M. E. Bacon, US.

Pictures:
Comments: Park Ward & Co. stock. Engine owned by J. B. Nethercutt, US, as spare.

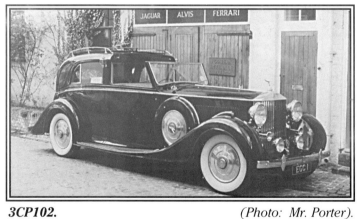

3CP100.

Coachbuilder:	Hooper.	**3CP100.**
Engine:		C98A.
Delivered:		8/16/37.
Body Style:		Limousine.
Design No:		6273.
Body No:		8882.
Registration:		Not listed.
First Owner:		Governor of Bombay, Sir (Lawrence) Roger Lumley, India.
Present Owner:		J. G. L. Spence, India (1951).

Pictures: Phantoms/389, RRB12.37/24 (Shown).
Comments:

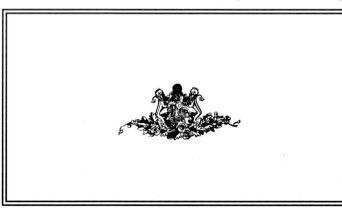

3CP102.   *(Photo: Mr. Porter).*

Coachbuilder:	Arthur Mulliner.	**3CP102.**
Engine:		H88U.
Delivered:		9/15/37.
Body Style:		Sedanca de ville.
Registration:		EGC 1.
First Owner:		Raymond Way, UK.
Present Owner:		J. G. Porter, UK.

Pictures: Phantoms/396.
Comments: Arthur Mulliner Ltd. stock. Featured in *The Motor*, 22 March 1938.

3CP104.

Coachbuilder:	Thrupp & Maberly.	**3CP104.**
Engine:		H98U.
Delivered:		7/27/37.
Body Style:		Sedanca de ville.
Design No:		Drawing SLE.1252.
Body No:		6634.
Registration:		ELA 504.
First Owner:		Major Colin Cooper, UK.
Present Owner:		F. J. Burnett, UK (1964).

Pictures:
Comments: Car Mart Ltd. stock.

3CP106.

Coachbuilder:	Hooper.
Engine:	C18A.
Delivered:	9/16/37.
Body Style:	Limousine.
Design No:	6443.
Body No:	8872.
Registration:	Not listed.
First Owner:	Henry McSweeney, US.
Present Owner:	E. Holzer, US.

Pictures: FL/3095 (Shown).
Comments: Original order by Joseph Cockshoot Ltd. as stock. Sold to Hooper & Co. as stock, July 1937.

3CP106.

3CP108.

Coachbuilder:	H. J. Mulliner.
Engine:	C38A.
Delivered:	9/1/37.
Body Style:	Saloon with division.
Design No:	Drawing 5937.
Body No:	4506.
Registration:	EGO 700.
First Owner:	Sir Francis Henry Granville Peek, Bart, UK.
Present Owner:	R. J. Depraetre, Belgium.

Pictures:
Comments: Jack Barclay Ltd. stock. Owned by George Formby, July 1938.

3CP108.   *(Photo: D. S. Archives).*

3CP110.

Coachbuilder:	Barker.
Engine:	C48A.
Delivered:	9/22/37.
Body Style:	Landaulet.
Registration:	Not listed.
First Owner:	Sir John Latta, Bart, UK.
Present Owner:	R. Marmoud, Switzerland (1960).

Pictures: Bird.
Comments: Latta also owned 3AX97, with a duplicate body. To Switzerland by 1950.

3CP110.   *(Photo: National Motor Museum, England).*

3CP112.

Coachbuilder:	Windovers.
Engine:	C58A.
Delivered:	6/22/37.
Body Style:	Sports saloon.
Body No:	6465.
Registration:	Not listed.
First Owner:	Maj. Gen. Sir Pratapsingh, Prince of Baroda, India.
Present Owner:	Unknown.

Pictures: B137/25, CORR/358 (Shown).
Comments: The Maharajah of Baroda owned 3BU106, said to have been upholstered at one time with leopard skins from animals he shot. The Maharanee owned 3AX201.

3CP112.

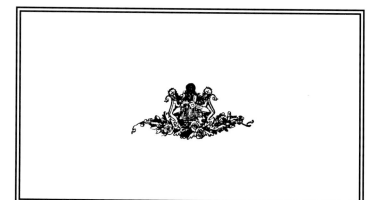

3CP114.

Coachbuilder:	Binder.	**3CP114.**
Engine:		C28A.
Delivered:		11/26/37.
Body Style:		Fixed-head cabriolet.
Registration:		Not listed.
First Owner:		N. Zographos, France.
Present Owner:		Unknown, US.

Pictures:
Comments: Paris Salon, 1937, Binder stand.

3CP116.   *(Photo: RROC Foundation).*

Coachbuilder:	Windovers.	**3CP116.**
Engine:		C68A.
Delivered:		2/16/38.
Body Style:		Cabriolet.
Design No:		6483.
Body No:		Not listed.
Registration:		Prince Azam Jah Berar of
First Owner:		Hyderbad, India.
Present Owner:		Dr. J. de Lacerda, Portugal.

Pictures: Bird/264, B137/8, B157/6.
Comments: Featured in *The Autocar*, 4 March 1938 and *The Motor*, 19 April 1938. Body amended by Hooper, c.1948. Currently in Museu do Caramulo, Portugal.

3CP118. Second body.   *(Photo: RROC Foundation).*

Coachbuilder:	Franay.	**3CP118.**
Engine:		C78A.
Delivered:		10/25/37.
Body Style:		(First) Limousine.
Registration:		Not listed.
First Owner:		Mme. E. Laguerre, France.
Present Owner:		Alfonso, Mexico.

Pictures: PIIITS/17.
Comments: Paris Salon, 1937. Owner 2: Pacha Marrakesh. Rebodied with Freestone & Webb coupé 1634, 1953.

3CP120.   *(Photo: Stuckey Collection).*

Coachbuilder:	Hooper.	**3CP120.**
Engine:		R18K.
Delivered:		9/23/37.
Body Style:		Limousine.
Design No:		6443.
Body No:		8871.
Registration:		ELF 360, VYN 513, AUY 10, APU 668 A.
First Owner:		F. Warren Pearl, UK.
Present Owner:		F. A. Frederick/ J. D. Lloyd, UK.

Pictures: B173/14, Phantoms\390.
Comments: Rolls-Royce Ltd. stock. Shipped to USA, returned to UK 1988.

3CP122.

Coachbuilder:	H. J. Mulliner.
Engine:	B28B.
Delivered:	9/6/37.
Body Style:	4-Light saloon with division.
Design No:	Drawing 5992.
Body No:	4525.
Registration:	BDW 1.
First Owner:	G. H. Latham, UK.
Present Owner:	W. P. Steinemann, Switzerland.

Pictures:

Comments:

3CP122.   *(Photo: Mr. Hans Enzler).*

3CP124.

Coachbuilder:	Inskip.
Engine:	T38J.
Delivered:	10/7/37.
Body Style:	(First) Limousine.
Registration:	Not listed.
First Owner:	Margaret, Mrs. D. A. Dunlop, US.
Present Owner:	For sale, UK dealer, 1993.

Pictures: CORR/431, deCampi/158, FL/130, FL/175.
Comments: Body to 3BU100, and rebodied with new Inskip close-coupled coupé, Feb. 1940.

3CP124. With coupé body.   *(Photo: Dr. James Stickley).*

3CP126.

Coachbuilder:	Hooper.
Engine:	B88B.
Delivered:	9/4/37.
Body Style:	Sports saloon.
Design No:	7052.
Body No:	8886.
Registration:	DKC 444.
First Owner:	W. Milligan, UK.
Present Owner:	For sale, UK Dealer, 1994.

Pictures: BA111/2.
Comments:

3CP126.   *(Photo: Mr. Mark Tuttle).*

3CP128.

Coachbuilder:	Park Ward.
Engine:	B58B.
Delivered:	9/18/37.
Body Style:	Touring limousine.
Body No:	4309.
Registration:	EGO 710.
First Owner:	V. Jobson, UK.
Present Owner:	Governor of Kibali-Ituri Province, Congo (1963).

Pictures: B168/67, FL/897 (Shown).
Comments: Jack Barclay Ltd. stock. In Uganda, 1959.

3CP128.

3CP130.

Coachbuilder:	Hooper.	**3CP130.**
Engine:		B48B.
Delivered:		10/28/37.
Body Style:		Sedanca de ville.
Design No:		7060.
Body No:		8890.
Registration:		DPO 900.
First Owner:		Miss Annie Jeffery, UK.
Present Owner:		W. P. White, US.

Pictures: Phantoms/391, FL/607 (Shown).
Comments: Hooper & Co. stock. Earl's Court Show, 1937, Hooper stand. Miss Jeffery also owned 3BU126.

3CP132.   *(Photo: Mr. Stevens).*

Coachbuilder:	Inskip.	**3CP132.**
Engine:		B68B.
Delivered:		1/8/38.
Body Style:		Limousine.
Registration:		Not listed.
First Owner:		Mrs. Albert J. Rhodes, US.
Present Owner:		**E. S. Stevens, US.**

Pictures:
Comments: For sale, June 1952, for $2,975, with a mileage of 33,000. The car was bought by Mr. Stevens' father in 1955 and has been in the family since then.

3CP134. With first body.   *(Photo: D. S. Archives).*

Coachbuilder:	Vanden Plas.	**3CP134.**
Engine:		B78B.
Delivered:		9/20/37.
Body Style:		(First) Drophead coupé.
Design No:		1379.
Body No:		3596.
Registration:		DKC 2.
First Owner:		Lawrence Durning Holt, UK.
Present Owner:		A. Warhol, US.

Pictures: TERR/233.
Comments: Rebodied as estate car after 1959.

3CP136.   *(Photo: Mr. Palfreyman).*

Coachbuilder:	Hooper.	**3CP136.**
Engine:		T18J.
Delivered:		12/3/37.
Body Style:		Limousine.
Design No:		6443.
Body No:		8930.
Registration:		ELF 358.
First Owner:		W. Graham Mutter, UK.
Present Owner:		M. T. Palfreyman, UK.

Pictures:
Comments: Being restored by Mr. Palfreyman.

3CP138. **Coachbuilder:** Barker.
Engine: T68J.
Delivered: 10/27/37.
Body Style: Sedanca de ville.
Registration: 300 CWF.
First Owner: Samuel Storey MP, UK.
Present Owner: Sir Richard Storey, Bart, UK.

Pictures:
Comments: Car in USA for some years. Current owner son of original owner.

3CP138. *(Photo: Sir Richard Storey).*

3CP140. **Coachbuilder:** Erdmann & Rossi.
Engine: B38B.
Delivered: 3/31/38.
Body Style: Limousine.
Registration: Not listed.
First Owner: Hans W. Behrens, Germany.
Present Owner: J. P. Pla, Spain (1947).

Pictures:
Comments:

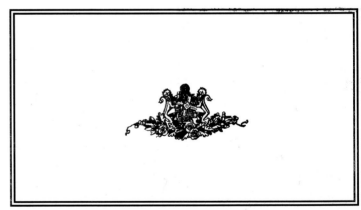

3CP140.

3CP142. **Coachbuilder:** Gurney Nutting.
Engine: T28J.
Delivered: 11/2/37.
Body Style: (First) Saloon.
Registration: EGO 130.
First Owner: Hubert C. Scott-Paine, UK.
Present Owner: Earl of Shrewsbury & Waterford, UK (1953).

Pictures:
Comments: Swapped body transferred to 3DL122, 1953.

3CP142.

3CP144. **Coachbuilder:** Vesters & Nierinck.
Engine: T48J.
Delivered: 2/5/38.
Body Style: 2-Door saloon.
Registration: M 6055219.
First Owner: Jean Francqui, Belgium.
Present Owner: **D. McCorkindale, US.**

Pictures: B111/36, FL/1074.
Comments: Brussels Show, 1938. Used by British Army on the Rhine, 1950.

3CP144. *(Photo: Mr. McCorkindale).*

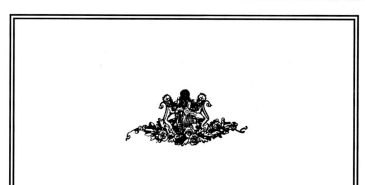

3CP146.

Coachbuilder:	H. J. Mulliner. **3CP146.**
Engine:	C88A.
Delivered:	9/21/37.
Body Style:	Saloon with division.
Design No:	Drawing 5937.
Body No:	4472.
Registration:	EJJ 20.
First Owner:	S. J. Field, Australia.
Present Owner:	**Probably Scrapped.**
Pictures:	

Comments: Jack Barclay Ltd. stock. Shipped to New York, driven to California, shipped to Sydney. Involved in accident with bus and written off. Body and gearbox to 3AZ204.

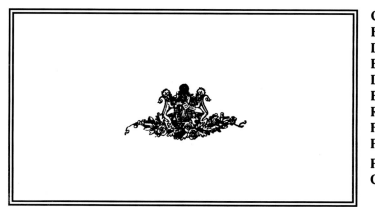

3CP148.

Coachbuilder:	Hooper. **3CP148.**
Engine:	B98B.
Delivered:	11/29/37.
Body Style:	Limousine.
Design No:	6443.
Body No:	8929.
Registration:	BGB 752.
First Owner:	Charles Marchant, UK.
Present Owner:	Unknown, UK (1977).
Pictures:	
Comments:	

3CP150.   *(Photo: RREC Photo Library).*

Coachbuilder:	Thrupp & Maberly. **3CP150.**
Engine:	T78J.
Delivered:	10/8/37.
Body Style:	Sports limousine.
Design No:	Drawing SLE.1245/F.
Body No:	6748.
Registration:	DT 9343.
First Owner:	Enos Smith, UK.
Present Owner:	Major Gollan, UK (1957).
Pictures:	

Comments: Earl's Court Show, 1937, Thrupp & Maberly stand.

3CP152 built as 3CM104.

3CP154.

Coachbuilder:	Barker.
Engine:	M98Q.
Delivered:	11/2/37.
Body Style:	Limousine.
Registration:	EGJ 50.
First Owner:	Mrs. R. J. Blackler, UK.
Present Owner:	**W. J. Blenko, US.**

Pictures: FL/1123 (Shown, at arrow).
Comments: Body duplicate of Barker's 1937 Earl's Court car.

3CP154.   *(Photo: Taken at Missouri Valley meet, 1969).*

3CP156 built as 3CM106.

3CP158.

Coachbuilder:	Vanvooren.
Engine:	M18Q.
Delivered:	12/12/38.
Body Style:	(First) Sedanca de ville.
Registration:	EYX 370.
First Owner:	Colonel Edward Treffry, UK (8/39).
Present Owner:	C. A. Baron, UK.

Pictures: TERR/301, FL/1202.
Comments: Paris Salon, 1937. Original order by André M. Embiricos, but cancelled. Phantom II used as trade-in by Treffry. Converted to limousine, 1939.

3CP158. As converted.   *(Photo: Mr. Cookson).*

3CP160.

Coachbuilder:	Rippon.
Engine:	M48Q.
Delivered:	10/27/37.
Body Style:	Pullman limousine.
Registration:	A 8281.
First Owner:	Roger Charlton Parr, UK.
Present Owner:	Middleton & Wood Ltd., UK (1948).

Pictures: Garnier/108 (Interior only).
Comments: Earl's Court Show, 1937, Rippon stand.

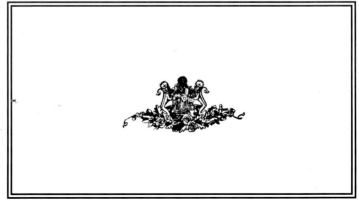

3CP160.

3CP162.   *(Photo: Mr. Peake).*

Coachbuilder:	H. J. Mulliner.	**3CP162.**
Engine:		M28Q.
Delivered:		9/22/37.
Body Style:		Sedanca de ville.
Design No:		Drawing 5960.
Body No:		4529.
Registration:		MG 5513, KMN 3.
First Owner:	Lt. Colonel James Nockells-Horlick, UK.	
Present Owner:		G. Peake, UK.

Pictures:
Comments:

3CP164.   *(Photo: The Real Car Company, England).*

Coachbuilder:	Windovers.	**3CP164.**
Engine:		M38Q.
Delivered:		10/26/37.
Body Style:		Limousine.
Body No:		6480.
Registration:		EGW 655.
First Owner:	William Parkinson, UK.	
Present Owner:		P. D. Wardley.

Pictures: BA108/8 (Shown).
Comments: Earl's Court Show, 1937, Windovers stand. Parkinson also owned 3CM173. To UK from USA, 1991. For sale *The Flying Lady*, 1992.

3CP166.   *(Photo: Mr. Bourchier).*

Coachbuilder:	Barker.	**3CP166.**
Engine:		M68Q.
Delivered:		11/18/37.
Body Style:		Touring limousine.
Body No:		7341.
Registration:		EGJ 39.
First Owner:	Ralph L. Jump, UK.	
Present Owner:	C. D. Bourchier, UK.	

Pictures: Sotheby/'91.
Comments:

3CP168.

Coachbuilder:	Barker.	**3CP168.**
Engine:		M58Q.
Delivered:		11/24/37.
Body Style:		Limousine.
Registration:		GS 7577.
First Owner:	Major D. Mirrielees, UK.	
Present Owner:	T. W. Hughes, US.	

Pictures:
Comments:

3CP170.

Coachbuilder:	Hooper.
Engine:	M78Q.
Delivered:	9/29/37.
Body Style:	Sedanca de ville.
Design No:	6928.
Body No:	8905.
Registration:	Not listed.
First Owner:	Mrs. Olive Tudor-Hart, UK.
Present Owner:	Davis, US.

Pictures:
Comments:

3CP170.

3CP172.

Coachbuilder:	H. J. Mulliner.
Engine:	M88Q.
Delivered:	10/26/37.
Body Style:	Sedanca de ville.
Body No:	4530.
Registration:	EGT 6.
First Owner:	C. J. Donada, UK.
Present Owner:	**I. James, UK.**

Pictures: Ullyett/53, Phantoms/391.
Comments: Earl's Court Show, 1937, H. J. Mulliner stand.

3CP172. *(Photo: RREC Photo Library).*

3CP174.

Coachbuilder:	Windovers.
Engine:	A18C.
Delivered:	12/23/37.
Body Style:	Limousine.
Body No:	6499.
Registration:	Not listed.
First Owner:	C. W. Evans, UK.
Present Owner:	**C. L. Larson, US.**

Pictures:
Comments: Windovers Ltd. stock. Car in Jamaica, 1950's-1971.

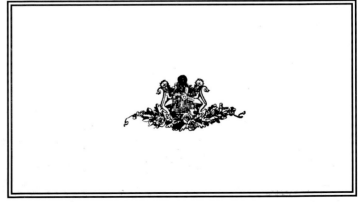
3CP174. *(Photo: Mr. Larson).*

3CP176.

Coachbuilder:	Arthur Mulliner.
Engine:	A38C.
Delivered:	9/29/37.
Body Style:	Limousine.
Registration:	559 HYX, JJH 1.
First Owner:	B. Westall, UK.
Present Owner:	F. M. Wilcock, UK.

Pictures:
Comments: Arthur Mulliner Ltd. stock. Chassis only, 1981.

3CP176.

3CP178.

Coachbuilder:	Barker.	**3CP178.**
Engine:		A28C.
Delivered:		11/10/37.
Body Style:		Sedanca de ville.
Registration:		EGJ 48.
First Owner:		G. S. Engle, UK.
Present Owner:		M. O. Johnson, US.

Pictures: FL/4189 (Shown).
Comments:

3CP180.   *(Photo: Mr. Gartner via RROC).*

Coachbuilder:	Hooper.	**3CP180.**
Engine:		A48C.
Delivered:		11/25/37.
Body Style:		Landaulet.
Design No:		6660.
Body No:		8943.
Registration:		EYV 212.
First Owner:		Leonora Margaret, Countess of Inchcape, UK.
Present Owner:		J. Reich, Switzerland.

Pictures:
Comments:

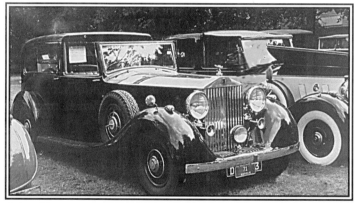

3CP182.   *(Photo: Mr. Adrian West).*

Coachbuilder:	Windovers.	**3CP182.**
Engine:		(Original) A58C.
Delivered:		10/22/37.
Body Style:		Limousine de ville.
Body No:		6502.
Registration:		DXO 773.
First Owner:		Sir Frederick Henry Richmond, Bart, UK.
Present Owner:		C. Raabe, US.

Pictures:
Comments: Windovers Ltd. stock. Later fitted with engine G88V ex 3BT31.

3CP184.   *(Photo: Dr. Cook).*

Coachbuilder:	Barker.	**3CP184.**
Engine:		A98C.
Delivered:		11/4/37.
Body Style:		Limousine de ville.
Registration:		RXB 750.
First Owner:		Mme Jacob Schick, Canada.
Present Owner:		R. A. Cook, US.

Pictures: Oldham/256c.
Comments: Earl's Court Show, 1937, Barker stand.

3CP186.
Coachbuilder:	Barker.
Engine:	A68C.
Delivered:	11/5/37.
Body Style:	Sedanca de ville.
Design No:	Drawing E11575.
Registration:	CWR 450.
First Owner:	Frederick Smith, UK.
Present Owner:	S. G. Thompson, UK.

Pictures: Oldham/256c, Hughes/18, Hughes/96.
Comments: Earl's Court Show, 1937, Rolls-Royce stand. Owned by Lord Mayor of London, 1962.

3CP186. *(Photo: Mr. Thompson).*

3CP188.
Coachbuilder:	Hooper.
Engine:	A78C.
Delivered:	11/1/37.
Body Style:	Limousine.
Design No:	6443.
Body No:	8835.
Registration:	ELP 86.
First Owner:	Lady Georgina Griggs, UK.
Present Owner:	Excess Insurance Co., UK (1951).

Pictures: Phantoms/392 (Shown).
Comments:

3CP188.

3CP190.
Coachbuilder:	Windovers.
Engine:	(Original) S28K.
Delivered:	11/8/37.
Body Style:	(First) Brougham de ville.
Body No:	6503.
Registration:	ELH 613.
First Owner:	Lionel, 6th Earl of Portarlington, UK.
Present Owner:	**K. F. Erbrecht, Germany.**

Pictures: B111/5, B127/10, B133/45, CORR/359 (Shown).
Comments: Windovers Ltd. Trials. Rebodied as hearse, 1951. Fitted with B80 engine, 1967. Rebodied as D.L. James drophead coupé, 1980's.

3CP190. The original body.

3CP192.
Coachbuilder:	Park Ward.
Engine:	A88C.
Delivered:	10/28/37.
Body Style:	Sedanca de ville.
Body No:	4372.
Registration:	CAK 15.
First Owner:	Gordon Waddilove, UK.
Present Owner:	J. R. G. Bunn, UK.

Pictures: TERR/187, Garnier/108, B176/58, B175/43 (Shown).
Comments: Earl's Court Show, 1937, Park Ward stand. Car in South Africa for many years.

3CP192.

3CP194. *(Photo: Mr. Raabe).*

Coachbuilder:	Hooper.	**3CP194.**
Engine:		(Original) S38K.
Delivered:		10/18/37.
Body Style:		Sedanca de ville.
Design No:		7083.
Body No:		8887.
Registration:		EGW 427.
First Owner:		Max Ausnit, Romania.
Present Owner:		**B. L. Raabe, US.**

Pictures: Schrader/131.
Comments: Later fitted with engine G38V ex 3BT43.

3CP196. *(Photo: Mr. E. A. Stern).*

Coachbuilder:	Mayfair.	**3CP196.**
Engine:		S18K.
Delivered:		10/21/37.
Body Style:		Limousine de ville.
Registration:		791 HLR.
First Owner:		M. V. Roberts, UK.
Present Owner:		C. Baron, UK.

Pictures:
Comments: Car in USA from 1950's to 1989.

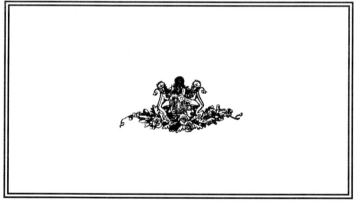

3CP198.

Coachbuilder:	Barker.	**3CP198.**
Engine:		S58K.
Delivered:		11/25/37.
Body Style:		Limousine.
Registration:		Not listed.
First Owner:		T. S. Curtis, UK.
Present Owner:		T. S. Curtis, UK (1951).

Pictures:
Comments: Scottish Show, 1937, Barker stand.
Barker & Co. stock.

3CP200. *(Photo: RROC Foundation).*

Coachbuilder:	Hooper.	**3CP200.**
Engine:		S78K.
Delivered:		11/10/37.
Body Style:		Sedanca de ville.
Design No:		Design 7060.
Body No:		8903.
Registration:		EXW 77.
First Owner:		Captain Alistair W. Mackintosh, UK.
Present Owner:		I. J. Gordon, UK.

Pictures: Bird, TERR/126, Eves/102, Car/1674.
Comments: Hooper & Co. stock. Owned from 1940 to 1977 by Mildred Mary, Hon. Mrs. Victor Bruce.

The CM Series
of
Phantom III Cars

The CM series is numbered odd, 3CM1
through 3CM203. Missing, of course, are 3CM13 and 3CM113.
Also missing are 3CM11, built as 3CM112; 3CM27, built
as 3CM110 and 3CM59, built as 3CM108. Added numbers
are 3CM92, ex 3AX102; 3CM104, ex 3CP152; 3CM106, ex 3CXP156;
3CM108, ex 3CM59; 3CM110, ex 3CM27; 3CM112, ex 3CM11 and
3CM114, ex 3CP90. The 104 CM series cars were
delivered in late 1937 and 1938.

3CM1.   *(Photo: Mr. Kolasa).*

Coachbuilder:	Windovers.	**3CM1.**
Engine:		S68K.
Delivered:		10/14/37.
Body Style:		Brougham de ville.
Body No:		6514.
Registration:		Not listed.
First Owner:		Nigel Colman, UK.
Present Owner:		B. J. Kolasa, US.

Pictures:
Comments:

3CM3.   *(Photo: Dr. Casteel).*

Coachbuilder:	H. J. Mulliner.	**3CM3.**
Engine:		S88K.
Delivered:		10/15/37.
Body Style:		Sedanca de ville.
Registration:		EYF 40.
First Owner:		Mrs. B. A. Horswell, UK.
Present Owner:		**J. S. Casteel, US.**

Pictures:
Comments: Car Mart Ltd. stock.

3CM5.   *(Photo: Mr. Atkinson).*

Coachbuilder:	Barker.	**3CM5.**
Engine:		(Original) S98K.
Delivered:		11/15/37.
Body Style:		Touring limousine.
Registration:		JT 21.
First Owner:		S. Lingard, UK.
Present Owner:		N. Atkinson, UK.

Pictures: TERR/54, FL/751, FL/860, B171/10.
Comments: Later fitted with Bentley Mark VI engine (by 1988).

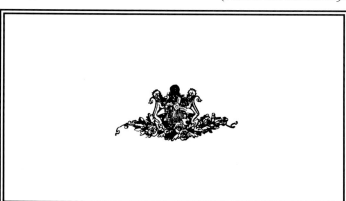

3CM7

Coachbuilder:	H. J. Mulliner.	**3CM7.**
Engine:		S48K.
Delivered:		11/29/37.
Body Style:		Limousine.
Design No:		Drawing 5999.
Body No:		4537.
Registration:		DRU 50.
First Owner:		Dr. J. L. Brownlie, UK.
Present Owner:		J. Little, UK .
		Dismantled.

Pictures:
Comments: Dismantled for spare parts, 1994.

3CM9. Coachbuilder: H.J. Muliner.
Engine: L18R.
Delivered: 10/20/37.
Body Style: Saloon with division.
Design No: Drawing 5962.
Body No: 4436.
Registration: FGH 99.
First Owner: Gustaaf H. Miesegaes, UK (10/38).
Present Owner: For sale, US dealer, 1994.
Pictures: FL/2032.
Comments: Car Mart Ltd. Trials (Major R. S. Grigg).
Modified coachwork and headlight mounting by H. J.
Mulliner, post-war.

3CM9. *(Photo: Mr. Richard Kughn).*

3CM11 built as 3CM112.

3CM15. Coachbuilder: Hooper.
Engine: L38R.
Delivered: 10/25/37.
Body Style: Limousine.
Design No: 6443.
Body No: 8928.
Registration: CAB 209.
First Owner: Mrs. J. Hamilton, UK.
Present Owner: T. G. Talbot, UK.
Pictures:
Comments: Scottish Show, 1937, Clyde Automobiles
stand. Rolls-Royce Ltd. Some reports have the car
rebodied with Park Ward limousine.

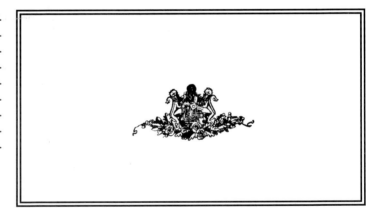

3CM15.

3CM17. Coachbuilder: Hooper.
Engine: L58R.
Delivered: 10/20/37.
Body Style: Limousine de ville.
Design No: 7088.
Body No: 8906.
Registration: EXW 78.
First Owner: Mrs. J. C. Williams, UK (6/38).
Present Owner: K. J. Thompson, Ireland.
Pictures: CORR/134.
Comments: Scottish Show, 1937, Hooper stand.
Hooper & Co. stock.

3CM17. *(Photo: Science Museum, London).*

3CM19.   *(Photo: Mr. McCormack).*

Coachbuilder:	H. J. Mulliner.	**3CM19.**
Engine:		L48R.
Delivered:		11/4/37.
Body Style:		Limousine.
Design No:		Drawing 6013.
Body No:		4547.
Registration:		LS 4154.
First Owner:		Alexander Shaw, 2nd Baron Craigmyle, UK.
Present Owner:		G. McCormack, US.

Pictures:
Comments: Probably at Scottish Show, 1937, John Croall stand. Baron Craigmyle also owned 3DL52. To USA, 1945; returned 1960's.

3CM21.

Coachbuilder:	H. J. Mulliner.	**3CM21.**
Engine:		(Original) L78R.
Delivered:		10/20/37.
Body Style:		Sedanca de ville.
Design No:		Drawing 5991.
Body No:		4516.
Registration:		ELF 313.
First Owner:		Gilbert Davis, UK.
Present Owner:		D. A. Benkelman, US.

Pictures: Phantoms/392 (Shown).
Comments: Later fitted with B80 engine number 57MK2.

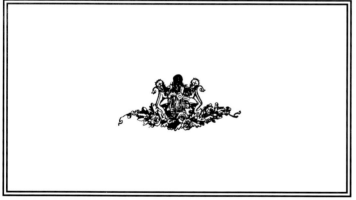

3CM23.

Coachbuilder:	Park Ward.	**3CM23.**
Engine:		L68R.
Delivered:		8/30/37.
Body Style:		Touring limousine.
Design No:		4376.
Registration:		GH 13.
First Owner:		Sir Harold Cecil Harmsworth, UK (1/38).
Present Owner:		**Destroyed in WWII bombing.**

Pictures:
Comments: Jack Barclay Ltd. Trials.

3CM25. The Hooper tourer.

Coachbuilder:	Windovers.	**3CM25.**
Engine:		L88R.
Delivered:		2/1/38 (4/16/46).
Body Style:		(First) Limousine.
Design No:		6505.
Registration:		Not listed.
First Owner:		King Abdul Aziz ibn Saud, Saudi Arabia (5/46).
Present Owner:		Saudi Government, Saudi Arabia.

Pictures: Bird, Brookland/51, Oldham/256h.(Shown).
Comments: Windovers Ltd. stock, unsold 1946. Rebodied with Hooper tourer No. 9171, 1946, first Hooper post-war body. Given to King Saud by the UK Government. Used by Emir Abdullah, the King's brother, from 1950. Featured *Autocar* 9/23/46.

3CM27 built as 3CM110.

3CM29.	**Coachbuilder:**	Hooper.
Engine:		L98R.
Delivered:		11/18/37.
Body Style:		Limousine de ville.
Design No:		7101.
Body No:		8936.
Registration:		Not listed.
First Owner:		Simon I Patino, France.
Present Owner:		**C. Teissier, France.**

Pictures: B193/1. See frontispiece for a photograph of this car in color.
Comments:

3CM29.   *(Photo: Mr. Klaus-Josef Rossfeldt).*

3CM31.	**Coachbuilder:**	Gurney Nutting.
Engine:		(Original) Z28D
Delivered:		12/21/37.
Body Style:		(First) Sedanca de ville.
Registration:		FLO 759.
First Owner:		Sir Herbert Smith, Bart, UK.
Present Owner:		B. L. Leverton, UK.

Pictures: P3TS/30.
Comments: H. R. Owen Ltd. stock. Smith also owned 3AZ168, 3BT81, 3DL104. Rebodied with Martell hearse. Engine later to 3AZ22, and fitted with B60 engine.

3CM31. *The Martell hearse.*   *(Photo: RREC Photo Library).*

3CM33.	**Coachbuilder:**	Windovers.
Engine:		Z38D.
Delivered:		11/30/37.
Body Style:		Limousine.
Body No:		6506.
Registration:		DUR 255.
First Owner:		Major John F. Harrison, UK.
Present Owner:		L. K. Keager, US.

Pictures: FL/829, FL/926, FL/1110.
Comments: Scottish Show, 1937, Windovers stand.

3CM33.   *(PIIITS Archives).*

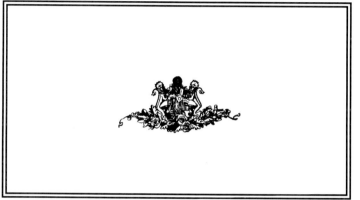

3CM35.   *(Photo: D. S. Archives).*

Coachbuilder:	H. J. Mulliner.	**3CM35.**
Engine:		Z48D.
Delivered:		11/12/37.
Body Style:		Sedanca de ville.
Body No:		4484.
Registration:		ELK 138.
First Owner:		Martin de Selincourt, UK.
Present Owner:		E. M. Pellkofer, US.

Pictures: Phantoms/393.
Comments: Jack Barclay Ltd. stock.

3CM37.

Coachbuilder:	Park Ward.	**3CM37.**
Engine:		R18L.
Delivered:		1/18/38.
Body Style:		Continental touring saloon.
Design No:		4390.
Body No:		Not listed.
Registration:		
First Owner:		Sir Umed Singh, Maharajah of Kotah, India.
Present Owner:		V. M. Molari, Italy.

Pictures:
Comments: Original order by J. S. Inskip as Trials car.

3CM39.   *(Photo: D.S. Archives).*

Coachbuilder:	H. J. Mulliner.	**3CM39.**
Engine:		(Original) Z78D.
Delivered:		1/11/37.
Body Style:		Sedanca de ville.
Design No:		Drawing 6012.
Body No:		4542.
Registration:		ELK 140.
First Owner:		Oscar Homolka, UK.
Present Owner:		**M. Tuttle, US.**

Pictures: Phantoms/393.
Comments: Jack Barclay Ltd. stock. Specified as "Show type chassis". To USA by 1961. Original engine Z78D later installed in 3BT65.

3CM41.

Coachbuilder:	Hooper.	**3CM41.**
Engine:		Z68D.
Delivered:		9/8/37.
Body Style:		Limousine de ville.
Design No:		7088.
Body No:		8907.
Registration:		Not listed.
First Owner:		Bernard Sunley, UK (4/38).
Present Owner:		Major O. R. H. Chichester, Palestine (1951).

Pictures:
Comments: Hooper & Co. stock.

3CM43.

Coachbuilder:	Erdmann & Rossi.
Engine:	Z88D.
Delivered:	12/17/38.
Body Style:	Limousine.
Body No:	3139.
Registration:	Not listed.
First Owner:	Geheimrat Kurt Elschner, Germany.
Present Owner:	Unknown.

Pictures:
Comments: Berlin Show, 1938, Erdmann & Rossi stand. Elschner also owned 3AX155.

3CM43.

3CM45.

Coachbuilder:	Windovers.
Engine:	Z58D.
Delivered:	6/22/38.
Body Style:	Saloon.
Body No:	6526.
Registration:	GCT 84.
First Owner:	S. Farrows, UK.
Present Owner:	L. J. Creery, Canada.

Pictures: Phantoms/410 (Shown).
Comments: Windovers Ltd. stock.

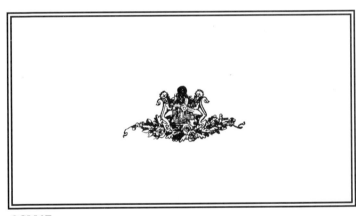
3CM45.

3CM47.

Coachbuilder:	Gurney Nutting.
Engine:	Z98D.
Delivered:	1/8/38.
Body Style:	Sedanca de ville.
Design No:	Drawing 245.
Registration:	Not listed.
First Owner:	HE Dimitri Tziracopoulos, Germany.
Present Owner:	L. J. Metcalfe, UK (1954).

Pictures:
Comments: First owner was Greek Minister to Germany.

3CM47.

3CM49.

Coachbuilder:	Barker.
Engine:	R38L.
Delivered:	12/9/37.
Body Style:	Saloon with division.
Registration:	ELP 87.
First Owner:	Captain C. L. O'Callaghan, UK.
Present Owner:	**G. Burkhardt, Australia.**

Pictures: B178/9, Phantoms/393 (Shown).
Comments: Rolls-Royce Trials. Phantom II 53TA used as trade-in. Car shipped to Australia 1989, having been in the USA.

3CM49.

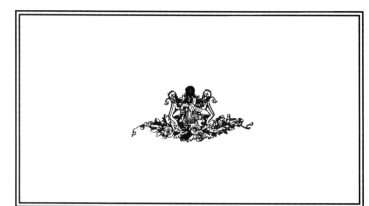

3CM51.

Coachbuilder:	H. J. Mulliner.	**3CM51.**
Engine:		R68L.
Delivered:		11/17/37.
Body Style:		Saloon with division.
Design No:		Drawing 5912.
Body No:		4545.
Registration:		EXW 487.
First Owner:		R. O. Hambro, UK.
Present Owner:		P&A Wood, UK.

Pictures:
Comments: Jack Barclay Ltd. stock.

3CM53.   *(Photo: RROC Foundation).*

Coachbuilder:	Vanden Plas.	**3CM53.**
Engine:		R48L.
Delivered:		1/5/38.
Body Style:		Limousine.
Design No:		1478/1.
Body No:		3614.
Registration:		Not listed.
First Owner:	Count Dr. Johann Larisch-Monnich,	
		Austria.
Present Owner:		D. Roberts, US.

Pictures: TERR/234, FL/3635.
Comments:

3CM55.

Coachbuilder:	Barker.	**3CM55.**
Engine:		R58L.
Delivered:		12/30/37.
Body Style:		Landaulet.
Body No:		7277.
Registration:		XN 6655.
First Owner:	Lady Cara Leland Fairhaven, UK.	
Present Owner:		G. Hosier, UK.

Pictures: BA100/69 (Shown).
Comments: Lady Fairhaven's son owned 3BU168.

3CM57.   *(Photo: Mr. G. R. Gilbert).*

Coachbuilder:	Hooper.	**3CM57.**
Engine:		R78L.
Delivered:		1/22/38.
Body Style:		Sports limousine.
Design No:		6665.
Body No:		8954.
Registration:		ELH 563.
First Owner:		Dr. R. Scott-Mason, UK.
Present Owner:		B. McIlroy, New Zealand.

Pictures: B170/68, B171/68, P3TS/8.
Comments: Scott-Mason also owned 3AX63, which was exchanged for this car. To New Zealand by 1961.

3CM59 built as 3CM108.

3CM61.   Coachbuilder: Park Ward.
Engine: R98L.
Delivered: 12/24/37.
Body Style: Sedanca de ville.
Body No: 4377.
Registration: ELN 7.
First Owner: J. D. Clarke, UK
Present Owner: Blackhawk Collection, US.

Pictures:
Comments:

3CM61.   *(Photo: Blackhawk Collection).*

3CM63.   Coachbuilder: Hooper.
Engine: R28L.
Delivered: 1/5/38.
Body Style: Limousine.
Design No: 7149.
Body No: 8967.
Registration: Not listed.
First Owner: King Farouk, Egypt.
Present Owner: Unknown.

Pictures:
Comments: King Farouk also owned 3DL182. Car still in Cairo, 1955.

3CM63.   *(Photo: Science Museum, London).*

3CM65.   Coachbuilder: H. J. Mulliner.
Engine: K48S.
Delivered: 12/6/37.
Body Style: Saloon with division.
Design No: Drawing 5912.
Body No: 4546.
Registration: EYY 333.
First Owner: T. C. Maryon-Wilson, UK
Present Owner: For sale, E. Hook, US, 1994.

Pictures: Shoup/23, TS/28, FL/1397, FL/4868.
Comments: Car Mart Ltd. stock.

3CM65.   *(Photo: Mrs. Hook).*

3CM67.

Coachbuilder:	H. J. Mulliner.	**3CM67.**
Engine:		K18S.
Delivered:		12/8/37.
Body Style:		Sedanca de ville.
Body No:		4543.
Registration:		DXE 1, UCH 1.
First Owner:	Madeline, Mrs. S. W. Tanfield, UK.	
Present Owner:		**F. F. Guyton, US.**

Pictures: FL/688 (Shown).
Comments: Jack Barclay Ltd. stock. Mrs. Tanfield also owned 3BT51. To USA, 1961.

3CM69.   *(Photo: Mr. Messier).*

Coachbuilder:	Hooper.	**3CM69.**
Engine:		K28S.
Delivered:		3/11/38.
Body Style:		Limousine.
Design No:		7240.
Body No:		8985.
Registration:		VJ 5712.
First Owner:		William Boyd, UK.
Present Owner:		R. L. Messier, US.

Pictures:
Comments: Windovers Ltd. stock.

3CM71.

Coachbuilder:	Hooper.	**3CM71.**
Engine:	(Original) K38S.	
Delivered:		1/12/38.
Body Style:		Landaulet.
Design No:		7165.
Body No:		8965.
Registration:		Not listed.
First Owner:	Lady Lucy Marianne Brunner, UK.	
Present Owner:		**P. L. Jessen, US.**

Pictures: FL4308-10 (Shown).
Comments: Fitted with invalid chair. Engine later fitted to 3CM165. Landau opening sealed pre-1970, and reopened 1986.

Coachbuilder:	Chapron.	**3CM73.**
Engine:		K58S.
Delivered:		12/30/37.
Body Style:		Saloon.
Registration:		ELT 17.
First Owner:	Edward S. Weisblat, France.	
Present Owner:		J. Peel, US.

Pictures: Harvey-Bailey/71 (Shown).
Comments: Fitted with flexible steering wheel.

3CM73.

3CM75.

Coachbuilder:	Park Ward.
Engine:	(Original) K68S.
Delivered:	12/9/37.
Body Style:	Touring limousine.
Body No:	4380.
Registration:	EXE 241, VML 14.
First Owner:	J. Marshall Vernham, UK.
Present Owner:	For sale, US dealer, 1994.

Pictures: CORR/260.
Comments: Park Ward & Co. stock. 20/25 GNC30 used as trade-in. Replacement engine fitted by Rolls-Royce, 1960. To USA, 1966.

3CM75. *(Photo: Mr. G. M. H. Stein).*

3CM77.

Coachbuilder:	Thrupp & Maberly.
Engine:	K78S.
Delivered:	11/27/37.
Body Style:	Sports limousine.
Design No:	Drawing SLE.1245/F.
Body No:	6771.
Registration:	EOG 1, 960 YBF, HEE 246.
First Owner:	J. H. James, UK.
Present Owner:	D. M. Heathcote, UK.

Pictures: TERR/222.
Comments: Rootes Ltd. stock. Featured in *The Motor*, 4 January 1938. For sale, to second owner, August 1958 for £875.

3CM77. *(Photo: Mr. Heathcote).*

3CM79.

Coachbuilder:	Hooper.
Engine:	K88S.
Delivered:	12/22/37.
Body Style:	Limousine.
Design No:	6443.
Body No:	8958.
Registration:	DRU 368, CXW 488.
First Owner:	Mrs. E. W. Parrington, UK.
Present Owner:	Florian, US.

Pictures: Science Museum, London (Interior only).
Comments:

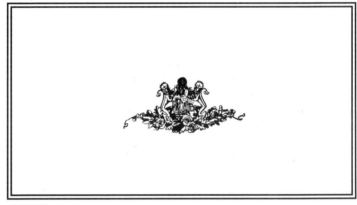

3CM79.

3CM81.

Coachbuilder:	Vanvooren.
Engine:	Y28E.
Delivered:	4/15/38.
Body Style:	Sports cabriolet.
Registration:	GS 9987.
First Owner:	Stefan Czarnecki, France/Poland.
Present Owner:	**W. J. Harwood, US.**

Pictures: Phantoms/394.
Comments: No rear seat fitted to allow for luggage storage. Owner 2: General Sikorski, Poland. To UK 1941. New engine installed at 45,000 miles. To US, 1969.

3CM81. *(Photo: Mr. Harwood).*

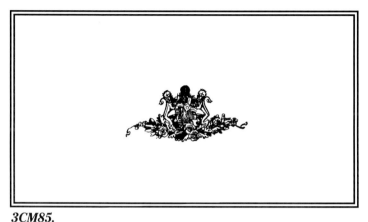

3CM83.

Coachbuilder:	Barker.	**3CM83.**
Engine:		Y18E.
Delivered:		10/30/37.
Body Style:		Sedanca de ville.
Registration:		Not listed.
First Owner:		Mrs. Corrigan, France.
Present Owner:		Don A. F. Canales, Spain (1948).

Pictures:
Comments: Returned to London, 1940.

3CM85.

Coachbuilder:	Hooper.	**3CM85.**
Engine:		Y48E.
Delivered:		1/10/38.
Body Style:		Limousine.
Design No:		6443.
Body No:		8959.
Registration:		GS 7692.
First Owner:		Sir James Denby Roberts, Bart, UK.
Present Owner:		Unknown.

Pictures:
Comments: Windovers Ltd. stock.

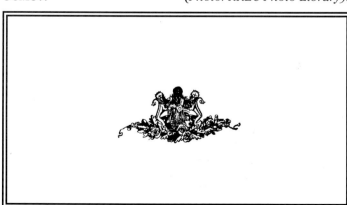

3CM87.   *(Photo: RREC Photo Library).*

Coachbuilder:	Park Ward.	**3CM87.**
Engine:		K98S.
Delivered:		11/29/37.
Body Style:		Touring limousine.
Body No:		4379.
Registration:		ELP 83.
First Owner:		Rolls-Royce Ltd., UK.
Present Owner:		D. J. Holland, US.

Pictures: Brookland/15, Brookland/22.
Comments: Company Trials until July 1942. Sold via Jack Barclay Ltd., 1942 to Gray's Holdings.

3CM89.

Coachbuilder:	Mann Egerton.	**3CM89.**
Engine:		Y38E.
Delivered:		2/23/38.
Body Style:		Limousine.
Registration:		Not listed.
First Owner:		Mrs. Mary Hooker Dole, US (6/41).
Present Owner:		**F. P. Meserow, US.**

Pictures:
Comments: Mann Egerton Ltd. stock. Chassis only since 1979.

3CM91.   Coachbuilder: Franay.
Engine: Y58E.
Delivered: 3/18/38.
Body Style: Sedanca de ville.
Registration: Not listed.
First Owner: Karl Thiel, Switzerland.
Present Owner: W. Lyon, US.

Pictures: CORR/5, FL/672.
Comments: Paris Salon, 1938, Franay stand. In Harrah's Automobile Collection, 1961-1986.

3CM91.   *(Photo: Harrah Collection via P3TS).*

3CM92.   Coachbuilder: Barker.
Engine: L28PX.
Delivered: 8/31/37.
Body Style: Touring saloon.
Design No: Drawing SF11495A.
Body No: 7311.
Registration: ELN 1, VYY 251.
First Owner: Sir George MacPherson-Grant, Bart, UK.
Present Owner: **M. A. Sysak, US.**
Pictures: Oldham/136g, FL/1694, FL/4289-91.
Comments:

3CM92.   *(Photo: Mr. Sysak).*

3CM93.   Coachbuilder: Barker.
Engine: Y68E.
Delivered: 3/21/38.
Body Style: Sedanca de ville.
Registration: ELR 507.
First Owner: Mark Ostrer, UK.
Present Owner: P. S. Liebert, US.

Pictures: FL/1192.
Comments: Featured in *The Autocar*, 20 May 1938, *The Motor*, 26 July 1938.

3CM93.   *(Photo: Mr. Liebert).*

3CM95.   Coachbuilder: Park Ward.
Engine: Y78E.
Delivered: 12/16/37.
Body Style: Touring limousine.
Body No: 4385.
Registration: AV 9900, KAV 426.
First Owner: D. C. Stewart, UK.
Present Owner: A. D. M. Allen, UK.

Pictures: TERR/187.
Comments:

3CM95.   *(Photo: D. S. Archives).*

3CM97.   (Photo: Mr . Mason).

Coachbuilder:	H. J. Mulliner.	**3CM97.**
Engine:		Y88E.
Delivered:		2/25/38.
Body Style:		Limousine.
Design No:		Drawing 6040.
Body No:		4567.
Registration:		EXE 242.
First Owner:	Sir (Samuel) Hardman Lever, Bart, UK.	
Present Owner:	T. Mason, UK.	

Pictures:

Comments: Ordered without mascot or front bumper bar.

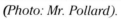

3CM99.

Coachbuilder:	Barker.	**3CM99.**
Engine:		Y98E.
Delivered:		2/9/38.
Body Style:		Saloon with division.
Body No:		7368.
Registration:		FRF 659.
First Owner:	William Humble Eric, 3rd Earl of Dudley, UK.	
Present Owner:	**G. Spitzak, US.**	

Pictures:

Comments: Phantom II 88MY used as trade-in.

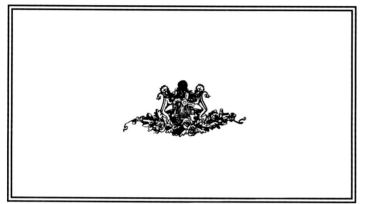

3CM101.   (Photo: Mr. Pollard).

Coachbuilder:	Hooper.	**3CM101.**
Engine:		(Original) Q18M.
Delivered:		2/4/38.
Body Style:		Limousine de ville.
Design No:		7202.
Body No:		8973.
Registration:		Not listed.
First Owner:	Mrs. Judith Solares, UK.	
Present Owner:	**G. B. Pollard, US.**	

Pictures: Schrader/132.

Comments. Later fitted with engine Y58D ex 3BU182.

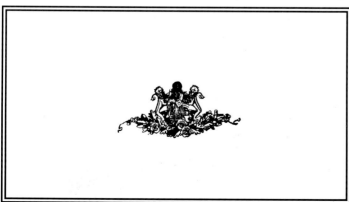

3CM103.

Coachbuilder:	Arthur Mulliner.	**3CM103.**
Engine:		Q28M.
Delivered:		1/28/38.
Body Style:		Limousine.
Design No:		Drawing 1677.
Registration:		Not listed.
First Owner:	James Campbell, UK.	
Present Owner:	**Destroyed.**	

Pictures:

Comments: Arthur Mulliner Ltd. stock. Destroyed by WWII bombing, March 1944.

3CM104.

Coachbuilder:	Arthur Mulliner.
Engine:	T88J.
Delivered:	12/13/37.
Body Style:	Limousine.
Registration:	Not listed.
First Owner:	Serge Karlinski, UK.
Present Owner:	Unknown.

Pictures:
Comments: Chassis ex 3CP152.

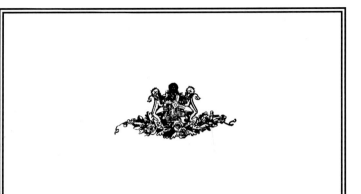
3CM104.

3CM105.

Coachbuilder:	Hooper.
Engine:	Q38M.
Delivered:	2/26/38.
Body Style:	Limousine.
Design No:	7176.
Body No:	8984.
Registration:	Not listed.
First Owner:	J. Spedan Lewis, UK.
Present Owner:	Nakajima, Japan.

Pictures: P/76, P/167, P/169.
Comments:

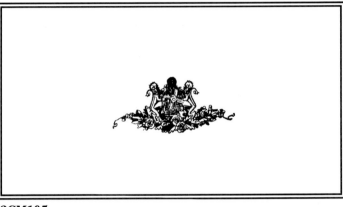
3CM105.

3CM106.

Coachbuilder:	Park Ward.
Engine:	T98J.
Delivered:	1/31/38.
Body Style:	Touring limousine.
Body No:	4310.
Registration:	EXX 13.
First Owner:	Clifford Whitely, UK (4/38).
Present Owner:	**M. Tuttle, US.**

Pictures:
Comments: Chassis ex 3CP156. Jack Barclay Ltd. stock.

3CM106.   *(Photo: Mrs. Penny Pollard).*

3CM107.

Coachbuilder:	Barker.
Engine:	Q48M.
Delivered:	1/29/38.
Body Style:	Saloon with division.
Body No:	7369.
Registration:	EYX 365.
First Owner:	Robert Young Eaton, Canada (9/39).
Present Owner:	Unknown, Australia.

Pictures:
Comments: Major Len Cox (CX) Trials. Phantom II 83XJ used by Eaton as trade-in. Returned to UK, 1958; to USA 1960, to Australia, 1993.

3CM107.   *(Photo: Mr. Mark Tuttle).*

3CM108.

Coachbuilder:	Park Ward. **3CM108.**
Engine:	R88L.
Delivered:	1/17/38.
Body Style:	Touring limousine.
Body No:	4335.
Registration:	CGO 9, NGN 587.
First Owner:	Lt-Colonel C. J. Odling, UK.
Present Owner:	J. L. L. Rodiger, Netherlands.

Pictures: B146/5, TERR/188 (Shown).
Comments: Chassis ex 3CM59. Jack Barclay Ltd. stock.

3CM109.

Coachbuilder:	H. J. Mulliner. **3CM109.**
Engine:	(Original) Q58M.
Delivered:	1/31/38.
Body Style:	Touring limousine.
Design No:	Drawing 6041.
Body No:	4568.
Registration:	ELP 85.
First Owner:	Mrs. Smalley, UK.
Present Owner:	**R. Feller, US.**

Pictures: FL/857, Phantoms/395 (Shown).
Comments: Later fitted with B80 engine.

3CM110.   *(Photo: Stuckey Collectiom).*

Coachbuilder:	Hooper. **3CM110.**
Engine:	Z18D.
Delivered:	12/16/37.
Body Style:	Limousine.
Design No:	6443.
Body No:	8957.
Registration:	7340 CC.
First Owner:	Gabriel, Duque de Maura, Portugal.
Present Owner:	W. L. Tucker, US.

Pictures:
Comments: Chassis ex 3CM27. Amsterdam and Geneva Shows, 1938.

3CM111.   *(Photo: Rev. Gray).*

Coachbuilder:	Rippon. **3CM111.**
Engine:	Q68M.
Delivered:	3/16/38.
Body Style:	Limousine.
Registration:	CKU 686.
First Owner:	Mayor of Bradford Corporation, UK.
Present Owner:	**J. J. Gray, US.**

Pictures:
Comments: Rippon Bros. stock.

3CM112.   Coachbuilder: H. J. Mulliner.
Engine: L28R.
Delivered: 4/4/38.
Body Style: Limousine de ville.
Design No: Drawing 6043.
Body No: 4570.
Registration: EXU 3.
First Owner: William Henry Collins, UK.
Present Owner: Sir C. J. Harman, UK (1965).

Pictures:
Comments: Chassis ex 3CM11. Collins also owned
3AX3, which was used as trade-in for £1,810.
Featured in *The Autocar*, 20 May 1938.

3CM112   *(Photo: Quadrant Picture Library, England).*

3CM114.   Coachbuilder: Arthur Mulliner.
Engine: H18U.
Delivered: 2/19/38.
Body Style: Sports limousine.
Registration: Not listed.
First Owner: A. F. England, UK.
Present Owner: Unknown.

Pictures:
Comments: Chassis ex 3CP90, which was ordered as
a Fernandez et Darrin sedanca de ville for Count
Maurice de Bosdari, France.

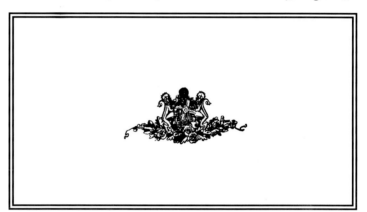

3CM114.

3CM115.   Coachbuilder: Gurney Nutting.
Engine: Q98M.
Delivered: 2/26/38.
Body Style: Sports saloon.
Registration: ELL 585.
First Owner: Sir Ernest Cain, Bart, UK.
Present Owner: D. B. Greenwood, UK.

Pictures:
Comments: H. R. Owen Ltd. stock. Bought by Mr.
Greenwood's grandfather in 1940 and remained in
the family until about 1955, then passed through a
variety of hands until repurchased in 1979. Now in
daily use.

3CM115. When purchased in 1940. (Photo: Mr. Greenwood).

3CM117.   Coachbuilder: H. J. Mulliner.
Engine: Q78M.
Delivered: 1/7/38.
Body Style: Touring limousine.
Body No: 4485.
Registration: ELR 498.
First Owner: A. J. D. Whitehead, UK.
Present Owner: R. W. Adkins, US.

Pictures: PIIITS/17.
Comments: Jack Barclay Ltd. stock.

3CM117.   *(Photo: Mr. Norman J. Kapson).*

3CM119.   *(Photo: Mr. Belden).*

Coachbuilder:	H. J. Mulliner.	**3CM119.**
Engine:		Q88M.
Delivered:		1/7/38.
Body Style:		Sedanca de ville.
Design No:		Drawing 5812.
Body No:		4544.
Registration:		EXC 200.
First Owner:		John Maxwell, UK.
Present Owner:		M. B. Belden, US.

Pictures:
Comments: Jack Barclay Ltd. stock.

3CM121.   *(Photo: Mr. Rose).*

Coachbuilder:	Barker.	**3CM121.**
Engine:		J18T.
Delivered:		3/26/38.
Body Style:		Limousine.
Registration:		Not listed.
First Owner:		Lady Alice Sedgwick Ludlow, UK.
Present Owner:		B. Rose, US.

Pictures:
Comments: Barker & Co. stock.

3CM123. *On the annual Vintage Car Tour, RROC, 1979.*

Coachbuilder:	Arthur Mulliner.	**3CM123.**
Engine:		J28T.
Delivered:		2/22/38.
Body Style:		Sedanca de ville.
Registration:		Not listed.
First Owner:		Roy Gibson, UK.
Present Owner:		J. N. Van Praag, US.

Pictures: FL/2145, FL/2146 (Shown).
Comments:

3CM125.   *(Photo: Mr. Klaus-Josef Rossfeldt).*

Coachbuilder:	H. J. Mulliner.	**3CM125.**
Engine:		J48T.
Delivered:		2/22/38.
Body Style:		Sedanca de ville.
Design No:		Drawing 6051.
Body No:		4562.
Registration:		EXC 194.
First Owner:		Rudolph Meyer, UK.
Present Owner:		**J. Sangster, UK.**

Pictures: TERR/158, FL/315, FL/3008.
Comments: In the USA 1956-1987, West Germany 1988-1989.

3CM127.

Coachbuilder:	Barker.
Engine:	J58T.
Delivered:	5/19/38.
Body Style:	Limousine de ville.
Registration:	Not listed.
First Owner:	Edna, Mrs. B. G. Barnard, US.
Present Owner:	Fairwood, US.

Pictures:
Comments: Reportedly rebodied by Brewster.

3CM127.

3CM129.

Coachbuilder:	Windovers.
Engine:	J68T.
Delivered:	3/3/38.
Body Style:	Saloon.
Body No:	6543.
Registration:	COT 420.
First Owner:	Jeremiah Colman, UK.
Present Owner:	D. L. Shore, UK.

Pictures: B154/23, B164/28.
Comments:

3CM129. *(Photo: Mr. Shore).*

3CM131.

Coachbuilder:	Hooper.
Engine:	J78T.
Delivered:	2/23/38.
Body Style:	Sports limousine.
Design No:	7239.
Body No:	8982.
Registration:	EUU 2.
First Owner:	H. Smith, UK.
Present Owner:	M. R. Stephenson, UK.

Pictures: Bishop/35, Bishop/40, Car/1674.
Comments: Road tested in *Motor Sport*, July 1958.

3CM131. *(Photo: Mr. Stephenson).*

3CM133.

Coachbuilder:	H. J. Mulliner.
Engine:	(Original) J38T.
Delivered:	3/3/38.
Body Style:	Saloon with division.
Design No:	Drawing 5912.
Body No:	4580.
Registration:	EXC 199.
First Owner:	A. C. Morrell, UK.
Present Owner:	S. Elman, US.

Pictures: Phantoms/397, B67/12.
Comments: Later fitted with B80 engine.

3CM133. *(Photo Mr. Ken Batchelor).*

3CM135.   *(Photo: Illustrated London News).*

Coachbuilder:	H. J. Mulliner. **3CM135.**
Engine:	J88T.
Delivered:	17/2/38.
Body Style:	Sedanca de ville.
Body No:	4560.
Registration:	EXO 1, JNB 306.
First Owner:	H. J. Caro, UK.
Present Owner:	D. Heyworth, UK.

Pictures:
Comments: Jack Barclay Ltd. stock. Ordered without mascot. Caro also owned 3BT65.

3CM137.

Coachbuilder:	Hooper. **3CM137.**
Engine:	J98T.
Delivered:	4/6/38.
Body Style:	Limousine.
Design No:	6850.
Body No:	8993.
Registration:	DNY 3.
First Owner:	Lady Magdalene Anne Llewellyn, UK.
Present Owner:	W. D. Peden, UK.

Pictures:
Comments:

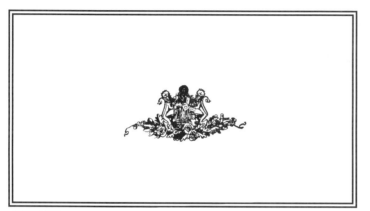

3CM139. *A very old and faded photograph.* *(Photo: RROC).*

Coachbuilder:	Thrupp & Maberly. **3CM139.**
Engine:	W18G.
Delivered:	2/3/38.
Body Style:	Limousine.
Design No:	Drawing SLE.1334.
Body No:	6799.
Registration:	FLY 111.
First Owner:	Sir (Alfred) Robert McAlpine, Bart, UK (1/39).
Present Owner:	J. F. Limoncelli, US.

Pictures:
Comments: Rootes Ltd. stock. Later owned by Montague Grahame-White.

3CM141.   *(Photo: Mr. Chaplar).*

Coachbuilder:	Thrupp & Maberly. **3CM141.**
Engine:	W28G.
Delivered:	3/30/38.
Body Style:	Sedanca de ville.
Design No:	Drawing SLE.1331.
Body No:	6800.
Registration:	EMP 938.
First Owner:	Frank Smith, UK.
Present Owner:	**R. R. Chaplar, US.**

Pictures: P3TS/16
Comments: Rootes Ltd. stock. Found in Egypt 1962.

3CM143.
Coachbuilder: Windovers.
Engine: W38G.
Delivered: 3/1/38.
Body Style: Limousine.
Body No: 6541.
Registration: EMN 49.
First Owner: A. E. Mallandain, UK.
Present Owner: Ranick, US.

Pictures: Schrader/128.
Comments: Cadillac fenders fitted post-war.

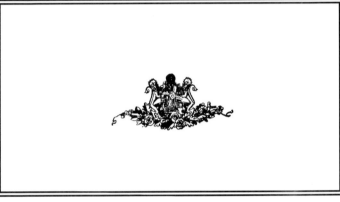

3CM143. *(Photo: Mr. Glyn Morris).*

3CM145.
Coachbuilder: Hooper.
Engine: W48G.
Delivered: 4/10/38.
Body Style: Limousine.
Design No: 7186.
Body No: 8968.
Registration: Not listed.
First Owner: D. C. Bowser, UK.
Present Owner: Queen Nafisa, Iraq (1954).

Pictures:
Comments: Ordered without mascot. To Prince Regent of Iraq, 1945.

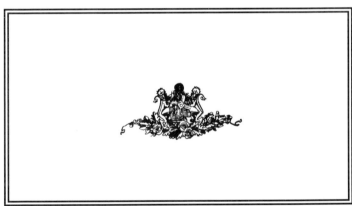

3CM145.

3CM147.
Coachbuilder: Hooper.
Engine: W58G.
Delivered: 3/18/38.
Body Style: Sports limousine.
Design No: 7225.
Body No: 8983.
Registration: Not listed.
First Owner: Thomas S. Short, UK.
Present Owner: M. J. Russell, UK (1963).

Pictures:
Comments:

3CM147.

3CM149.
Coachbuilder: Windovers.
Engine: W68G.
Delivered: 12/11/37.
Body Style: Limousine.
Body No: 6540.
Registration: APN 757.
First Owner: Z. G. Michalinos, UK.
Present Owner: P. A. Owram , UK.

Pictures: BS116/31.
Comments:

3CM149. *(Photo: Mr. G. C. Munton).*

3CM151.　　　　　(Photo: Mr. Charles Crail).

Coachbuilder:	Barker.	**3CM151.**
Engine:		W78G.
Delivered:		3/25/38.
Body Style:		Sports saloon.
Registration:		CTJ 421.
First Owner:		G. D. Gregson, UK.
Present Owner:		Unknown, UK.

Pictures: R&T/35, FL/355.
Comments: Featured in *Road & Track*, January 1958.

3CM153.

Coachbuilder:	Windovers.	**3CM153.**
Engine:		W88G.
Delivered:		5/17/38.
Body Style:		Limousine.
Body No:		6542.
Registration:		EXY 672.
First Owner:		Captain R. L. Jolliffe, UK.
Present Owner:		Mr. Hodgson, UK (1958).

Pictures: TERR/247 (Shown).
Comments: Jolliffe also owned, used, 3AZ40.

3CM155.

Coachbuilder:	H. J. Mulliner.	**3CM155.**
Engine:		W98G.
Delivered:		3/22/38.
Body Style:		Limousine de ville.
Body No:		4581.
Registration:		Not listed.
First Owner:		Arthur Croft, UK.
Present Owner:		J. L. L. Rodiger, Netherlands.

Pictures:
Comments: Ordered without mascot.

3CM157.　　　　(Photo: Mr. Charles Wright via RROC).

Coachbuilder:	Hooper.	**3CM157.**
Engine:		P18N.
Delivered:		3/21/38.
Body Style:		Limousine.
Design No:		6443.
Body No:		8962.
Registration:		GRE 140.
First Owner:		E. R. Corn, UK.
Present Owner:		P. Tamblyn, Australia.

Pictures: Rossfeldt/109, P/102, FL/1256.
Comments:

3CM159.
Coachbuilder:	H. J. Mulliner.
Engine:	P28N.
Delivered:	2/15/38.
Body Style:	Sedanca de ville.
Body No:	4554.
Registration:	EXC 192, 6593 SF.
First Owner:	Miss Nora H. MacCaw, UK.
Present Owner:	A. Porter, UK.

Pictures: B158/56, B170/48, TERR/159 (Shown).
Comments: Ordered without mascot.

3CM159.

3CM161.
Coachbuilder:	Barker.
Engine:	P38N.
Delivered:	5/7/38.
Body Style:	Limousine.
Registration:	DL 4374.
First Owner:	H. D. Clark, UK.
Present Owner:	W. J. Forrest, UK.

Pictures: FL/1609, Auto Quarterly 17/2 (Shown).
Comments: (Completed by Hooper). Watson Ltd. stock. Owned 1945 by Dr. A. H. Rice, who owned 3DL62.

3CM161. When owned by R. D. LaPenta.

3CM163.
Coachbuilder:	Thrupp & Maberly.
Engine:	P48N.
Delivered:	3/23/38.
Body Style:	Special saloon.
DesignNo:	Drawing SLS.1348/A.
Body No:	6805.
Registration:	EXV 770.
First Owner:	Major H. R. White, UK.
Present Owner:	B. J. Dubas, UK.

Pictures: TERR/221.
Comments:

3CM163. *(RREC Photo Library).*

3CM165.
Coachbuilder:	Barker.
Engine:	(Original) P58N.
Delivered:	3/29/38.
Body Style:	Limousine.
Registration:	FBC 999, 740 HRY.
First Owner:	Miss J. Laing, UK.
Present Owner:	Bryant, US.

Pictures:
Comments: Later fitted with engine K38S ex 3CM71.

3CM165. *(Photo: Mr. Bryant).*

3CM167.

Coachbuilder: James Young. **3CM167.**
Engine: P68N.
Delivered: 5/20/38.
Body Style: Sports saloon with division.
Registration: EYH 406.
First Owner: Hon. Philip Henderson, UK.
Present Owner: **D. C. F. Bartlet, UK.**

Pictures: TERR/260, B63/17 (Shown).
Comments: Jack Barclay Ltd. stock. Henderson also owned 3AZ136.

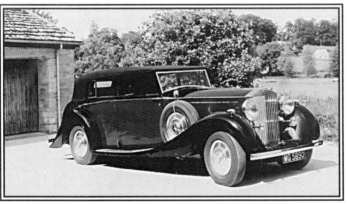

3CM169. *(Photo: Mr. Corser).*

Coachbuilder: Barker. **3CM169.**
Engine: P78N.
Delivered: 4/8/38.
Body Style: Limousine.
Design No: 7293.
Body No: 9001.
Registration: HF 7976.
First Owner: A. Bruce Wallis, UK.
Present Owner: G. B. Corser, UK.

Pictures: Robinson/'82.
Comments:

3CM171. *The cabriolet.*

Coachbuilder: Park Ward. **3CM171.**
Engine: P88N.
Delivered: 3/18/38.
Body Style: (First) Limousine.
Body No: 4408.
Registration: MG 5890.
First Owner: Weetman, 3rd Viscount Cowdray.
Present Owner: A. H. Goddard , UK.

Pictures:
Comments: Car in Canada for some years. Converted to cabriolet.

3CM173. *(Photo: Mr. Young).*

Coachbuilder: Hooper. **3CM173.**
Engine: P98N.
Delivered: 3/30/38.
Body Style: Fixed-head coupé.
Design No: 7289.
Body No: 9000.
Registration: AFV 1, 11 DPW.
First Owner: William Parkinson, UK.
Present Owner: J. A. Young, UK.

Pictures: P3TS/44, B158/13, B176/54.
Comments: Parkinson also owned 3CP164.

3CM175.

Coachbuilder:	Rippon.
Engine:	D 18Z.
Delivered:	6/27/38.
Body Style:	Limousine.
Registration:	CWX 320.
First Owner:	George Peter Norton, UK.
Present Owner:	E. G. Cheeseman, UK.

3CM175.   *(Photo: Stuckey Collection).*

Pictures: Phantoms.
Comments: Rippon Bros. stock. Car in Iraq between 1953 and 1963.

3CM177.

Coachbuilder:	H.J. Mulliner.
Engine:	D28Z.
Delivered:	1/29/38.
Body Style:	Saloon with division.
Design No:	Drawing 5937.
Body No:	4586.
Registration:	AUT 555.
First Owner:	Frank Morris, UK.
Present Owner:	**A. S. Hazzah, US.**

3CM177.   *(Photo: Mr. C. M. Streat).*

Pictures: FL/826.
Comments:

3CM179.

Coachbuilder:	Windovers.
Engine:	D38Z.
Delivered:	4/25/38.
Body Style:	Limousine.
Body No:	6548.
Registration:	EXW 488.
First Owner:	Mrs. S. G. Wilkenson, UK.
Present Owner:	Lohéac Museum, France.

3CM179.

Pictures: CORR/356 (Shown).
Comments: Car in Iraq, 1956.

3CM181.

Coachbuilder:	Park Ward.
Engine:	D48Z.
Delivered:	4/20/38.
Body Style:	Touring saloon.
Body No:	4410.
Registration:	AFU 209.
First Owner:	G. H. Bowser, UK.
Present Owner:	D. Browne, UK.

3CM181.

Pictures: Phantoms/398 (Shown).
Comments: Park Ward & Co. stock. On display at National Motor Museum, England, 1991.

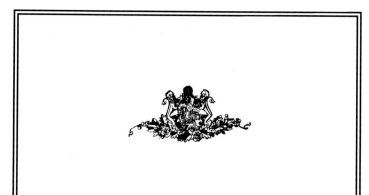

3CM183.

Coachbuilder:	Park Ward.	**3CM183.**
Engine:		D58Z.
Delivered:		4/29/38.
Body Style:		Limousine.
Design No:		Drawing 13111.
Body No:		4411.
Registration:		EXE 247.
First Owner:		H. F. Brand, UK.
Present Owner:		A. B. Mitchell, US.

Pictures:
Comments: 25/30 GRM63 used as trade-in. To USA, 1962. Chassis only.

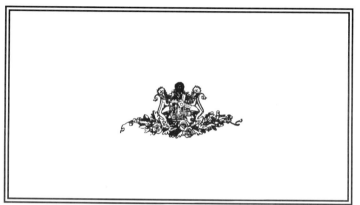

3CM185.

Coachbuilder:	Park Ward.	**3CM185.**
Engine:		D68Z.
Delivered:		4/13/38.
Body Style:		(First) Touring limousine.
Body No:		4412.
Registration:		DPX 999.
First Owner:		Colonel Evelyn William Margesson CMG, UK.
Present Owner:		R. M. Whitaker, US.

Pictures:
Comments: Margesson also owned 3AZ120. Rebodied as Royt limousine.

3CM187.

Coachbuilder:	Kellner.	**3CM187.**
Engine:		D78Z.
Delivered:		6/15/38.
Body Style:		Saloon with division.
Registration:		Not listed.
First Owner:		Princess J. L. de Faucigny-Lucinge, France.
Present Owner:		A. Surmain, Spain.

Pictures: FL/1046 (Shown).
Comments: La Princesse also owned 3AZ206. Car in UK, 1960, and USA, 1966.

3CM189.   *(Photo: Mr. Hans Enzler).*

Coachbuilder:	Hooper.	**3CM189.**
Engine:		D88Z.
Delivered:		4/30/38.
Body Style:		Limousine.
Design No:		Design 7302.
Body No:		9008.
Registration:		Not listed.
First Owner:		Carl Abegg-Stockar, Switzerland.
Present Owner:		Musée de l'Automobile, France.

Pictures: Drehsen/168.
Comments: Reportedly later owned by Charlie Chaplin. Shown with a patina of dust from the Musée white rock floor covering.

3CM191.

Coachbuilder:	H. J. Mulliner.
Engine:	(Original) D98Z.
Delivered:	5/4/38.
Body Style:	Limousine.
Design No:	Drawing 6087.
Body No:	4590.
Registration:	EXX 514.
First Owner:	Harry Flatau, UK.
Present Owner:	D. P. McClelland, UK.

Pictures:

Comments: Ordered without mascot. Later fitted with B80 engine.

3CM191. *(Photo: Mr. McClelland).*

3CM193.

Coachbuilder:	Hooper.
Engine:	E18Y.
Delivered:	5/13/38.
Body Style:	Limousine.
Design No:	Design 7282.
Body No:	9004.
Registration:	ANV 254.
First Owner:	Alice Katherine, Viscountess Wimborne, UK.
Present Owner:	Flournoy, US.

Pictures:

Comments:

3CM193. *(Photo: Sotheby 's).*

3CM195.

Coachbuilder:	Barker.
Engine:	E28Y.
Delivered:	5/2/38.
Body Style:	Sports saloon with division.
Body No:	7370.
Registration:	EXY 685.
First Owner:	A. R. Porter, UK.
Present Owner:	J. Pilø, UK.

Pictures: Phantoms/398, B117/35.
Comments: Barker & Co. stock.

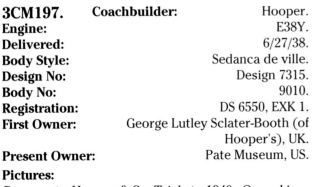

3CM195. *(Photo: Mr. Pilø).*

3CM197.

Coachbuilder:	Hooper.
Engine:	E38Y.
Delivered:	6/27/38.
Body Style:	Sedanca de ville.
Design No:	Design 7315.
Body No:	9010.
Registration:	DS 6550, EXK 1.
First Owner:	George Lutley Sclater-Booth (of Hooper's), UK.
Present Owner:	Pate Museum, US.

Pictures:

Comments: Hooper & Co. Trials to 1940. Owned in 1945 by Prince Regent of Iraq.

3CM197. *(Photo: RREC Photo Library).*

3CM199. *(Photo: Science Museum, London).*

Coachbuilder:	Hooper.	**3CM199.**
Engine:		E48Y.
Delivered:		5/26/38.
Body Style:		Limousine de ville.
Design No:		Design 7284.
Body No:		9012.
Registration:		EYE 795.
First Owner:		Jakob Heinrich Frey, Switzerland.
Present Owner:		M. Brugger, Switzerland.

Pictures:
Comments:

3CM201. *(Photo: Mr. Webb).*

Coachbuilder:	Park Ward.	**3CM201.**
Engine:		E58Y.
Delivered:		5/30/38.
Body Style:		Touring saloon.
Body No:		4416.
Registration:		EXT 4.
First Owner:		Mrs. C. W. Allen, UK.
Present Owner:		S. P. Webb, Canada.

Pictures: B148/25, FL/3084, FL/3333.
Comments:

3CM203. *(Photo: Mr. Barton).*

Coachbuilder:	Park Ward.	**3CM203.**
Engine:		E68Y.
Delivered:		4/12/38.
Body Style:		Touring limousine.
Design No:		Drawing 12899.
Body No:		4384.
Registration:		FLD 96.
First Owner:		A. L. Humes, US (5/40).
Present Owner:		**W. K. Barton, US.**

Pictures: FL/2632, FL/2652.
Comments: Rolls-Royce Ltd. stock, then used by Inspection Department.

The DL Series
of
Phantom III Cars

The DL series consists of 99 cars, numbered even,

3DL2 through 3DL200, less 3DL80, which was built as 3DH9.

Several changes were introduced in this series, including a

redesign of the cylinder heads and deletion of the hydraulic tappets.

Overdrive gearboxes were fitted beginning with 3DL172.

The DL series cars were delivered in late 1938 and 1939.

3DL2.   *(Photo: Stuckey Collection).*

Coachbuilder:	Hooper.	**3DL2.**
Engine:		E78Y.
Delivered:		5/5/38.
Body Style:		Limousine.
Design No:		Design 6443.
Body No:		8963.
Registration:		EXE 248.
First Owner:		W. Shakespeare, UK.
Present Owner:		Nakajima Collection, Japan.

Pictures: P/100, P/283.
Comments: Owned 1941 by the Governor of South Australia, 1945. Bought by Australian Government as Governor-General's car, 1947.

3DL4.

Coachbuilder:	Park Ward.	**3DL4.**
Engine:		E88Y.
Delivered:		5/4/38.
Body Style:		Touring limousine.
Design No:		Drawing 12899.
Body No:		4381.
Registration:		CS 8671.
First Owner:		Major J. Mann Thomson, UK.
Present Owner:		Unknown, UK.

Pictures:
Comments: Park Ward Ltd. stock.

3DL6. *The Wilkinson roadster.*   *(Photo: Mr. Mathews).*

Coachbuilder:	Arthur Mulliner.	**3DL6.**
Engine:		E98Y.
Delivered:		6/3/38.
Body Style:		(First) Limousine.
Registration:		KBC 344, FSU 122.
First Owner:		Eric S. Fox, UK.
Present Owner:		P. J. Mathews, UK.

Pictures: P/1311, B170/54, B176/50.
Comments: Arthur Mulliner Ltd. stock. Rebodied by Wilkinson in style of Brewster Henley roadster, 1977.

3DL8.   *(Photo: Mr. Waites).*

Coachbuilder:	Hooper.	**3DL8.**
Engine:		C18B.
Delivered:		5/17/38.
Body Style:		Limousine.
Design No:		Design 7317.
Body No:		9011.
Registration:		EYE 792.
First Owner:		H. E. Walters, UK.
Present Owner:		**L. Waites, US.**

Pictures:
Comments: Phantom II 1TA used as trade-in.

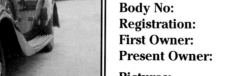

3DL10.
Coachbuilder: Arthur Mulliner.
Engine: C28B.
Delivered: 5/18/38.
Body Style: Saloon with division.
Registration: ANV 481.
First Owner: J. T. Barnard, UK.
Present Owner: B. Grant, UK.

Pictures: Phantoms/399 (Shown).
Comments: Arthur Mulliner Ltd. stock.

3DL10.

3DL12.
Coachbuilder: Windovers.
Engine: C38B.
Delivered: 3/29/38.
Body Style: Sedanca de ville.
Body No: 6525.
Registration: ͰYP 912.
First Owner: Sir (Mark Tatton) Richard Sykes, Bart, UK.
Present Owner: Atkins, US.
Pictures:
Comments: Windovers Ltd. stock, then taken over by Jack Barclay Ltd.

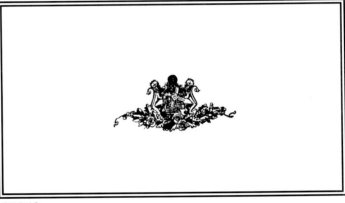
3DL12.

3DL14.
Coachbuilder: ,Rippon.
Engine: C48B.
Delivered: 5/13/38.
Body Style: Limousine.
Registration: BCX 200, KM 24458 (Australia).
First Owner: Mayor of Huddersfield, UK.
Present Owner: **J. Walter, Australia.**

Pictures:
Comments: Rippon Bros. stock. Shipped to Australia, 1989, after having been in the USA.

3DL14. *(Photo: Mr. Walter).*

3DL16.
Coachbuilder: Hooper.
Engine: C58B.
Delivered: 6/21/38.
Body Style: Sports saloon.
Design No: Design 7334.
Body No: 9014.
Registration: Not listed.
First Owner: George Ross, UK.
Present Owner: Unknown.

Pictures:
Comments:

3DL16. *(Photo: Science Museum, London).*

3DL18.   *(Photo: Mr. Baron).*

Coachbuilder:	Hooper.	**3DL18.**
Engine:		C68B.
Delivered:		6/8/38.
Body Style:		Limousine.
Design No:		Design 7327.
Body No:		9013.
Registration:		EUU 236.
First Owner:		Sir John William Lorden, UK.
Present Owner:		C. A. Baron, UK.

Pictures:

Comments: Ordered without mascot. Car returned to UK after having been in the USA.

3DL20.   *(Photo: Mr. Rosenberg).*

Coachbuilder:	Inskip.	**3DL20.**
Engine:		C78B.
Delivered:		8/8/38.
Body Style:		Limousine.
Registration:		Not listed.
First Owner:		Mrs. John H. Miller, US.
Present Owner:		**R. Rosenberg, US.**

Pictures: deCampi/164.
Comments:

3DL22.   *(Photo: Frank Dale & Stepsons).*

Coachbuilder:	Thrupp & Maberly.	**3DL22.**
Engine:		C88B.
Delivered:		6/18/38.
Body Style:		Touring limousine.
Design No:		Drawing SLF.1376.
Body No:		6814.
Registration:		FKJ 123.
First Owner:		Stanley Johnson, UK.
Present Owner:		**J. Ferguson, New Zealand.**

Pictures: CORR/312.
Comments:

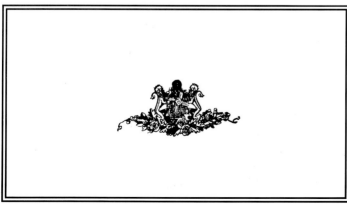

3DL24.

Coachbuilder:	Hooper.	**3DL24.**
Engine:		C98B.
Delivered:		5/25/38.
Body Style:		Limousine.
Design No:		Design 6443.
Body No:		8964.
Registration:		DPX 111.
First Owner:		J. J. Morgan, UK.
Present Owner:		Central Garage, Croydon, UK (1954).

Pictures:
Comments:

3DL26.
Coachbuilder:	Thrupp & Maberly.
Engine:	R18M.
Delivered:	7/6/38.
Body Style:	Cabriolet.
Design No:	Drawing SLE.1368.
Body No:	6815.
Registration:	DNU 1.
First Owner:	Krishnachandra, Rajah of Parla Kimedi, India.
Present Owner:	P. Wichard, US.

Pictures: FL/2329, CORR/315 (Shown, misnumbered 3AZ172).
Comments: Owned by Raja Saheb of Bilkha, 1946-1954.

3DL26. *(Photo: Mr. R. M. Bowers).*

3DL28.
Coachbuilder:	Hooper.
Engine:	R28M.
Delivered:	7/13/38.
Body Style:	Sports saloon.
Design No:	Design 7372.
Body No:	9022.
Registration:	Not listed.
First Owner:	W. Fielden, UK.
Present Owner:	D. Z. de Ferranti, Ireland.

Pictures:
Comments: Car dismantled, awaiting restoration.

3DL28.

3DL30.
Coachbuilder:	Rippon.
Engine:	(Original) R38M.
Delivered:	10/4/38.
Body Style:	Limousine.
Registration:	JX 6888.
First Owner:	Percy Horsfall, UK.
Present Owner:	M. D. Parker, UK.

Pictures: B143/18, B152/51, B166/50, TERR/198.
Comments: Rippon Bros. stock. Later fitted with B80 engine.

3DL30. *(Photo: RREC Photo Library).*

3DL32.
Coachbuilder:	H. J. Mulliner.
Engine:	R48M.
Delivered:	6/30/38.
Body Style:	Sedanca de ville.
Design No:	Drawing 6012.
Body No:	4585.
Registration:	FGO 123.
First Owner:	Manuel Gomez Waddington, UK.
Present Owner:	W. J. Harnett, US.

Pictures: FL/595.
Comments: Jack Barclay Ltd. stock.

3DL32. *(Photo: Illustrated London News).*

3DL34.   *(Photo: D. S. Archives).*

Coachbuilder:	H. J. Mulliner.	**3DL34.**
Engine:		R58M.
Delivered:		7/9/38.
Body Style:		Sedanca de ville.
Body No:		4584.
Registration:		CC 7938, AYX 701 T.
First Owner:		Sir Ernest Oppenheimer, South Africa.
Present Owner:		Spencer, UK.

Pictures: Phantoms/400, TS/29, FL/618.
Comments: Jack Barclay Ltd. stock.

3DL36.

Coachbuilder:	Park Ward.	**3DL36.**
Engine:		R68M.
Delivered:		5/23/38.
Body Style:		Limousine.
Design No:		Drawing 13133.
Body No:		4419.
Registration:		EXE 250.
First Owner:		Mrs. Mabel S. Luck, UK.
Present Owner:		**Scrapped.**

Pictures: CORR/260 (Shown).
Comments: Phantom II 64UK used as trade-in.
Scrapped in USA; last owner was J. B. Nethercutt.

3DL38.

Coachbuilder:	Park Ward.	**3DL38.**
Engine:		R78M.
Delivered:		6/24/38.
Body Style:		Touring limousine.
Body No:		4336.
Registration:		EYU 310, JW 45.
First Owner:		William Murray, UK.
Present Owner:		A. J. Wilkins, UK.

Pictures: FL/885 (Shown).
Comments: Jack Barclay Ltd. stock. Owned by Lord Beaverbrook, 1949.

3DL40.   *(Photo: Mr. Possehl).*

Coachbuilder:	Hooper.	**3DL40.**
Engine:		R88M.
Delivered:		9/30/38.
Body Style:		Limousine.
Design No:		7412.
Body No:		9035.
Registration:		Not listed.
First Owner:		F. Ambrose Clark, US (7/40).
Present Owner:		J. H. Possehl, US.

Pictures: FL/745, FL/908.
Comments: Hooper & Co. stock.

3DL42.
Coachbuilder: Park Ward.
Engine: R98M.
Delivered: 7/4/38.
Body Style: Touring limousine.
Body No: 4337.
Registration: FYF 95.
First Owner: H. H. Harjes, UK (8/39).
Present Owner: **J. H. Fisher, US.**

Pictures: Phantoms/400.
Comments: Jack Barclay Ltd. stock.

3DL42. *(Photo: Dr. Fisher).*

3DL44.
Coachbuilder: H. J. Mulliner.
Engine: H18W.
Delivered: 8/3/38.
Body Style: Sedanca de ville.
Body No: 4603.
Registration: Not listed.
First Owner: Mrs. Kathleen Moody, UK.
Present Owner: Harold Radford Hire, UK (1951).

Pictures:
Comments: Rolls-Royce Ltd. stock.

3DL44.

3DL46.
Coachbuilder: H. J. Mulliner.
Engine: H28W.
Delivered: 7/6/38.
Body Style: Saloon with division.
Design No: Drawing 5912.
Body No: 4564.
Registration: FGO 124.
First Owner: Harold Butler, UK.
Present Owner: **D. Bennett, US.**

Pictures:
Comments: Jack Barclay Ltd. stock.

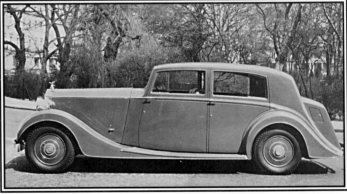

3DL46. *(Photo: Stuckey Collection).*

3DL48.
Coachbuilder: Salmons.
Engine: H38W.
Delivered: 8/17/38.
Body Style: Sports saloon.
Registration: Not listed.
First Owner: John White, UK.
Present Owner: D. R. Coleman, UK (1956).

Pictures:
Comments:

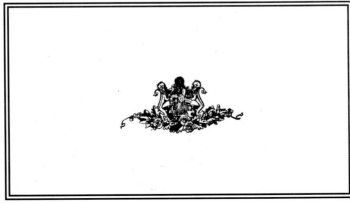

3DL48.

3DL50.   *(Photo: Mr. Margulies).*

Coachbuilder:	H. J. Mulliner.	**3DL50.**
Engine:		H48W.
Delivered:		9/8/38.
Body Style:		6-Light saloon with division.
Body No:		4617.
Registration:		Not listed.
First Owner:		Sir Charles Hyde, Bart, UK.
Present Owner:		D. Margulies, UK.

Pictures:
Comments: Rolls-Royce Ltd. Trials. Owned by Ministry of War Transport, 1943.

3DL52.   *(Photo: RREC Photo Library).*

Coachbuilder:	Hooper.	**3DL52.**
Engine:		H58W.
Delivered:		7/21/38.
Body Style:		Limousine.
Design No:		7253.
Body No:		9017.
Registration:		16 YF 70.
First Owner:		Alexander Shaw, 2nd Baron Craigmyle, UK.
Present Owner:		R. B. Chamberlain, UK.

Pictures: FL/897, FL/1369.
Comments: Hooper & Co. stock. Craigmyle also owned 3CM19. Donated to Scottish Command, 1940. Presented to Junior Tradesmen's Regiment, 1960's.

3DL54.   *(Photo: Mr. Croutcher).*

Coachbuilder:	Park Ward.	**3DL54.**
Engine:		H68W.
Delivered:		8/15/38.
Body Style:		Sedanca de ville.
Body No:		4427.
Registration:		EYT 8.
First Owner:		S. C. Millenstead, UK.
Present Owner:		D. L. Croutcher, US.

Pictures: FL/1395, FL/1502.
Comments:

3DL56. *The HJM cabriolet..*   *(Photo: Mr. Yardumian).*

Coachbuilder:	Hooper.	**3DL56.**
Engine:		H78W.
Delivered:		9/9/38.
Body Style:		(First) Limousine.
Design No:		7253.
Body No:		9018.
Registration:		ODL 82.
First Owner:		Dr. (William) Lombard Murphy, Ireland.
Present Owner:		**H. S. Yardumian, US.**

Pictures: Phantoms/401.
Comments: Hooper & Co. stock. Rebodied 1952 as H. J. Mulliner cabriolet 5149.

3DL58.   **Coachbuilder:**   Binder.
Engine: H88W.
Delivered: 6/14/38.
Body Style: Close-coupled saloon.
Registration: Not listed.
First Owner: Robert Suel, France (5/39).
Present Owner: R. Suel, France (1951).

Pictures:
Comments: Rolls-Royce Ltd. Continental Trials.
Body to 3DL176, 1939.

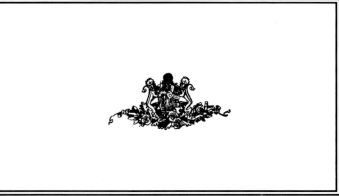

3DL58.

3DL60.   **Coachbuilder:**   Barker.
Engine: H98W.
Delivered: 8/16/38.
Body Style: Saloon with division.
Registration: FGX 820.
First Owner: Charles A. Lundy, UK (12/38).
Present Owner: W. J. Harnett, US.

Pictures:
Comments: Original order by Erdmann & Rossi, but
reverted to stock.

3DL60.   *(Photo: Mr. Harnett).*

3DL62.   **Coachbuilder:**   Hooper.
Engine: B18C.
Delivered: 11/1/38.
Body Style: Sedanca de ville.
Design No: Design 7390.
Body No: 9027.
Registration: FLX 59, MAN 5326, P 111 MAN.
First Owner: Dr. Alexander Hamilton Rice,
France (2/39).
Second Owner: S. Barraclough, UK.
Pictures: Bishop/41, B146/40, B160/39, B152/36 (Shown).
Comments: Earl's Court Show, 1938, Hooper stand.
Hooper & Co. stock. Rice also owned, used, 3CM161.

3DL62.

3DL64.   **Coachbuilder:**   Hooper.
Engine: B28C.
Delivered: 9/20/38.
Body Style: Limousine.
Design No: Design 7253.
Body No: 9019.
Registration: Not listed.
First Owner: Mrs. Mary K. Ellis, US (1/40).
Present Owner: B. Edlund, US.

Pictures:
Comments: Rolls-Royce Ltd. stock. Sent on consign-
ment to Inskip.

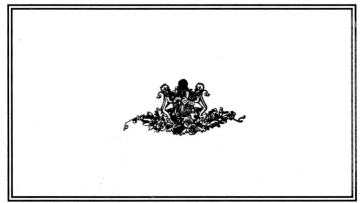

3DL64.

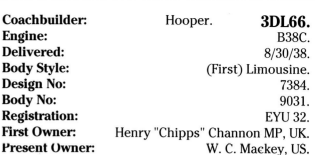

3DL66. *Roadster by Wilkinson.*   *(Photo: Mr. Mackey).*

Coachbuilder:	Hooper.	**3DL66.**
Engine:		B38C.
Delivered:		8/30/38.
Body Style:		(First) Limousine.
Design No:		7384.
Body No:		9031.
Registration:		EYU 32.
First Owner:	Henry "Chipps" Channon MP, UK.	
Present Owner:	W. C. Mackey, US.	

Pictures: TS/40.
Comments: Body to 3AX15, Mar 1973. Rebodied by Wilkinson in style of Brewster Henley roadster, 1973.

3DL68.   *(RREC Photo Library).*

Coachbuilder:	Hooper.	**3DL68.**
Engine:	(Original) B48C.	
Delivered:		9/16/38.
Body Style:		Pullman limousine.
Design No:		7393.
Body No:		9025.
Registration:		EYV 220.
First Owner:	Harold Sidney, 1st Viscount Rothermere, UK.	
Present Owner:	**C. L. Doyle, US.**	

Pictures: Phantoms/402, P3TS/30.
Comments: Rolls-Royce Ltd. stock. Later fitted with B60 engine.

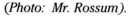

3DL70.   *(Photo: Mr. Rossum).*

Coachbuilder:	Hooper.	**3DL70.**
Engine:		B58C.
Delivered:		12/12/38.
Body Style:		Limousine.
Design No:		7408.
Body No:		9038.
Registration:		MCO 88.
First Owner:	Louis Nicholas, UK.	
Present Owner:	**J. R. Rossum, US.**	

Pictures: TERR/128.
Comments: Hooper & Co. stock. Body originally allocated to this chassis placed on 3DL140.

3DL72.

Coachbuilder:	Park Ward.	**3DL72.**
Engine:		B68C.
Delivered:		8/22/38.
Body Style:		Touring limousine.
Body No:		4382.
Registration:		EYE 799.
First Owner:	Mrs. Victor G. Walker, UK.	
Present Owner:	H. G. Anderson, US.	

Pictures: TERR/190 (Shown).
Comments: Rolls-Royce Ltd. stock. Phantom II 84PY and 20/25 GBA39 used as trade-ins. Major Walker owned 3AX41.

3DL74. Coachbuilder: Hooper.
Engine: B78C.
Delivered: 11/2/38.
Body Style: Limousine de ville.
Design No: Design 7421.
Body No: 9036.
Registration: ADA 999, J 190, J 277, MAC 222, ECJ 156.
First Owner: Ada, Mrs. Harry Scribbans, UK.
Present Owner: Sir James Cayzer, Bart, UK.

Pictures: CORR/130, Sotheby/'89, Phantoms/402 (Shown).
Comments: Earl's Court Show, 1938, Rolls-Royce stand.

3DL74.

3DL76. Coachbuilder: Thrupp & Maberly.
Engine: B88C.
Delivered: 10/25/38.
Body Style: Touring limousine.
Design No: Drawing SLE.1414.
Body No: 6831.
Registration: ANV 688.
First Owner: Mrs. C. Sears, UK.
Present Owner: J. G. Sears, UK.

Pictures: Tubbs/37, Ullyett/33, Hugo/184, Car/1675, Phantoms/206 (Shown).
Comments: Earl's Court Show, 1938, Rolls-Royce stand. Owned, 1952, by Stanley E. Sears, (who also owned 3AZ38.)

3DL76.

3DL78. Coachbuilder: Rippon.
Engine: (Original) B98C.
Delivered: 8/12/38.
Body Style: Touring limousine.
Registration: EYG 194.
First Owner: J. H. Robinson, UK (1946).
Present Owner: T. S. Barnes, US.

Pictures:
Comments: Earl's Court Show, 1938, Rippon stand. Used by Lord Mayor of Rochdale, 1955. Now with Cadillac engine.

3DL78. *(Photo: RREC Photo Library).*

3DL80 built as 3DH9.

3DL82.   *(Photo: Mr. Price).*

Coachbuilder:	H. J. Mulliner.	**3DL82.**
Engine:		Q28N.
Delivered:		8/29/38.
Body Style:		Touring saloon.
Body No:		4583.
Registration:		FXP 479.
First Owner:		Lady Ethel Lindesay, UK (5/39).
Present Owner:		G. D. A. Price, UK.

Pictures: CORR/194.
Comments: Jack Barclay Ltd. stock.

3DL84.   *(Photo: Mr. John Wallerich via RROC).*

Coachbuilder:	Park Ward.	**3DL84.**
Engine:		Q38N.
Delivered:		11/2/38.
Body Style:		Touring limousine.
Body No:		4604.
Registration:		FLC 694.
First Owner:		Sir George Augustus Sutton; Bart, UK.
Present Owner:		K. Takihana, Japan.

Pictures: CORR/262, FL/507, FL1190.
Comments: Earl's Court Show, 1938, Park Ward stand. To USA, 1960; Japan, 1990.

3DL86.   *(Photo: RROC Foundation).*

Coachbuilder:	James Young.	**3DL86.**
Engine:		Q48N.
Delivered:		10/28/38.
Body Style:		2-Door saloon coupé.
Design No:		Design 4531R.
Registration:		JB 1, HPC 111.
First Owner:		R. C. Graseby, UK.
Present Owner:		**F. F. Guyton, US.**

Pictures: Ullyett/53, CORR/366, Oldham/256c.
Comments: Earl's Court Show, 1938, James Young stand. Parallel opening doors. Later fitted with overdrive by Norris Allen.

3DL88.   *(Photo: PIIITS Archives).*

Coachbuilder:	H. J. Mulliner.	**3DL88.**
Engine:		Q58N.
Delivered:		10/24/38.
Body Style:		Sedanca de ville.
Design No:		Drawing 6194.
Body No:		4595.
Registration:		EXP 73, HPE 174.
First Owner:		Park Royal Stadium Ltd.,UK.
Present Owner:		Unknown, Germany.

Pictures: TERR/158, P/1345, P/1359.
Comments: Earl's Court Show, 1938, H. J. Mulliner stand. John Croall & Son stock, then Jack Barclay Ltd. stock. Shipped to Australia from the USA in 1984.

3DL90.

Coachbuilder:	Park Ward.
Engine:	Q68N.
Delivered:	9/15/38.
Body Style:	Touring limousine.
Body No:	4383.
Registration:	FXX 100.
First Owner:	Issac Agnew, UK (6/42).
Present Owner:	C. E. Lindros, US.

Pictures: FL/3214.
Comments: To Bombay for use as Allied Motors Trials Oct. 1938, then returned as Jack Barclay Ltd. stock.

3DL90. *(Photo: Mr. Lindros).*

3DL92.

Coachbuilder:	Vesters & Neirinck.
Engine:	Q78N.
Delivered:	12/15/38.
Body Style:	Saloon with division.
Registration:	Not listed.
First Owner:	Baron Brugmann de Walzin, Belgium.
Present Owner:	C. Mahy, Belgium.

Pictures: B136/7 (Shown).
Comments:

3DL92.

3DL94.

Coachbuilder:	Freestone & Webb.
Engine:	Q88N.
Delivered:	12/29/38.
Body Style:	Cabriolet.
Design No:	1971.
Body No:	1317.
Registration:	FKN 1.
First Owner:	Kenneth L. Bilbrough, UK.
Present Owner:	**J. R. Fisher, US.**

Pictures: Oldham/256d, CORR/79 (Shown).
Comments: Built with centre gearchange, and ordered without mascot. Featured in *The Autocar*, 21 July 1939. To USA, 1962.

3DL94.

3DL96.

Coachbuilder:	Park Ward.
Engine:	Q98N.
Delivered:	11/28/38.
Body Style:	Sports tourer.
Body No:	4605.
Registration:	GBL 157.
First Owner:	Maharajah Lukhdhirji of Morvi, India.
Present Owner:	C. Howard. UK.

Pictures: CORR/262, FL/272, FL/1381.
Comments: Featured in *The Motor*, 17 January 1939. To USA, 1956, to UK 1992.

3DL96. *(Photo: Stuckey Collection).*

3DL98. The Worblaufen saloon.   *(Photo: Mr. W. Richey).*

Coachbuilder:	Hooper.	**3DL98.**
Engine:		E18Z.
Delivered:		9/10/38.
Body Style:		(First) Sports limousine.
Design No:		7419.
Body No:		9043.
Registration:		CGO 100 B.
First Owner:		Benjamin Guinness, France.
Present Owner:		**T. M. Long, US.**

Pictures: Phantoms/403.
Comments: Guinness also owned 3AZ110 and 3AZ150. Rebodied as Worblaufen saloon.

3DL100.   *(Photo: RROC Foundation).*

Coachbuilder:	H. J. Mulliner.	**3DL100.**
Engine:		E28Z.
Delivered:		11/18/38.
Body Style:		Sedanca de ville.
Body No:		4639.
Registration:		Not listed.
First Owner:		Thomas F. Hamilton, US (9/40).
Present Owner:		J. R. Watkins, US.

Pictures: Phantoms/403.
Comments: Car Mart Ltd. stock. Featured in The Autocar, 29 November 1940.

3DL102.

Coachbuilder:	H. J. Mulliner.	**3DL102.**
Engine:		E38Z.
Delivered:		11/15/38.
Body Style:		(First) Saloon with division.
Body No:		4642.
Registration:		FLD 95.
First Owner:		Theodore P. Cozzika, Egypt.
Present Owner:		A. S. Andreadis, Greece.

Pictures:
Comments: Rolls-Royce Ltd. Trials. Cozzika also owned 3DL142. First body to 3AZ98. Rebodied with Hooper cabriolet 9621, fitted 1950 while owned by King George II of Greece.

3DL104.   *(Photo: Mr. Tom Clarke).*

Coachbuilder:	H. J. Mulliner.	**3DL104.**
Engine:		E48Z.
Delivered:		11/22/38.
Body Style:		Sedanca de ville.
Design No:		Drawing 6043.
Body No:		4635.
Registration:		FLX 885.
First Owner:		Sir Herbert Smith, Bart, UK.
Present Owner:		Unknown, UK.

Pictures: TERR/158.
Comments: H. J. Mulliner & Co. stock. Smith also owned 3AZ168, 3BT81 and 3CM31. 3BT81 used as trade-in on 3DL104. To Australia from the USA, 1988; to UK, 1990. Engine for sale, 1994, UK.

3DL106.
Coachbuilder:	Hooper.
Engine:	E58Z.
Delivered:	8/19/38.
Body Style:	Landaulet.
Design No:	Design 7417.
Body No:	9044.
Registration:	EYV 218.
First Owner:	Lady Patricia Florence Susan Guinness, UK.
Present Owner:	L. Weinstein, US.

Pictures: FL/3055 (Shown).
Comments: Original order by A. Stern. Owned by Lord Iveagh, 1954.

3DL106.

3DL108.
Coachbuilder:	Park Ward.
Engine:	E68Z.
Delivered:	10/4/38.
Body Style:	Touring limousine.
Body No:	4338.
Registration:	FGW 388, MWB 832.
First Owner:	J. H. Clement-Ansell, UK.
Present Owner:	Unknown, France.

Pictures: Bennett/39, FL/897, P/100.
Comments: Jack Barclay Ltd. stock. Body modernised by Park Ward, c.1954. Sold to France via Hong Kong, 1990.

3DL108. *(Photo: RROC Foundation).*

3DL110.
Coachbuilder:	H. J. Mulliner.
Engine:	E78Z.
Delivered:	10/31/38.
Body Style:	Sedanca de ville.
Design No:	Drawing 6123.
Body No:	4604.
Registration:	CGD 1.
First Owner:	Robert H. Carlaw, UK.
Present Owner:	K. W. Shodeen, US.

Pictures:
Comments: Scottish Show, 1938, John Croall stand. Rolls-Royce Ltd. stock.

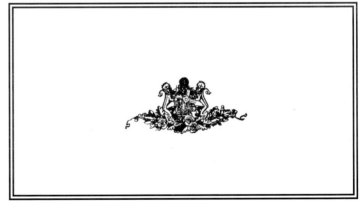

3DL110.

3DL112.
Coachbuilder:	
Engine:	E88Z.
Delivered:	9/10/38.
Body Style:	Under construction.
Registration:	Not listed.
First Owner:	Erdmann & Rossi Gmbh, Germany.
Present Owner:	J. B. Nethercutt, US.

Pictures: FL/1408 (Chassis only) (Shown).
Comments: Sold to Erdmann & Rossi for fitting of a saloon body. The chassis never carried coachwork and was discovered after having been bricked into a cellar during World War II.

3DL112. The chassis as found. A replica body is being built.

3DL114.

Coachbuilder:	Hooper.	**3DL114.**
Engine:		E98Z.
Delivered:		12/30/38.
Body Style:		Sedanca de ville.
Design No:		7390.
Body No:		9049.
Registration:		DAC 257.
First Owner:		J. T. Brockhouse, UK.
Present Owner:		A. P. Zafer, UK.

Pictures:
FL/721, TERR/126 (Shown).
Comments: Scottish Show, 1938, Hooper stand.
Hooper & Co. stock.

3DL116. After conversion to tourer.   (Photo: Mr. Harris).

Coachbuilder:	Hooper.	**3DL116.**
Engine:		Z18E.
Delivered:		11/5/38.
Body Style:		(First) Landaulet.
Design No:		6660.
Body No:		8944.
Registration:		Not listed.
First Owner:		J. A. Salz, US.
Present Owner:		Unknown, Germany.

Pictures: FL/89.
Comments: Converted to tourer by Mazzara &
Meyer, 1952. To Germany, 1992.

3DL118.

Coachbuilder:	Park Ward.	**3DL118.**
Engine:		Z28E.
Delivered:		1/28/39.
Body Style:		Cabriolet.
Body No:		4607.
Registration:		HPF 129.
First Owner:	Hon. Peter Randolph Louis Beatty,	
		UK.
Present Owner:		R. R. Wilke, US.

Pictures: CORR/263 (Shown).
Comments: Beatty's brother owned 3AZ92. Car in
Rhodesia, 1951-1962: to USA, 1962.

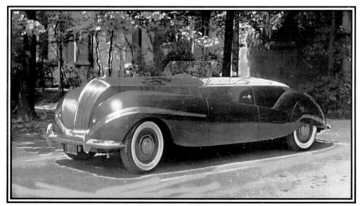

3DL120. The Labourdette tourer. (Photo: RROC Foundation).

Coachbuilder:	Hooper.	**3DL120.**
Engine:		Z38E.
Delivered:		1/3/39.
Body Style:		(First) Limousine de ville.
Design No:		7421.
Body No:		9056.
Registration:		Not listed.
First Owner:	Oscar Greenwald, US (2/40).	
Present Owner:		H. Boyer, US.

Pictures: CORR/433, Oldham/256f, FL/1507.
Comments: Brussels, Amsterdam, Geneva Shows,
1939, Rolls-Royce stand; New York World's Fair,
1939. Body to 3DL180. Owner 2: Louie Ritter.
Rebodied as Labourdette tourer, 1947.

3DL122.
Coachbuilder:	See comments.
Engine:	Z48E.
Delivered:	2/3/39.
Body Style:	(First) Touring limousine.
Design No:	Drawing E11468.
Registration:	FXV 707.
First Owner:	Colonel Jack D. Olding, UK (5/40).
Present Owner:	**K. R. Karger, US.**

Pictures: CORR/87, Rossfedlt/113, FL/894.
Comments: Barker(completed Hooper). Hooper & Co. stock. Rebodied with Gurney Nutting saloon ex 3CP142, 1953. Barker body for sale, 1957. Owned by Earl of Shrewsbury & Waterford, 1953.

3DL122.   *(Photo: Mr. Karger).*

3DL124.
Coachbuilder:	Hooper.
Engine:	W18H.
Delivered:	12/13/38.
Body Style:	Limousine.
Design No:	7438.
Body No:	9046.
Registration:	DPX 911, CUE 909, 199 MAN.
First Owner:	L. T. White, UK.
Present Owner:	S. Barraclough, UK.

Pictures: B160/39.
Comments: Scottish Show, 1938, Hooper stand. Rolls-Royce Ltd. stock.

3DL124.   *(Photo: Mr. Barraclough).*

3DL126.
Coachbuilder:	H. J. Mulliner.
Engine:	E78A.
Delivered:	1/5/39.
Body Style:	Saloon with division.
Body No:	4614.
Registration:	CGD 849.
First Owner:	Miss. E. W. Thomson, UK.
Present Owner:	S. J. Gilbert, US.

Pictures: Phantoms/410.
Comments: Miss Thomson also owned 3AZ74. HJM "High-vision" windscreen, with rear doors fully wood panelled.

3DL126.   *(Photo: Mr. Gilbert).*

3DL128.
Coachbuilder:	Hooper.
Engine:	W58H.
Delivered:	3/17/39.
Body Style:	Limousine de ville.
Design No:	7477.
Body No:	9074.
Registration:	HPJ 1, TYF 867.
First Owner:	Oliver Edwin Simmonds MP, UK.
Present Owner:	S. B. Girdler, US.

Pictures: TERR/128, P3TS/13.
Comments:

3DL128.   *(Photo: Mr. Girdler).*

3DL130.

Coachbuilder:	H. J. Mulliner.	**3DL130.**
Engine:		Z88E.
Delivered:		3/30/39.
Body Style:		4-light saloon.
Design No:		Drawing 5867.
Body No:		4669.
Registration:		Not listed.
First Owner:		Sir Edmund Frank Crane, UK.
Present Owner:		M. F. Crookes, South Africa.
		(1957).

Pictures:
Comments: Sir Edmund also owned 3AX181.
Ordered without mascot.

3DL132.   *(Photo: National Motor Museum, England).*

Coachbuilder:	James Young.	**3DL132.**
Engine:		Z98E.
Delivered:		2/16/39.
Body Style:		2-light saloon coupé.
Design No:		4531R.
Registration:		154 FYV.
First Owner:		Francis V. duPont, US (4/39).
Present Owner:		J. C. Owen, US.

Pictures: The Car/1672, FL1492.
Comments: Jack Barclay Ltd. stock. Parallel opening doors. To France 1948, to UK, 1963. In UK 1994, for engine overhaul.

3DL134.   *(Photo: Mr. Wallace Donoghue).*

Coachbuilder:	Hooper.	**3DL134.**
Engine:		N18Q.
Delivered:		1/10/39.
Body Style:		Limousine.
Design No:		7438.
Body No:		9047.
Registration:		Not listed.
First Owner:		Lyman Candee (11/39), US.
Present Owner:		D. J. Ehrlich, US.

Pictures:
Comments: Rolls~Royce Ltd. stock.

3DL136.   *(Photo: RROC Foundation).*

Coachbuilder:	Brewster.	**3DL136.**
Engine:		W68H.
Delivered:		12/13/38.
Body Style:		Trouville town car.
Body No:		5992.
Registration:		Not listed.
First Owner:		J. S. Inskip, US.
Present Owner:		A. L. Shaw, US.

Pictures: deCampi 23/161.
Comments: Body ex 69W. Inskip Inc. Trials. Front opening later sealed and divison removed by Inskip.

3DL138. Coachbuilder: Park Ward.
Engine: N38Q.
Delivered: 1/20/38.
Body Style: Touring limousine.
Design No: Drawing 13361.
Body No: 4619.
Registration: Not listed.
First Owner: HIH Shahinshah Reza Pahlevi, Iran.
Present Owner: Government of Iran.

Pictures:
Comments:

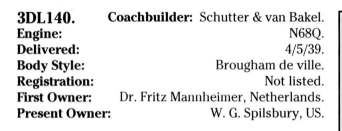

3DL138.

3DL140. Coachbuilder: Schutter & van Bakel.
Engine: N68Q.
Delivered: 4/5/39.
Body Style: Brougham de ville.
Registration: Not listed.
First Owner: Dr. Fritz Mannheimer, Netherlands.
Present Owner: W. G. Spilsbury, US.

Pictures: Oldham/256G, FL/278, FL/1723, FL/1724.
Comments:

3DL140. *(Photo: Mr. Spilsbury).*

3DL142. Coachbuilder: H. J. Mulliner.
Engine: W48H.
Delivered: 12/20/38.
Body Style: Saloon with division.
Design No: Drawing 6304.
Body No: 4698.
Registration: Not listed.
First Owner: Theodore P. Cozzika, Egypt (8/39).
Present Owner: Ex-King Constantine, Greece.

Pictures:
Comments: Originally ordered as a Sodomka-bodied 2/3 seater cabriolet for Joseph Trachta of Czechoslovakia, but canceled. Cozzika also owned 3DL102.

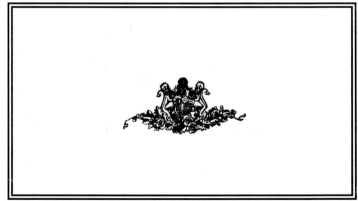

3DL142.

3DL144. Coachbuilder: Binder.
Engine: H28Q.
Delivered: (Guarantee) 5/6/39.
Body Style: Sedanca de ville.
Registration: Not listed.
First Owner: Khedive Abbas Hilmi II, France.
Present Owner: Emara, Canada.

Pictures:
Comments:

3DL144.

3DL146. *(Photo: Mrs. Pryer).*

Coachbuilder:	H. J. Mulliner.	**3DL146.**
Engine:		W78H.
Delivered:		1/23/39.
Body Style:		Sedanca de ville.
Body No:		4643.
Registration:		FLD 97.
First Owner:		Mrs. Winkworth, France.
Present Owner:		**H. Pryer, Australia.**

Pictures: P/23, P/102.
Comments: Rolls-Royce Ltd. Trials. Returned to the UK Oct. 1952. Shipped to Australia, June 1968.

3DL148. *(Photo: Mr. Dameyer).*

Coachbuilder:	Hooper.	**3DL148.**
Engine:		W88H.
Delivered:		5/18/39.
Body Style:		Sports limousine.
Design No:		7520.
Body No:		9106.
Registration:		GV 7128.
First Owner:		William James, 1st Baron Glanely, UK.
Present Owner:		L. Smith, UK.

Pictures: CORR/135, B124/19, P3TS/17.
Comments: Glanely also owned 3BU132. To USA, 1963. Car owned in Canada in 1970's and 1980's.

3DL150. *(Photo: Mr. Kinloch).*

Coachbuilder:	Hooper.	**3DL150.**
Engine:		N98Q.
Delivered:		4/3/39.
Body Style:		Sedanca de ville.
Design No:		7516.
Body No:		9077.
Registration:		FUW 1.
First Owner:		Lupino Lane, UK.
Present Owner:		**A. Kinloch, Australia.**

Pictures: B166/51.
Comments:

3DL152. *(Photo: Dr. Nickels).*

Coachbuilder:	Barker.	**3DL152.**
Engine:		E18A.
Delivered:		6/5/39.
Body Style:		Touring limousine.
Registration:		FLX 886.
First Owner:		HE Sir Noel Hughes Charles, Bart, Brazil (10/41).
Present Owner:		J. H. Nickels, US.

Pictures: Oldham/208e, FL/854, FL/3144, P3TS/43.
Comments: Body ex 39EX. New York World's Fair, 1939. Sir Charles was UK Minister to Brazil. Ambassadorial car in Cairo 1949-1952 and Rangoon 1953-1956. To US, 1968.

3DL154. Coachbuilder: Freestone & Webb.
Engine: E28A.
Delivered: 6/2/39.
Body Style: Touring limousine.
Design No: 2026.
Body No: 1334.
Registration: FXM 7.
First Owner: Sir John Leigh, Bart, M. P., UK.
Present Owner: **J. J. D. Altman, Australia.**

Pictures: CORR/79, P/1174, P1253.
Comments: Leigh also owned 3AZ68, 3BU136, 3BT99.
Shipped to Australia, 1985.

3DL154. *(Photo: Mr. Altman).*

3DL156. Coachbuilder: Hooper.
Engine: M18R.
Delivered: 3/13/39.
Body Style: Limousine de ville.
Design No: 7421A.
Body No: 9081.
Registration: Not listed.
First Owner: Mrs. Blanche J. Parks, US (2/40).
Present Owner: C. Bryant, US.

Pictures: FL/718, FL/795, CORR/135.
Comments: Displayed at New York World's Fair,
1939.

3DL156. *(Photo: Mr. Bryant).*

3DL158. Coachbuilder: H. J. Mulliner.
Engine: W98H.
Delivered: 7/13/39.
Body Style: Limousine de ville.
Design No: Drawing 6282.
Body No: 4695.
Registration: Not listed.
First Owner: Prince Regent Aditya Dhipya
Present Owner: **Scrapped.**

Pictures: B152/8 (Shown).
Comments:

3DL158.

3DL160. Coachbuilder: H. J. Mulliner.
Engine: M28R.
Delivered: 7/4/39.
Body Style: Saloon with division.
Design No: Drawing 6289.
Body No: 4692.
Registration: FXO 6.
First Owner: Mrs. Wise, UK.
Present Owner: Unknown, Japan.

Pictures:
Comments: Ordered without mascot, and with special gear lever. To Japan from USA, 1990.

3DL160. *(Photo: RREC Photo Library).*

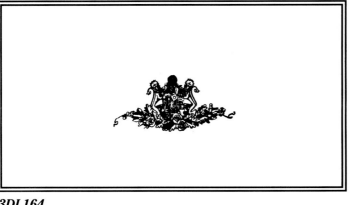

3DL162.   *(Photo: Mr. Nilsson).*

Coachbuilder:	Wiklunds Nordbergs. **3DL162.**
Engine:	M38R.
Delivered:	6/13/39.
Body Style:	Limousine.
Registration:	Not listed.
First Owner:	Mrs. Anton Ohlsson, Sweden.
Present Owner:	O. K. Nilsson, Sweden.

Pictures: B134/25.
Comments:

3DL164.

Coachbuilder:	Binder. **3DL164.**
Engine:	M48R.
Delivered:	9/23/39.
Body Style:	Saloon with division.
Registration:	Not listed.
First Owner:	E. Boucherit, France.
Present Owner:	Unknown.

Pictures:
Comments: Phantom II 5UK used as trade-in.

3DL166.   *(Photo: Mr. Cullen).*

Coachbuilder:	Windovers. **3DL166.**
Engine:	M58R.
Delivered:	6/23/39.
Body Style:	Limousine.
Body No:	6512.
Registration:	FXE 868.
First Owner:	Andrew Weir, 1st Baron Inverforth, UK.
Present Owner:	J. T. Cullen, UK.

Pictures: B144/11,P3TS/42.
Comments: Windovers Ltd. stock. Recovered, derelict, in London, 1982 and fully restored.

3DL168.

Coachbuilder:	Hooper. **3DL168.**
Engine:	M68R.
Delivered:	9/26/39.
Body Style:	Limousine.
Design No:	7503.
Body No:	9061.
Registration:	Not listed.
First Owner:	Annie M, Mrs. L. V. Bell, US (1/40).
Present Owner:	**J. Weideman, US.**

Pictures: FL/2452 (Shown).
Comments: Rolls-Royce Ltd. stock.

3DL170.
Coachbuilder:	Hooper.
Engine:	M78R.
Delivered:	6/30/39.
Body Style:	Limousine.
Design No:	7438.
Body No:	9048.
Registration:	Not listed.
First Owner:	A. S. Hutchins, US (1/40).
Present Owner:	**L. Daniels, US.**

Pictures:
Comments: Rolls-Royce Ltd. stock.

3DL170. *(Photo: Mrs. Daniels).*

3DL172.
Coachbuilder:	Gurney Nutting.
Engine:	Z68E.
Delivered:	8/23/39.
Body Style:	Saloon with division.
Registration:	MPE 2.
First Owner:	S. L. Groom, UK.
Present Owner:	L. Smith, UK.

Pictures: FL/760, FL/3244, FL/3545.
Comments: First chassis fitted with overdrive gear-box as standard.

3DL172. *(Photo: Mr. Smith).*

3DL174.
Coachbuilder:	H. J. Mulliner.
Engine:	Z58E.
Delivered:	8/31/39.
Body Style:	Sedanca de ville.
Body No:	4708.
Registration:	JPC 298.
First Owner:	J. D. Titler, UK.
Present Owner:	**Scrapped.**

Pictures:
Comments: Chassis only in 1968, and later scrapped. Last owner, B. D. Gordon, UK.

3DL174.

3DL176.
Coachbuilder:	Binder.
Engine:	Z78E.
Delivered:	11/30/39.
Body Style:	Close-coupled saloon.
Registration:	Not listed.
First Owner:	Raymond Patenotre, France.
Present Owner:	Musée de l'Automobile , France.

Pictures: Drehsen/166, Phantoms/405.
Comments: Body ex 3DL58. Rolls-Royce Ltd.
Continental Trials. The dust from the white crushed rock floor of the Musée is evident on the car.

3DL176. *(Photo: Mr. Hans Enzler).*

3DL178. The Ropner/Royle tourer.

Coachbuilder:	Park Ward.	**3DL178.**
Engine:		N48Q.
Delivered:		12/8/39.
Body Style:		(First) Cabriolet.
Body No:		4625.
Registration:		JYH 83.
First Owner:	Mrs. Alice W. Webb, US (6/40).
Present Owner:	K. J. M. Kjellqvist, UK.

Pictures: B159/41, Phantoms/406 (Shown).
Comments: Original order by Polish Government. Rolls-Royce Ltd. stock. Returned to UK 1948 (as saloon). Rebodied with replica tourer by Ropner/Royle, 1986.

3DL180. The Hooper sedanca.   *(Photo: Mr. Bullock).*

Coachbuilder:	Inskip.	**3DL180.**
Engine:		N58Q.
Delivered:		8/15/40.
Body Style:		(First) Limousine.
Registration:		Not listed.
First Owner:	Mrs. Edith L. Worden, US (8/40).
Present Owner:	M. Y. Bullock, US.

Pictures: deCampi/164, FL/1621, FL/3439.
Comments: Original order by Mrs. Edith deLong, who died. Rebodied with Hooper limousine de ville 9056 ex 3DL120, Oct. 1947.

3DL182.

Coachbuilder:	Charlesworth.	**3DL182.**
Engine:		N78Q.
Delivered:		4/4/40.
Body Style:		Limousine.
Registration:		Not listed.
First Owner:	King Farouk, Egypt.
Present Owner:	Unknown, Austria.

Pictures:
Comments: King Farouk also owned 3CM63.

3DL184.   *(Photo: Mr. Thill).*

Coachbuilder:	H. J. Mulliner.	**3DL184.**
Engine:		N88Q.
Delivered:		4/8/40.
Body Style:		Touring limousine.
Design No:		4689.
Body No:		Not listed.
Registration:	Alice H, Mrs. Arthur C. Burrage, US
First Owner:	(7/40).
Present Owner:	**W. F. Thill, US.**

Pictures:
Comments: Prepared for 1939 Scottish Show, H. J. Mulliner stand. Mrs. Burrage also owned 3BU100.

3DL186.

Coachbuilder:	Thrupp & Maberly.
Engine:	E38A.
Delivered:	4/12/40.
Body Style:	Touring limousine.
Design No:	Drawing SLE.1520.
Body No:	6925.
Registration:	Not listed.
First Owner:	W. Wallace Potter, US.
Present Owner:	R. C. Bacon, US (1951).

Pictures:
Comments: Prepared for 1939 Earl's Court Show, Rolls-Royce stand. Sent to USA unpainted 15 Dec. 1939.

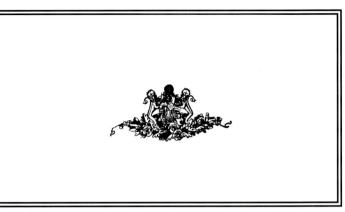
3DL186.

3DL188.

Coachbuilder:	Hooper.
Engine:	E48A.
Delivered:	10/6/39.
Body Style:	Sedanca de ville.
Design No:	7690.
Body No:	9135.
Registration:	Not listed.
First Owner:	Davis H. Marks, US.
Present Owner:	M. D. Tims, Canada.

Pictures: FL/2013 (Shown).
Comments: Prepared for 1939 Earl's Court Show, Rolls-Royce stand.

3DL188.

3DL190.

Coachbuilder:	James Young.
Engine:	E58A.
Delivered:	3/12/40.
Body Style:	Sports limousine.
Registration:	Not listed.
First Owner:	Dr. Dennestoun M. Bell, US (4/45).
Present Owner:	**C. W. Curtin, US.**

Pictures: FL/686, FL/3084, FL/3333.
Comments: To be used at 1939 Earl's Court Show, 1939, Hooper stand, but sold to James Young. To USA June, 1940, J. S. Inskip Inc. stock. Body not completed until 1945. Mrs. Bell also owned 3BU2.

3DL190.   *(Photo: Mr. Curtin).*

3DL192.

Coachbuilder:	James Young.
Engine:	E68A.
Delivered:	1/22/40.
Body Style:	Sedanca de ville.
Registration:	GGT 1.
First Owner:	H. G. Barlow, UK (10/41).
Present Owner:	Unknown.

Pictures: TERR/260, Brookland/11, FL/816.
Comments: Prepared for 1939 Earl's Court Show, James Young stand. Featured in *The Motor*, 6 March 1940.

3DL192.   *(Photo: Mr. Victor Ehrenberg).*

3DL194.   *(Photo: Mr. Hirsch).*

Coachbuilder:	H. J. Mulliner.	**3DL194.**
Engine:		E88A.
Delivered:		12/2/39.
Body Style:		Limousine de ville.
Body No:		4706.
Registration:		GGW 724.
First Owner:		Messrs. Henry Meadows Ltd., UK (9/41).
Present Owner:		G. Hirsch, US.

Pictures: Phantoms/406, FL/1482.
Comments: Prepared for 1939 Earl's Court Show, H. J. Mulliner stand.

3DL196.

Coachbuilder:	Hooper.	**3DL196.**
Engine:		E98A.
Delivered:		3/15/40.
Body Style:		Limousine.
Design No:		7503.
Body No:		9062.
Registration:		Not listed.
First Owner:		Samuel Robinson, US (6/40).
Present Owner:		**Dismantled.**

Pictures:
Comments: Original order by Rippon Bros. for their stand, 1939 Earl's Court Show. Car dismantled for parts, 1974, by Acme Garage, California.

3DL198.   *(Photo: Mr. Hirsch).*

Coachbuilder:	H. J. Mulliner.	**3DL198.**
Engine:		W38H.
Delivered:		1/27/40.
Body Style:		Limousine de ville.
Body No:		4697.
Registration:		Not listed.
First Owner:		Mrs. Evelyn Mendelssohn, US (1/40).
Present Owner:		G. Hirsch, US.

Pictures: Auto Quarterly/148, Auto Quarterly/164, PIIITS/35.
Comments: Original order as Allied Motors, Bombay, Trials car. Sent to USA unfinished.

3DL200.

Coachbuilder:	Park Ward.	**3DL200.**
Engine:		W28H.
Delivered:		11/11/39.
Body Style:		Coupé cabriolet.
Design No:		Drawing 13704.
Body No:		4633.
Registration:		Not listed.
First Owner:		King Zahir Shah, Afghanistan.
Present Owner:		Undetermined, Afghanistan.

Pictures: CORR/262 (Shown).
Comments: Polished aluminum coachwork. Delivered to the High Commissioner for India for presentation to the Shah. See Gallery pages for 3DL200's current circumstance.

The DH Series
of
Phantom III Cars

The DH series consists of only six chassis
as war preparations curtailed motorcar production.
Several cars were sent to the US for coachwork.
All the cars were sold to US owners in and after 1940.

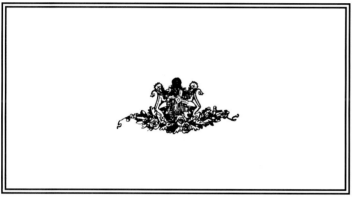

3DH1.   *(Photo: RREC Photo Library).*

3DH3.

3DH5.

3DH7. Still a chassis only.   *(Photo: Uncertain Origin).*

Coachbuilder:	Hooper.	**3DH1.**
Engine:		M88R.
Delivered:		2/12/40.
Body Style:		Sedanca de ville.
Design No:		7704.
Body No:		9145.
Registration:		Not listed.
First Owner:		Marquise Marie Suzanne de Villeroy, US (4/42).
Present Owner:		Unknown, UK (1975).

Pictures:
Comments: Prepared for 1939 Earl's Court Show, Hooper stand. The Marquis owned 3BU94 (in France).

Coachbuilder:	Hooper.	**3DH3.**
Engine:		M98R.
Delivered:		4/17/40.
Body Style:		Limousine.
Design No:		7503.
Body No:		9063.
Registration:		Not listed.
First Owner:		Robert C. Taylor, US (6/40).
Present Owner:		J. W. Flaherty, US.

Pictures:
Comments:

Coachbuilder:	Park Ward.	**3DH5.**
Engine:		D18B.
Delivered:		5/24/40.
Body Style:		Sedanca de ville.
Body No:		4627.
Registration:		Not listed.
First Owner:		Mrs. Mary L. L. Mauran, US (9/40).
Present Owner:		Unknown, France.

Pictures: FL/1963 (Shown).
Comments: New York World's Fair, 1940. Featured in *The Autocar*, 14 June 1940. Car displayed in the Harrah Collection, USA, for some years.

Coachbuilder:	Hooper.	**3DH7.**
Engine:		D28B.
Delivered:		2/28/40.
Body Style:		(First) Limousine.
Registration:		Not listed.
First Owner:		P. Fischbacher, US (10/45).
Present Owner:		Le Mans Museum, France.

Pictures:
Comments: To USA November 1940, body incomplete. J. S. Inskip Inc. stock. Body to 3AX57 1949. Rebodied with Inskip limousine ex 3BT53, 1941. Chassis only from 1970's.

3DH9.

Coachbuilder:	Windovers.
Engine:	Q18N.
Delivered:	11/3/38.
Body Style:	Limousine de ville.
Body No:	6513.
Registration:	Not listed.
First Owner:	Mme. Gertrude Voronoff, US (5/41).
Present Owner:	E. C. Amorim, Portugal.

Pictures:
Comments: Chassis ex 3DL80, which was at Earl's Court Show, 1938, Windovers stand. Chassis unsold, recalled and modernised.

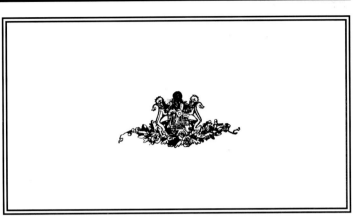

3DH9.

3DH11.

Coachbuilder:	H. J. Mulliner.
Engine:	D38B.
Delivered:	11/24/39.
Body Style:	Limousine.
Registration:	Not listed.
First Owner:	Mrs. Helen MacKay, US.
Present Owner:	D. J. McIntyre, US.

Pictures: CORR/196, PIIITS/17.
Comments: Sent to US late 1939 and interior completed by J. S. Inskip Inc..

3DH11. *(Photo: Mr. McIntyre).*

The Appendix

The Phantom III Tools

The complement of tools supplied with the Phantom III was unusually comprehensive, even for Rolls-Royce. It varied, depending on chassis number and the requirements of the owner; a typical assortment is pictured below. Not shown are the usually-supplied Spencer-Moulton steel-handled rubber mallet, road wheel removal spanner (G54861) and the Ace wheel disc spanner and its valve extension key, generally stowed beneath the bonnet.

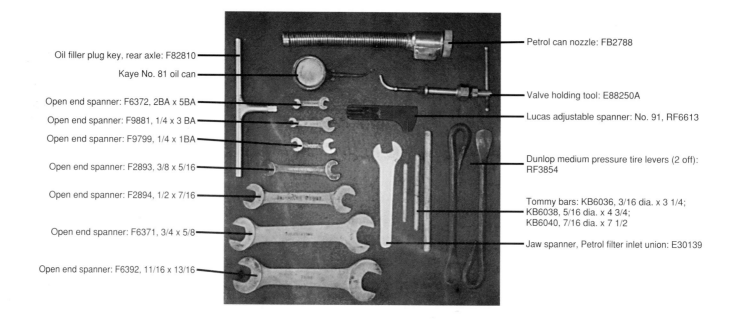

Oil filler plug key, rear axle: F82810

Kaye No. 81 oil can

Open end spanner: F6372, 2BA x 5BA

Open end spanner: F9881, 1/4 x 3 BA

Open end spanner: F9799, 1/4 x 1BA

Open end spanner: F2893, 3/8 x 5/16

Open end spanner: F2894, 1/2 x 7/16

Open end spanner: F6371, 3/4 x 5/8

Open end spanner: F6392, 11/16 x 13/16

Petrol can nozzle: FB2788

Valve holding tool: E88250A

Lucas adjustable spanner: No. 91, RF6613

Dunlop medium pressure tire levers (2 off): RF3854

Tommy bars: KB6036, 3/16 dia. x 3 1/4; KB6038, 5/16 dia. x 4 3/4; KB6040, 7/16 dia. x 7 1/2

Jaw spanner, Petrol filter inlet union: E30139

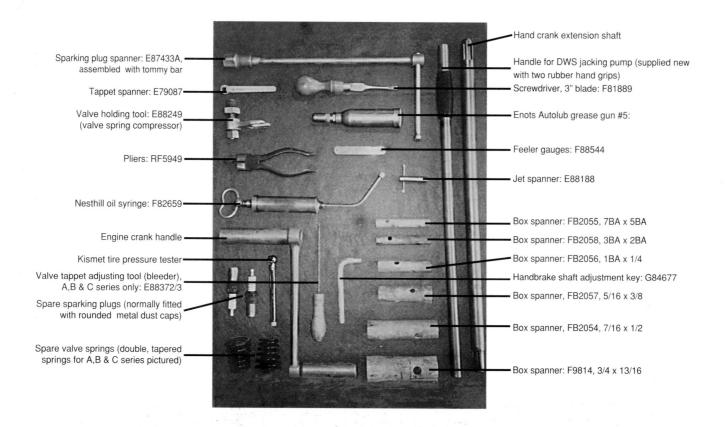

Sparking plug spanner: E87433A, assembled with tommy bar

Tappet spanner: E79087

Valve holding tool: E88249 (valve spring compressor)

Pliers: RF5949

Nesthill oil syringe: F82659

Engine crank handle

Kismet tire pressure tester

Valve tappet adjusting tool (bleeder), A,B & C series only: E88372/3

Spare sparking plugs (normally fitted with rounded metal dust caps)

Spare valve springs (double, tapered springs for A,B & C series pictured)

Hand crank extension shaft

Handle for DWS jacking pump (supplied new with two rubber hand grips)

Screwdriver, 3" blade: F81889

Enots Autolub grease gun #5:

Feeler gauges: F88544

Jet spanner: E88188

Box spanner: FB2055, 7BA x 5BA

Box spanner: FB2058, 3BA x 2BA

Box spanner: FB2056, 1BA x 1/4

Handbrake shaft adjustment key: G84677

Box spanner, FB2057, 5/16 x 3/8

Box spanner, FB2054, 7/16 x 1/2

Box spanner: F9814, 3/4 x 13/16

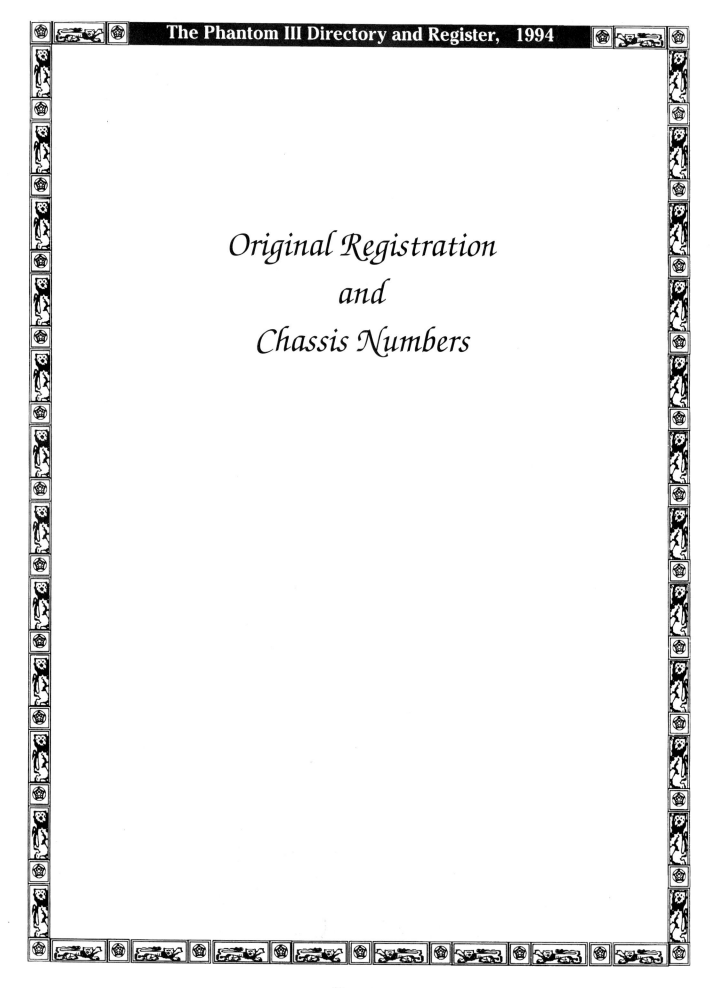

Original Registration
and
Chassis Numbers

Original Registration and Chassis Numbers

Reg	Chassis	Reg	Chassis	Reg	Chassis	Reg	Chassis
11 DPW	3CM173	CAX 15	3CP192	DGT 367	38EX	DYH 140	3BT5
122 CBP	3BT73	CBJ 717	3BU10	DGT 369	3AZ226	DYK 474	3BU152
154 FYV	3DL132	CC 7340	3CM110	DGT 398		DYK 481	3BU166
199 MAN	3DL124	CFG 8	3BT135	DGW 555	3AZ222	DYK 487	3BU76
2 T KM	3BT135	CGD 1	3DL110	DGX 3	3AZ84	DYK 490	3BU174
345 GOT	3BT67	CGO 9	3CM108	DGX 133	3AZ232	DYL 200	3BT69
454 YKR	3AZ124	CLF 419		DGX 136	3AX63	DYM 4	3BT125
559 HYX	3CP176	CLJ 600	3AZ146	DGY 1	3AZ186	DYM 799	3AX71
570 EGX	3CP88	CLL 789	3AX195	DJJ 6	3AZ98	DYN 424	3CP44
5545 RH	3AZ186	CNX 596		DJJ 180	3AZ136	DYO 333	3BT151
5942 DH	3BU134	COR 501		DJJ 401	3AZ138	DYO 953	3BU70
6593 SF	3CM159	COT 420	3CM129	DKB 300		DYR 6	3BU162
740 HRY	3CM165	COV 999	3AZ224	DKC 2	3CP134	DYR 65	3BT59
800 HRY	3AZ102	CPT 251	3BT167	DKT 2	3BU30	DYR 232	3BT121
844 HWR	3CP80	CS 2	3AZ178	DKX 410	3AX115	DYR 620	3AZ176
873 HPX	3CP84	CS 6128	3BT127	DLA 133	3AZ170	DYR 671	3BT79
960 YBF	3CM77	CS 8671	3DL4	DLA 136	3AZ116	DYR 672	3BT89
A 351	3AZ106	CTJ 42	3BT179	DLA 137		DYR 688	3BU186
ADA 999	3DL74	CTJ 421	3CM151	DLA 600	3AX3	DYR 689	3BT179
AFU 209	3CM181	CUE 909	3DL124	DLA 762	3AZ94	DYR 699	3BT155
AHS 79	3CM181	CWR 450	3CP186	DLA 777	3BT45	DYV 8	3BT101
AJF 242	3AZ238	CWX 320	3CM175	DLB 1	3AZ166	DYV 100	3BT85
AJH 532	3AZ104	CXU 976	3AZ38	DLB 5	3AZ172	DYX 643	
AMO 249	3BT19	CXW 488	3CM179	DLB 450	3AZ162	DYX 861	3CP30
ANJ 496	3AX161	CYE 300	3AX53	DLD 580	3AZ128	DYX 864	3BU138
ANV 688	3DL76	CYL 327	3BU150	DLF 66	3AZ220	DYX 867	3CP52
APN 757	3CM149	CYP 1	3AZ43	DLF 740	3AX45	DYX 870	3CP10
ASC 345	3AX9	CYP 921	3AZ22	DLF 928	3AZ218	EGC 1	3CP102
ASF 707	3AX151	CYP 922	3AZ44	DLJ 11	3CP4	EGC 665	3CP6
ASR 902	3CP56	CYP 927	3AZ102	DLK 610	3AX199	EGC 666	3CP12
AUT 555	3CM177	CYP 930	3AZ76	DLK 959	3AZ156	EGF 1	3BT65
AV 9900	3CM95	CYV 781	3AZ26	DLL 155	3AX109	EGF 541	3BT139
AWD 578	3AZ54	CYX 437	3AZ46	DLM 953	3AX19	EGH 513	
AYE 1	3BU78	CYX 523	3AZ72	DLN 470	3AX201	EGH 514	3BT41
BAC 44	3AX91	CYY 2	3AZ36	DLP 720	3AX175	EGH 723	3CP22
BAC H21	3AX69	DAC 257	3DL114	DLR 369	3AZ230	EGJ 39	3CP166
BAH 717	3AZ80	DAK 820	3CP72	DLT 426	3AX73	EGJ 40	3BT171
BDW 1	3CP122	DBB 623	3BU144	DLU 998	3BU18	EGJ 44	3CP86
BFG 909	3AX43	DBP 500	3BU126	DLW 644		EGJ 48	3CP178
BGA 111	3CP32	DCH 1	3CM67	DLW 656	3AX61	EGJ 50	3CP154
BGA 119	3CP8	DGF 998	3AZ78	DLX 320/330	3AX179	EGO 126	3CP70
BGB 752	3CP148	DGH 2		DLY 380	3AZ168	EGO 130	3CP142
BH 44	3AZ52	DGH 7	3AZ68	DMJ 600	32EX	EGO 178	3CP46
BNM 600	3BT197	DGJ 28	3AZ70	DMY 996	3AX169	EGO 700	3CP108
BPW 1	3BT73	DGK 43	3AZ92	DNY 3	3CM137	EGO 710	3CP128
BTE 1	3AX83	DGO 3	3AZ62	DOF 474	3AZ184	EGT 6	3CP172
BTJ 918	3BU116	DGO 750	3AZ88	DOV 817	3AX123	EGW 427	3DL74
BUE 165	3BT111	DGP 300	3AZ96	DPO 900		EGW 654	3BU152
BUU 700	3CP82	DGP 500	3AZ32	DPX 111	3DL24	EJJ 20	3CP146
CAA 566	3BU60	DGT 361	3AZ124	DPX 911	3DL124	EKE 316	3BT83
CAB 209	3CM15	DGT 364	3AX23	DYH 1	3CP58	EKL 596	3BT45

Original Registration and Chassis Numbers

DPX 999	3CM185	ELF 319	3BT61	EYH 406	3CM167	GV 7128	3DL148
DRU 368	3CM79	ELF 351	3BT143	EYP 488	3CP68	HF 7976	3CM169
DS 180	3BT169	ELF 352	3CP94	EYP 912	3DL10	HLR 791	3CP196
DS 6550	3CM197	ELF 357	3CP72	EYT 8	3DL54	HLT 1	3AZ132
DTK/DTR 65	3BU158	ELF 358	3CP136	EYU 310	3DL38	HPC 111	3DL86
DTT 656	3BT195	ELF 360	3CP120	EYU 32	3DL66	HPE 174	3DL88
DTV 700	3BT203	ELH 563	3CM57	EYV 218	3DL106	HPF 129	3DL118
DUC 314	3AZ174	ELH 613	3CP190	EYX 365	3CM107	HPJ 1	3DL128
DUC 635	3AX41	ELK 131	3CP96	EYX 370	3CP158	HPP 10 G	3AX199
DUL 353	3AX99	ELK 138	3CM35	EYX 514	3CM191	J 190	3DL74
DUL 359	3BU40	ELK 140	3CM39	EYY 333	3CM65	J 376	3AZ146
DUL 360	3AX5	ELL 584	3CP62	FBC 999	3CM165	JB 1	3CP34
DUL 362	3BU14	ELL 585	3CM115	FDH 59	3CM9	JB 1	3DL86
DUL 363	3BU80	ELN 1	3CM92	FGO 123	3DL32	JB 9999	3AZ28
DUL 366	3AX157	ELN 7	3CM61	FGO 124	3DL46	JBY 20	3BU194
DUL 370	3BU46	ELP 83	3CM87	FGW 388	3DL108	JJ 5614	3AX61
DUL 532	3AX133	ELP 85	3CM109	FGX 820	3DL60	JPC 298	3DL174
DUL 591	3AZ152	ELP 86	3CP188	FKJ 123	3DL22	JT 21	3CM5
DUL 600	3BU48	ELP 87	3CM49	FKN 1	3DL94	JW 45	3DL38
DUR 255	3CM33	ELR 498	3CM117	FLC 694	3DL84	JX 6888	3DL30
DUU 628	3BU110	ELR 507	3CM93	FLD 95	3DL102	JYH 83	3DL178
DUV 5	3AX105	ELR 519	3AX33	FLD 96	3CM203	KAV 426	3CM95
DUV 26	3AX159	ELT 17	3CM73	FLD 97	3DL146	KLP 49	3AX55
DUV 553	3AX79	EMF 929	3AZ112	FLO 759	3CM31	KOL 888	3AZ28
DVK 894	3AX59	EMN 49	3CM143	FLX 59	3DL62	KUM 1	
DWX 648	3BU84	EOG 1	3CM77	FLX 855	3DL104	LEL 159	3CP60
DXA 9	3BU130	ERF 35	3AX183	FLX 886	3DL152	LGY 408	3AX195
DXB 496	3BU128	EUC 7	3BT191	FML 7	3BU114	LKH 869	3BT147
DXE 1	3CM67	EUU 2	3CM131	FML 191	3AX51	LRU 583	3BT179
DXE 274	3AX171	EVY 200	3DL68	FOY 1	3CP38	LS 4154	3CM19
DXF 505	3BT91	EWY 585	3BT121	FPA 1	3AX29	LYU 822	3AZ142
DXF 777	3BU146	EXC 192	3CM159	FPB 221	3BU28	MAN 5326	3DL62
DXH 4	3BU86	EXC 194	3CM125	FRF 659	3CM99	MF 3366	3AZ236
DXM 471	3BU56	EXC 199	3CM133	FSV 146	3AX193	MG 5890	3CM171
DXM 473	3BU160	EXC 200	3CM119	FXE 868	3DL166	MMD 114 C	3BT105
DXM 476	3BU42	EXE 241	3CM75	FXM 7	3DL154	MMD 116 C	3BT51
DXN 909	3BU88	EXE 242	3CM97	FXP 479	3DL82	MN 6000	3BU6
DXO 773	3CP182	EXE 243	3CP48	FXV 707	3DL122	MPE 2	3DL172
DXO 776	3BT11	EXE 247	3CM183	FXX 100	3DL90	MWB 832	3DL108
DXP 115	3BU188	EXE 248	3DL2	FYF 95	3DL42	ONE 1	3BT107
DXR 555	3BU50	EXE 250	3DL36	FYT 1	3BU126	P 111 MAN	3DL62
DXT 224	3BT107	EXO 1	3CM135	G 541	3BT133	PUF 3	3AZ86
DXV 604	3BU164	EXP 110	3BT81	GBL 157	3DL96	PB 4600	35EX
DXW 647	3BT23	EXT 4	3CM201	GCT 84	3CM45	RC 2406	30EX
DXW 662	3BU92	EXU 3	3CM112	GF 7826	3CP186	RC 2406	31EX
DXX 125	3BT103	EXV 770	3CM163	GGT 1	3DL192	RC 2545	32EX
DXX 126	3BT115	EXW 77	3CP200	GGW 724	3DL194	RC 3054	30EX
DXX 128	3BU190	EXW 78	3CM17	GH 13	3CM23	RC 3055	31EX
DXX 130	3BT137	EXW 487	3CM51	GO 45	3AZ158	RC 3168	33EX
DYE 22	3BT33	EXW 488	3CM179	GRE 140	3CM157	RC 3169	34EX
DYE 810	3BU20	EXX 13	3CM106	GS 7196	3BT29	RC 3170	35EX
DYF 860	3BU178	EXX 514	3CM19	GS 7577	3CP168	RC 3695	36EX
ELA 504	3CP104	EXY 685	3CM195	GS 7692	3CM85	RC 4090	37EX
ELD 678	3CP76	EXE 792	3DL8	GS 9987	3CM81	RC 4922	39EX
ELF 313	3CM21	EYE 799	3DL72	GV 5351	3BU132	RH 1	3BT147

Original Registration and Chassis Numbers

RJ 500	3BT151
RRP 111	
RRR 939	3BT63
SN 8162	3BT141
SUL 739	3BT47
T 5400	3AX199
TH 9299	3BT169
TL 5947	3AZ132
TL 6730	3BT145
TYF 867	
UA 1	3BU16
UD 9009	3CP60
UOC 1	3AX135
US 65	3AX191
VG 9136	3AX17
VJ 5712	3CM69
VML 14	3CM75
VYN 513	3CP120
VYY 251	3CM92
WG 6000	3BU6
WKO 251	3AX65
WYF 111	3BT149
XH 8888	3AX195
XOB 460	3BU184
YBL 999	3AX107
YJ 4455	3AX145

3BT 125 FPF6

Original Engine Numbers
and
Chasssis Numbers

Page 232

Engine	Chassis	Engine	Chassis	Engine	Chassis	Engine	Chassis
1, 3, 4	30EX	B44Y	3AZ210	C68Y	3AX171	E28Y	3CM195
13	32EX	B48A	3BU66	C68Z	3CP62	E28Z	3DL100
15	38EX	B48B	3CP130	C78A	3CP118	E38A	3DL186
2, 10	31EX	B48C	3DL68	C78B	3DL20	E38W	3AX109
6	33EX	B48Z	3BU64	C78Y	3AX175	E38X	3BT143
7	34EX	B54Y	3AX97	C78Z	3CP76	E38Y	3CM197
8	36EX	B58A	3BU72	C88A	3CP146	E38Z	3DL102
8, 11	35EX	B58B	3CP128	C88B	3DL22	E48A	3DL188
9	37EX	B58C	3DL70	C88Y	3BU58	E48W	3AX105
		B58Z	3BU18	C88Z	3CP66	E48X	3BT147
A14A	3AZ30	B64Y	3AX75	C98A	3CP100	E48Y	3CM199
A14Z	3AZ126	B68A	3BU92	C98B	3DL24	E48Z	3DL104
A18C	3CP174	B68B	3CP132	C98Y	3AX189	E58A	3DL190
A24A	3AZ26	B68C	3DL72	C98Z	3CP64	E58W	3AX115
A24Z	3AZ128	B68Z	3BU22	D14W	3AZ66	E58X	3BT149
A28C	3CP178	B74Y	3AX85	D18B	3DH5	E58Y	3CM201
A34A	3AZ38	B78A	3BU28	D18Y	3BT187	E58Z	3DL106
A34Z	3AZ130	B78B	3CP134	D18Z	3CM175	E68A	3DL192
A38C	3CP176	B78C	3DL74	D24W	3AZ76	E68W	3AX117
A44A	3AZ34	B78Z	3BU68	D28B	3DH7	E68X	3BT155
A44Z	3AZ132	B84Y	3AX87	D28Y	3BT201	E68Y	3CM203
A48C	3CP180	B88A	3BU94	D28Z	3CM177	E68Z	3DL108
A54A	3AZ20	B88B	3CP126	D34W	3AZ60	E78A	3DL126
A54Z	3AZ134	B88C	3DL76	D38B	3DH11	E78W	3AX149
A58C	3CP182	B88Z	3BU30	D38Y	3BT199	E78X	3BT139
A64A	3AZ24	B94Y	3AX73	D38Z	3CM179	E78Y	3DL2
A64Z	3AZ136	B98A	3BU102	D44W	3AZ58	E78Z	3DL110
A68C	3CP186	B98B	3CP148	D48Y	3BT203	E88A	3DL194
A74A	3AZ32	B98C	3DL78	D48Z	3CM181	E88W	3AX167
A74Z	3AZ138	B98Z	3BU24	D54W	3AZ48	E88X	3BT151
A78C	3CP188			D58Y	3CP12	E88Y	3DL4
A84A	3AZ28	C18A	3CP106	D58Z	3CM183	E88Z	3DL112
A84Z	3AZ142	C18B	3DL8	D64W	3AZ70	E98A	3DL196
A88C	3CP192	C18Y	3AX157	D68Y	3CP16	E98W	3AX79
A94A	3AZ36	C18Z	3CP56	D68Z	3CM185	E98X	3BT109
A94Z	3AZ194	C28A	3CP114	D74W	3AZ68	E98Y	3DL6
A98C	3CP184	C28B	3DL10	D78Y	3CP4	E98Z	3DL114
		C28Y	3AX169	D78Z	3CM187		
B14Y	3AX59	C28Z	3CP54	D84W	3AZ72	F18V	3BU166
B18A	3BU52	C38A	3CP108	D88Y	3CP6	F18W	3BT89
B18B	3CP70	C38B	3DL12	D88Z	3CM189	F28V	3BU164
B18C	3DL62	C38Y	3AX161	D94W	3AZ78	F28W	3BT101
B18Z	3BU14	C38Z	3CP52	D98Y	3CP32	F38V	3BU160
B24Y	3AX53	C48A	3CP110	D98Z	3CM191	F38W	3BT93
B28A	3BU34	C48B	3DL14			F48V	3BU168
B28B	3CP122	C48Y	3AX165			F48W	3BT81
B28C	3DL64	C48Z	3CP20	E18A	3DL152	F58V	3BU162
B28Z	3BU88	C58A	3CP112	E18W	3AX99	F58W	3BT99
B34Y	3AX155	C58B	3DL16	E18X	3BT129	F68V	3BU172
B38A	3BU86	C58Y	3AX173	E18Y	3CM193	F68W	3BT95
B38B	3CP140	C58Z	3CP58	E18Z	3DL98	F78V	3BT25
B38C	3DL66	C68A	3CP116	E28A	3DL154	F78W	3BT105
B38Z	3BU62	C68B	3DL18	E28W	3AX111	F88V	3BU170
				E28X	3BT145		

Engine	Chassis	Engine	Chassis	Engine	Chassis	Engine	Chassis
F88W	3BT103	J18R	3BU110	K58R	3BT197	M18R	3DL156
F98V	3BU174	J18S	3CP38	K58S	3CM73	M24N	3AX39
F98W	3BT107	J18T	3CM121	K64P	3AZ82	M28P	3BT63
		J24Q	3AZ180	K68Q	3BU48	M28Q	3CP162
G14T	3AZ232	J28R	3BU130	K68R	3BT185	M28R	3DL160
G18V	3BT39	J28S	3CP50	K68S	3CM75	M34N	3AX37
G24T	3AZ234	J28T	3CM123	K74P	3AZ86	M38P	3BT75
G28V	3BT37	J34Q	3AZ222	K78Q	3BU44	M38Q	3CP164
G34T	3AZ236	J38R	3BU128	K78R	3BT193	M38R	3DL162
G38V	3BT43	J38S	3CP42	K78S	3CM77	M44N	3AX41
G44T	3AZ238	J38T	3CM133	K84P	3AZ92	M48P	3BT67
G48V	3BT33	J44Q	3AZ106	K88Q	3BU100	M48Q	3CP160
G54T	3AX1	J48R	3BU114	K88R	3BT195	M48R	3DL164
G58V	3BT69	J48S	3CP40	K88S	3CM79	M54N	3AX45
G64T	3AX3	J48T	3CM125	K94P	3AZ94	M58P	3BT61
G68V	3BT45	J54Q	3AZ110	K98Q	3BU54	M58Q	3CP168
G74T	3AX11	J58R	3BU116	K98R	3BT189	M58R	3DL166
G78V	3BT29	J58S	3CP22	K98S	3CM87	M64N	3AX33
G84T	3AX51	J58T	3CM127			M68P	3BT91
G88V	3BT31	J68R	3BU154	L18P	3AX177	M68Q	3CP166
G94T	3AX5	J68S	3CP34	L18Q	3BT115	M68R	3DL168
G98V	3BT47	J68T	3CM129	L18R	3CM9	M74N	3AX49
		J74Q	3AZ122	L28PX	3AX203	M78P	3BT87
H14S	3AZ172	J78R	3BU78	L28PX	3AX179	M78Q	3CP170
H18U	3CP90	J78S	3CP44	L28PX	3CM92	M78R	3DL170
H18U	3CM114	J78T	3CM131	L28Q	3BT175	M84N	3AX55
H18W	3DL44	J84Q	3AZ116	L28R	3CM112	M88P	3BT97
H24S	3AZ176	J88R	3BU104	L28R	3CM11	M88Q	3CP172
H28U	3CP84	J88S	3CP60	L38P	3AX131	M88R	3DH1
H28W	3DL46	J88T	3CM135	L38Q	3BT123	M94N	3AX47
H34S	3AZ178	J94Q	3AZ124	L38R	3CM15	M98P	3BT83
H34U	3CP88	J98R	3BU132	L48P	3AX201	M98Q	3CP154
H38W	3DL48	J98S	3CP26	L48Q	3BT131	M98R	3DH3
H44S	3AZ192	J98T	3CM137	L48R	3CM19		
H48U	3CP96			L58Q	3BT133	N14M	3AZ226
H48W	3DL50	K14P	3AZ88	L58R	3CM17	N18N	3AX135
H54S	3AZ216	K18Q	3BU26	L59P	3BU6	N18Q	3DL134
H58U	3CP92	K18R	3BT179	L68P	3BU10	N24M	3AZ200
H58W	3DL52	K18S	3CM67	L68Q	3BT137	N28N	3AX145
H64S	3AZ182	K24P	3AZ90	L68R	3CM23	N28Q	3DL144
H68U	3CP94	K28Q	3BU80	L78P	3BU8	N34M	3AX23
H68W	3DL54	K28R	3BT177	L78Q	3BT191	N38N	3AX147
H74S	3AX9	K28S	3CM69	L78R	3CM21	N38Q	3DL138
H78U	3CP98	K34P	3AZ74	L88P	3BU4	N44M	3AZ214
H78W	3DL56	K38Q	3BU46	L88Q	3BT135	N48N	3AX141
H84S	3AX7	K38R	3BT181	L88R	3CM25	N48Q	3DL178
H88U	3CP102	K38S	3CM71	L98P	3BU16	N54M	3AZ220
H88W	3DL58	K44P	3AZ80	L98Q	3BT141	N58N	3AX121
H94S	3AZ162	K48Q	3BU12	L98R	3CM29	N58Q	3DL180
H98U	3CP104	K48R	3BT183			N64M	3AZ228
H98W	3DL60	K48S	3CM65	M14N	3AX27	N68N	3AX183
		K54P	3AZ84	M18P	3BT79	N68Q	3DL140
J14Q	3AZ108	K58Q	3BU38	M18Q	3CP158	N74M	3AZ198

Engine	Chassis	Engine	Chassis	Engine	Chassis	Engine	Chassis
N78N	3AX151	Q44J	3AZ120	R68L	3CM51	T74G	3AZ224
N78Q	3DL182	Q48K	3BU96	R68M	3DL36	T78H	3BU32
N84M	3AZ218	Q48L	3BT5	R78J	3BU134	T78J	3CP150
N88N	3AX163	Q48M	3CM107	R78K	3CP86	T84G	3AX31
N88Q	3DL184	Q48N	3DL86	R78L	3CM57	T88H	3BU36
N94M	3AZ230	Q54J	3AZ104	R78M	3DL38	T88J	3CP152
N98N	3AX159	Q58K	3BU152	R88J	3BU90	T88J	3CM104
N98Q	3DL150	Q58L	3BT23	R88K	3CP74	T94G	3AX35
		Q58M	3CM109	R88L	3CM59	T98H	3BU40
P14K	3AZ146	Q58N	3DL88	R88L	3CM108	T98J	3CP156
P18L	3AX57	Q64J	3AZ112	R88M	3DL40	T98J	3CM106
P18N	3CM157	Q68K	3BU122	R98J	3BU112		
P24K	3AZ144	Q68L	3BT27	R98K	3CP48	U18H	3BT153
P28L	3AX153	Q68M	3CM111	R98L	3CM61	U28H	3BT159
P28N	3CM159	Q68N	3DL90	R98M	3DL42	U38H	3BT163
P34K	3AZ154	Q74J	3AZ114			U48H	3BT161
P38L	3AX65	Q78K	3BU138	S18J	3CP8	U58H	3BT165
P38N	3CM161	Q78L	3BT17	S18K	3CP196	U68H	3BT167
P44K	3AZ158	Q78M	3CM117	S28J	3CP10	U78H	3BT171
P48L	3AX61	Q78N	3DL92	S28K	3CP190	U88H	3BT169
P48N	3CM163	Q84J	3AZ150	S38J	3CP2	U98H	3BT173
P54K	3AZ160	Q88K	3BU106	S38K	3CP194		
P58L	3AX93	Q88L	3BT35	S48J	3CP14	V18F	3AX181
P58N	3CM165	Q88M	3CM119	S48K	3CM7	V18G	3BT157
P64K	3AZ170	Q88N	3DL94	S58J	3CP36	V28F	3AX187
P68L	3AX95	Q89K	3BU158	S58K	3CP198	V28G	3BT117
P68N	3CM167	Q98J	3AZ164	S68J	3CP24	V38F	3AX199
P74K	3AZ184	Q98L	3BT41	S68K	3CM1	V38G	3BT111
P78L	3AX107	Q98M	3CM115	S78J	3CP28	V48F	3AX191
P78N	3CM169	Q98N	3DL96	S78K	3CP200	V48G	3BT119
P84K	3AZ166			S88J	3CP30	V58F	3AX193
P88L	3AX89	R18J	3BU74	S88K	3CM3	V58G	3BT77
P88N	3CM171	R18K	3CP120	S98J	3CP18	V68F	3AX197
P94K	3AZ168	R18L	3CM37	S98K	3CM5	V68G	3BT121
P98L	3AX103	R18M	3DL26			V78F	3AX185
P98N	3CM173	R28J	3BU188	T14G	3AX19	V78G	3BT127
		R28K	3CP68	T18H	3BU76	V88F	3AX195
Q14J	3AZ100	R28L	3CM63	T18J	3CP136	V88G	3BT85
Q18K	3BU142	R28M	3DL28	T24G	3AX15	V98F	3BU2
Q18L	3BT3	R38J	3BU82	T28H	3BU42	V98G	3BT125
Q18M	3CM101	R38K	3CP78	T28J	3CP142		
Q18N	3DH9	R38L	3CM49	T34G	3AX17	W14D	3AX43
Q18N	3DL80	R38M	3DL30	T38H	3BU84	W18E	3AX127
Q24J	3AZ148	R48J	3BU98	T38J	3CP124	W18F	3BT51
Q28K	3BU108	R48K	3CP80	T44G	3AX29	W18G	3CM139
Q28L	3BU186	R48L	3CM53	T45G	3AX25	W18H	3DL124
Q28M	3CM103	R48M	3DL32	T48H	3BU50	W24D	3AZ186
Q28N	3DL82	R58J	3BU70	T48J	3CP144	W28E	3AX91
Q34J	3AZ118	R58K	3CP72	T58H	3BU56	W28F	3BT53
Q38K	3BU148	R58L	3CM55	T58J	3CP46	W28G	3CM141
Q38L	3BT21	R58M	3DL34	T64G	3AX21	W28H	3DL200
Q38M	3CM105	R68J	3BU60	T68H	3BU20	W34D	3AZ196
Q38N	3DL84	R68K	3CP82	T68J	3CP138	W38E	3AX83

Engine	Chassis	Engine	Chassis	Engine	Chassis
W38F	3BT49	Y38C	3AX67	Z68C	3BU120
W38G	3CM143	Y38D	3BU192	Z68D	3CM41
W38H	3DL198	Y38E	3CM89	Z68E	3DL172
W44D	3AZ188	Y44B	3AZ56	Z74A	3AZ50
W48E	3AX133	Y48C	3AX71	Z78C	3BU150
W48F	3BT59	Y48D	3BU176	Z78D	3CM39
W48G	3CM145	Y48E	3CM85	Z78E	3DL176
W48H	3DL142	Y54B	3AZ206	Z84A	3AZ44
W54D	3AZ174	Y58C	3AX77	Z88C	3BU156
W58E	3AX139	Y58D	3BU182	Z88D	3CM43
W58F	3BT55	Y58E	3CM91	Z88E	3DL130
W58G	3CM147	Y64B	3AZ96	Z94A	3AZ64
W58H	3DL128	Y68C	3AX81	Z98C	3BU136
W64D	3AZ152	Y68D	3BU180	Z98D	3CM47
W68E	3AX137	Y68E	3CM93	Z98E	3DL132
W68F	3BU184	Y74B	3AZ204		
W68G	3CM149	Y78C	3AX101		
W68H	3DL136	Y78D	3BT57		
W74D	3AZ190	Y78E	3CM95		
W78E	3AX123	Y84B	3AZ140		
W78F	3BT71	Y88C	3AX69		
W78G	3CM151	Y88D	3BU190		
W78H	3DL146	Y88E	3CM97		
W84D	3AZ156	Y89C	3AX129		
W88E	3AX125	Y94B	3AZ102		
W88F	3BT65	Y98D	3BU200		
W88G	3CM153	Y98E	3CM99		
W88H	3DL148				
W94D	3AZ202	Z14A	3AZ22		
W98E	3AX143	Z14B	3AZ40		
W98F	3BT73	Z18C	3BU126		
W98G	3CM155	Z18D	3CM110		
W98H	3DL158	Z18D	3CM27		
		Z18E	3DL116		
X18E	3BU198	Z24A	3AZ47		
X28E	3BT15	Z24A	3AZ46		
X38E	3BU196	Z28C	3BU124		
X48E	3BU194	Z28D	3CM31		
X58E	3BT7	Z28E	3DL118		
X68E	3BT19	Z34A	3AZ62		
X78E	3BT1	Z34B	3AZ52		
X88E	3BT11	Z38C	3BU146		
X98E	3BT9	Z38D	3CM33		
		Z38E	3DL120		
Y14B	3AZ98	Z44A	3AZ43		
Y18C	3AX63	Z48C	3BU140		
Y18D	3BU178	Z48D	3CM35		
Y18E	3CM83	Z48E	3DL122		
Y24B	3AZ212	Z54A	3AZ42		
Y28C	3AX119	Z58C	3BU144		
Y28D	3BU118	Z58D	3CM45		
Y28E	3CM81	Z58E	3DL174		
Y34B	3AZ208	Z64A	3AZ54		

Phantom III V-12 Engine Replacements

The Phantom III V-12 's coolant and lubrication needs were often poorly served during the car's early life. Even well-maintained engines were years ahead of the modern high pressure oils and corrosion inhibitors which would have eliminated most difficulties. Overhauls were, then as now, eyewateringly expensive and a number of these intrinsically smooth and silent powerplants were replaced by the Rolls-Royce straight eight B-80 or lesser lumps - temporarily, the Society hopes. The engine changes listed below have been reported but many are unconfirmed.

3AZ22   Z14A: replaced by Z28D, then B80.

3AZ36   A94A: to 3BT23.

3AZ48   D54W: to 3AEX36, May 1936.

3AZ70   D64W: replaced by 6 cyl. Bedford, then B80.

3AZ150 Q84J: replaced by J94Q, ex 3AZ124.

3AZ192 H44H: replaced by US V-8.

3AZ210 B44Y: replaced by unknown Phantom III V-12.

3AZ216 H54S: replaced by unknown engine.

3AZ33   M64N: for sale, 1991.

3AX34   M54N: replaced by Ford V-8.

3AX69   Y88C: replaced by Princess 4 litre.

3AX71   Y48C: replaced by B80 B1357WS

3AX131 L38P: replaced by Ford Thunderbird by 1973.

3AX157 C18Y: replaced, 1966.

3AX193 V58F: replaced by 1983.

3BU8   L78F: replaced by unknown Phantom III V-12.

3BU46   K38Q: replaced by Bentley 4 1/4 litre.

3BU84   T38H: replaced by B74Y, ex 3AX85, August '53.

3BU114 J48R: replaced by W58E, ex 3AX139.

3BU126 Z18C: replaced by J48R, ex 3BU114.

3BU138 Q78K: replaced by J94Q, then third engine.

3BU164 F18V: replaced by B80 4818 at 124,594 miles.

3BT9   X98E: replaced by J28S, ex 3CP50 in 1950's.

3BT15   X28E: to 3BT93, replaced with B80, 1962.

3BT23   Q58L: replaced by A94A, ex 3AZ36.

3BT29   G78V: replaced by B80.

3BT31   G88V: replaced by B80.

3BT35   Q88L, replaced by B80.

3BT41   Q98L, replaced by unknown engine by 1971.

3BT51   W18F: to 3BT135, replaced by Austin.

3BT57   Y78D: replaced by R-R Wraith.

3BT63   M28P: replaced by B80 B80654.

3BT65   W88F: replaced by Z78D, ex 3CM39.

3BT87   M78P: replaced by Canadian Chrysler.

3BT91   M68P: replaced by B80.

3BT93   F38W: replaced by X28E, ex 3BT15.

3BT135 L88Q: replaced by W18F, ex 3BT51.

3BT171 U78H: replaced by B80.

3CP10   S28J: replaced by Perkins diesel.

3CP20   C48Z: Cad V-8 replaced by W88F, ex 3BT65.

3CP46   T58J: replaced by Bentley 4 1/4 litre.

3CP50   J28S: replaced by X98E, ex 3BT9.

3CP52   C38Z: replaced by unknown engine by 1988.

3CP56   C18Z: replaced by B80 667MK1

3CP98   H78U: to Nethercutt Collection as spare.

3CP182 A58C: replaced by G88V, ex 3BT31.

3CP190 S28K: replaced by B80.

3CP194 S38K: replaced by G38V, ex 3BT43.

3CM5   S98K: replaced by Bentley Mark VI by 1988.

3CM21   L78R: replaced by B80 57MK2.

3CM31   Z28D: to 3AZ22, replaced by R-R B60.

3CM39   Z78D: to 3BT65, replaced by B68A, ex 3BU92.

3CM71   K38S: to 3CM165.

3CM75   K68S: replaced by unknown engine.

3CM101 Q18M: replaced by Y58D, ex 3BU182.

3CM109 Q58M: replaced by B80.

3CM133 J38T: replaced by B80.

3CM165 P58N: replaced by K38S, ex 3CM71.

3DL30   R38M: replaced by B80.

3DL68   B48C: replaced by R-R B60.

3DL78   B98C: replaced by Cadillac V-8.

3DL196 E98A: sold, with transmission, 1994.

Coachbuilders, Body Styles and Chassis Numbers

E. D. Abbott Ltd., Farnham Surrey

3AX153	Sports saloon
3AZ44	Limousine
3BT37	Saloon limousine

Allweather Motor Bodies Ltd.

3AZ64	Limousine
3AZ76	Cabriolet

Arthur Mulliner, Horhampton

3AX143	Sports saloon
3AX19	Landaulette
3AZ134	Limousine
3AZ180	Limousine
3AZ86	Coupé cabriolet
3BT101	Sedanca de ville
3BT139	Saloon with division
3BT153	Limousine
3BT157	Limousine
3BU114	Touring limousine
3BU118	4-Light limousine
3BU160	Sedanca de ville
3BU192	Limousine
3BU8	Saloon with division
3CM103	Limousine
3CM104	Limousine
3CM114	Sports limousine
3CM123	Sedanca de ville
3CM102	Sedanca de ville
3CP176	Limousine
3CP72	Limousine
3DL10	Limousine
3DL6	Limousine

Barker & Co. Ltd.

38EX	Touring limousine
3AX121	Limousine
3AX125	Limousine
3AX161	Limousine
3AX167	Limousine
3AX169	Limousine
3AX177	Drophead coupé
3AX179	Limousine
3AX185	Touring limousine
3AX187	Limousine
3AX195	Limousine
3AX25	Touring saloon
3AX27	Sedanca de ville
3AX33	Sports saloon
3AX45	Limousine
3AX61	Sedanca de ville
3AX67	Sedanca de ville
3AX77	Limousine

3AX87	Saloon limousine
3AX97	Landaulette
3AZ116	Limousine
3AZ142	Limousine
3AZ166	Touring saloon
3AZ178	Limousine
3AZ194	Touring limousine
3AZ210	Touring limousine
3AZ218	Sedancalette
3AZ222	Sports saloon
3AZ24	Sedanca de ville
3AZ38	Touring limousine
3AZ43	Touring limousine
3AZ74	Allweather
3AZ78	Landaulette
3AZ84	Saloon
3AZ92	Sedanca de ville
3BT1	Sedanca de ville
3BT111	Touring limousine
3BT119	Sedanca de ville
3BT143	Touring limousine
3BT149	Fixed-head sedanca coupé
3BT159	Limousine de ville
3BT167	Limousine
3BT169	Touring limousine
3BT17	Sedanca de ville
3BT171	Limousine
3BT181	Sports cabriolet
3BT183	Limousine
3BT21	Touring limousine
3BT49	Sedanca de ville
3BT73	Touring limousine
3BT95	Limousine
3BU10	Limousine
3BU110	Limousine
3BU112	Limousine
3BU122	Touring limousine
3BU124	Landaulette
3BU134	Tourer
3BU138	Saloon with division
3BU142	Sedanca de ville
3BU144	Limousine
3BU150	Limousine
3BU166	Limousine
3BU168	Sedanca de ville
3BU174	Landaulette
3BU176	Sedanca de ville
3BU190	Touring limousine
3BU2	Coupé limousine
3BU20	Limousine
3BU26	Limousine
3BU28	Sports saloon
3BU30	Sports saloon
3BU32	Sedanca de ville
3BU52	Limousine

3BU66	Sedanca de ville
3BU76	Sedanca de ville
3BU78	Sports saloon
3CM107	Saloon with division
3CM121	Limousine
3CM127	Limousine de ville
3CM151	Sports saloon
3CM161	Limousine
3CM165	Limousine
3CM195	Sports saloon with division
3CM49	Saloon with division
3CM5	Touring limousine
3CM55	Landaulette
3CM83	Sedanca de ville
3CM92	Touring saloon
3CM93	Sedanca de ville
3CM99	Saloon with division
3CP10	Touring limousine
3CP110	Landaulette
3CP138	Sedanca de ville
3CP154	Limousine
3CP166	Touring limousine
3CP168	Limousine
3CP178	Sedanca de ville
3CP184	Limousine de ville
3CP186	Sedanca de ville
3CP198	Limousine
3CP26	Touring limousine
3CP40	Touring limousine
3CP48	Sedanca de ville
3CP60	Touring limousine
3CP70	Limousine
3CP84	Limousine
3CP86	Cabriolet de ville
3CP94	Touring limousine
3DL60	Saloon with division
3DL122	Touring limousine
3DL152	Touring limousine

Binder

3AZ140	Touring saloon
3BT117	Saloon
3BT3	Saloon with division
3BU94	Sedanca de ville
3CP114	Fixed-head cabriolet
3CP88	Saloon with division
3DL144	Sedanca de ville
3DL164	Saloon with division
3DL176	Close-coupled saloon
3DL58	Close-coupled saloon

Brewster

3BT165	Newmarket sedan
3DL136	Trouville town car

Chapron

3CM73	Saloon

Charlesworth

3DL182	Limousine

Joseph Cockshoot

3BU96	Limousine

Cooper Motor Bodies, Putney

3AX123	Phaeton

Crosbie & Dunn

3AZ54	4-Light saloon

Erdmann & Rossi

3AX155	Cabriolet
3BU154	Cabriolet
3CM43	Limousine
3CP140	Limousine

Franay

3CM91	Sedanca de ville
3CP118	Limousine

Freestone & Webb

3AX131	Saloon limousine
3AX17	Limousine
3AX51	Limousine
3AX59	Sedanca de ville
3AZ174	Drophead sedanca coupé
3AZ186	Saloon with division
3AZ68	Sports saloon
3BT93	4-Light saloon
3BT99	Sports saloon
3BU136	Sedanca cabriolet
3BU58	Saloon with division
3CP2	Saloon with division
3DL154	Touring limousine
3DL94	Cabriolet

Gurney Nutting

3AX101	Sedanca de ville
3AX109	Sedanca de ville
3AX147	Limousine
3AX197	Sedanca de ville
3AX31	Sedanca coupé
3AX55	Sedanca de ville
3AX71	Sedanca de ville
3AZ154	Sedanca de ville
3AZ158	Drophead sedanca coupé
3AZ168	Sedanca de ville
3AZ182	Sports saloon w/ division
3AZ188	Sedanca de ville
3AZ196	Sports sedanca de ville
3AZ202	Sedanca de ville
3AZ228	Sports saloon
3AZ234	Sedanca de ville
3AZ32	Sports sedanca de ville
3AZ50	Drophead sedanca coupé
3AZ62	Sedanca de ville
3AZ98	Sedanca de ville
3BT35	Sports saloon
3BT81	Drophead sedanca coupé
3BU162	Sports sedanca de ville
3BU196	Sedanca de ville
3CM115	Sports saloon
3CM31	Sedanca de ville
3CM47	Sedanca de ville
3CP142	Saloon
3CP54	Sedanca de ville
3CP56	Sports saloon with division
3CP62	Sports sedanca de ville
3CP96	Limousine de ville
3DL172	Saloon with division

H. J. Mulliner, Chiswick

3AX1	Sedanca de ville
3AX105	Sedanca de ville
3AX151	Limousine
3AX157	Sedanca de ville
3AX41	Saloon with division
3AX7	Saloon with division
3AX73	Saloon with division
3AX79	Saloon with division
3AX9	Saloon with division
3AX95	Pullman limousine
3AX112	Sedanca de ville
3AZ132	Drophead coupe
3AZ136	4-Light saloon
3AZ152	Saloon with division
3AZ170	Sedanca de ville
3AZ176	Sedanca de ville

3AZ192	Saloon with division
3AZ20	Saloon with division
3AZ236	Sedanca de ville
3AZ28	Saloon with division
3AZ34	Saloon with division
3AZ46	Sedanca de ville
3AZ48	Saloon with division
3AZ58	6-Light saloon
3AZ60	Fixed-head sedanca coupé
3AZ88	Saloon with division
3AZ94	Saloon with division
3BT103	Fixed-head sedanca coupé
3BT155	Saloon with division
3BT179	Sedanca de ville
3BT203	Limousine
3BT23	Saloon with division
3BT29	Limousine
3BT65	Saloon with division
3BU108	Sedanca de ville
3BU128	Sedanca de ville
3BU130	Saloon with division
3BU182	Pullman limousine
3BU36	Allweather
3BU40	Saloon with division
3BU42	Saloon with division
3BU84	Saloon with division
3BU90	Limousine
3CM109	Touring limousine
3CM112	Limousine de ville
3CM117	Touring limousine
3CM119	Sedanca de ville
3CM125	Sedanca de ville
3CM133	Saloon with division
3CM135	Sedanca de ville
3CM155	Limousine de ville
3CM159	Sedanca de ville
3CM177	Saloon with division
3CM19	Limousine
3CM191	Limousine
3CM21	Sedanca de ville
3CM3	Sedanca de ville
3CM35	Sedanca de ville
3CM39	Sedanca de ville
3CM51	Saloon with division
3CM65	Saloon with division
3CM67	Sedanca de ville
3CM7	Limousine
3CM9	Saloon with division
3CM97	Limousine
3CP108	Saloon with division
3CP122	4-Light saloon with division
3CP146	Saloon with division
3CP162	Sedanca de ville
3CP172	Sedanca de ville

3CP22	Limousine de ville
3CP74	Limousine
3CP82	Saloon with Division
3DH11	Limousine
3DL100	Sedanca de ville
3DL102	Saloon with division
3DL104	Sedanca de ville
3DL110	Sedanca de ville
3DL126	Saloon with division
3DL130	4-Light saloon
3DL142	Saloon with division
3DL146	Sedanca de ville
3DL158	Limousine de ville
3DL160	Saloon with division
3DL174	Sedanca de ville
3DL184	Touring limousine
3DL194	Limousine de ville
3DL198	Limousine de ville
3DL32	Sedanca de ville
3DL34	Sedanca de ville
3DL44	Sedanca de ville
3DL46	Saloon with division
3DL50	6-Light saloon with division
3DL82	Touring saloon
3DL88	Sedanca de ville

Hooper & Co Ltd.

36EX	Limousine
3AX11	Sports limousine
3AX129	Sports limousine
3AX165	Limousine
3AX199	Sports saloon
3AX201	Limousine
3AX21	Landaulette
3AX23	Limousine de ville
3AX29	Limousine
3AX35	Limousine
3AX47	Saloon limousine
3AX49	Sedanca de ville
3AX5	Sports limousine
3AX53	Sports saloon
3AX63	Sports limousine
3AX69	Limousine
3AX75	Limousine
3AX89	Sports limousine
3AX93	Limousine
3AZ100	Landaulette
3AZ102	Limousine
3AZ104	Limousine
3AZ114	Sports limousine
3AZ122	Sports limousine
3AZ138	Limousine
3AZ144	Limousine
3AZ146	Limousine
3AZ160	Sports saloon

3AZ162	Limousine
3AZ164	Sedanca de ville
3AZ198	Limousine
3AZ200	Limousine
3AZ22	Limousine
3AZ224	Sports limousine
3AZ226	Limousine
3AZ232	Limousine
3AZ36	Sports limousine
3AZ47	Limousine
3AZ66	Sports limousine
3BT105	Limousine
3BT107	Limousine
3BT115	Limousine
3BT127	Limousine
3BT133	Sedanca de ville
3BT141	Sports limousine
3BT145	Limousine
3BT151	Sedanca de ville
3BT173	Sedanca de ville
3BT175	Cabriolet
3BT177	Sedanca de ville
3BT189	Limousine
3BT19	Landaulette
3BT193	Limousine
3BT201	Sports saloon
3BT25	Landaulette
3BT31	Limousine
3BT39	Limousine
3BT41	Limousine
3BT47	Sedanca de ville
3BT5	Sports limousine
3BT55	Sports limousine
3BT67	Allweather
3BT85	Sports limousine
3BT87	Limousine
3BT89	Sedanca de ville
3BT91	Limousine
3BT97	Limousine
3BU102	Limousine
3BU104	Limousine
3BU116	Sports limousine
3BU126	Sports limousine
3BU132	Limousine
3BU14	Limousine
3BU148	Limousine
3BU164	Limousine
3BU170	Saloon limousine
3BU172	Limousine
3BU18	Sports limousine
3BU24	Limousine
3BU34	Sports saloon
3BU44	Limousine
3BU46	Limousine
3BU60	Limousine

3BU68	Sedanca de ville
3BU82	Sedanca de ville
3BU92	Limousine
3CM101	Limousine de ville
3CM105	Limousine
3CM110	Limousine
3CM131	Sports limousine
3CM137	Limousine
3CM145	Limousine
3CM147	Sports limousine
3CM15	Limousine
3CM157	Limousine
3CM169	Limousine
3CM17	Limousine de ville
3CM173	Fixed-head coupé
3CM189	Limousine
3CM193	Limousine
3CM197	Sedanca de ville
3CM199	Limousine de ville
3CM29	Limousine de ville
3CM41	Limousine de ville
3CM57	Sports limousine
3CM63	Limousine
3CM69	Limousine
3CM71	Landaulette
3CM79	Limousine
3CM85	Limousine
3CP100	Limousine
3CP106	Limousine
3CP12	Landaulette
3CP120	Limousine
3CP126	Sports saloon
3CP130	Sedanca de ville
3CP136	Limousine
3CP148	Limousine
3CP170	Sedanca de ville
3CP180	Landaulette
3CP188	Limousine
3CP194	Sedanca de ville
3CP200	Sedanca de ville
3CP24	Sports limousine
3CP30	Limousine
3CP32	Limousine
3CP4	Limousine
3CP42	Limousine
3CP46	Limousine
3CP78	Limousine
3CP92	Limousine
3DH1	Sedanca de ville
3DH3	Limousine
3DH7	Limousine
3DL106	Sedancalette
3DL114	Sedanca de ville
3DL116	Landaulette
3DL120	Limousine de ville
3DL124	Limousine
3DL128	Limousine de ville

3DL134	Limousine
3DL148	Sports limousine
3DL150	Sedanca de ville
3DL156	Limousine de ville
3DL16	Sports saloon
3DL168	Limousine
3DL170	Limousine
3DL18	Limousine
3DL188	Sedanca de ville
3DL196	Limousine
3DL2	Limousine
3DL24	Limousine
3DL28	Sports saloon
3DL40	Limousine
3DL52	Limousine
3DL56	Limousine
3DL62	Sedanca de ville
3DL64	Limousine
3DL66	Limousine
3DL68	Pullman limousine
3DL70	Touring limousine
3DL74	Limousine de ville
3DL8	Limousine
3DL98	Sports limousine

J. S. Inskip Inc.

3AX119	5-Passenger limousine
3AX141	Convertible coupé
3AX85	5-Passenger limousine
3AZ190	5-Passenger limousine
3BT129	Sedanca coupé
3BT161	5-Passenger limousine
3BT163	Town car
3BT53	5-Passenger limousine
3BU100	Limousine
3BU64	Limousine
3CP124	Limousine
3CP132	Limousine
3CP18	Coupé convertible
3CP20	Fixed-head coupé
3CP36	5-Passenger sedan
3CP50	Touring limousine
3DL180	Limousine
3DL20	Limousine

Woolley of Nottingham

3AX15	Saloon limousine
3AX37	Limousine

James Young Ltd.

3AX135	Saloon
3AX193	Drophead coupé
3AZ184	Saloon with division
3AZ30	Sedanca de ville
3BT109	Saloon with division
3BT197	Limousine
3BT69	Saloon with division
3CM167	Sports saloon with division
3CP8	Limousine
3DL132	2-Door saloon coupé
3DL190	Sports limousine
3DL192	Sedanca de ville
3DL86	2-Door Saloon coupé

Kellner

3AZ206	Sedanca de ville
3AZ208	Sedanca de ville
3AZ212	Limousine
3AZ214	Landaulette
3BT9	Limousine
3BU106	Limousine
3CM187	Saloon with division

Lancefield Coachworks

3AX111	Limousine
3AZ126	Limousine

Mann, Egerton Ltd. Norwich

3AZ80	Touring saloon
3BT27	Limousine
3CM89	Limousine
3CP66	Limousine

Mayfair Carriage Company

3BT121	Drophead sedanca coupé
3CP196	Limousine de ville

Park Ward & Company

30EX	Limousine
31EX	Limousine
32EX	Continental touring saloon
33EX	Continental touring saloon
34EX	Limousine
35EX	Saloon with division
37EX	Saloon with division
38EX	Limousine
3AX107	Limousine
3AX115	Touring limousine
3AX133	Touring saloon

3AX139	Limousine
3AX145	Limousine
3AX159	Sedanca de ville
3AX171	Limousine
3AX183	Limousine
3AX191	Limousine de ville
3AX43	Sedanca de ville
3AX83	Limousine
3AX99	Limousine
3AZ106	Limousine
3AZ120	Touring saloon
3AZ128	Limousine
3AZ156	Sedanca de ville
3AZ230	Touring limousine
3AZ238	Touring saloon
3AZ52	Touring saloon
3AZ70	Limousine
3BT123	Limousine
3BT125	Brougham de ville
3BT137	Limousine
3BT147	Touring saloon
3BT195	Limousine
3BT33	Sedanca de ville
3BT7	Sedanca de ville
3BT79	Touring limousine
3BU16	Sedanca de ville
3BU178	Touring limousine
3BU186	Touring limousine
3BU188	Touring saloon
3BU48	Sedanca de ville
3BU56	Touring saloon
3BU6	Touring limousine
3BU70	4-Light limousine
3BU80	Touring saloon
3BU88	Limousine
3CM106	Touring limousine
3CM108	Touring limousine
3CM171	Limousine
3CM181	Touring saloon
3CM183	Limousine
3CM185	Touring limousine
3CM201	Touring saloon
3CM203	Touring limousine
3CM23	Touring limousine
3CM37	Continental touring saloon
3CM61	Sedanca de ville
3CM75	Touring limousine
3CM87	Touring limousine
3CM95	Touring limousine
3CP128	Touring limousine
3CP192	Sedanca de ville
3CP34	Touring limousine
3CP52	Limousine
3CP58	Limousine

3CP64	Limousine
3CP68	Limousine
3CP98	4-Light limousine
3DH5	Sedanca de ville
3DL108	Touring limousine
3DL118	Cabriolet
3DL138	Touring limousine
3DL178	Cabriolet
3DL200	Coupé cabriolet
3DL36	Limousine
3DL38	Touring limousine
3DL4	Touring limousine
3DL42	Touring limousine
3DL54	Sedanca de ville
3DL72	Touring limousine
3DL84	Touring limousine
3DL90	Touring limousine
3DL96	Sports tourer

Rippon Bros.

3AX137	Limousine
3AX189	Limousine
3AZ42	Limousine
3AZ82	Fixed-head coupe
3BT71	Limousine
3BU156	Limousine
3BU184	Limousine
3CM111	Limousine
3CM175	Limousine
3CP14	Limousine
3CP160	Pullman limousine
3CP80	Limousine
3DL14	Limousine
3DL30	Limousine
3DL78	Touring limousine

Salmons

3DL48	Sports saloon

Schutter van Bakel

3BU72	Saloon
3DL140	Brougham de ville

Thrupp & Maberly

3AX117	Sports saloon
3AX127	Sports saloon
3AX149	Limousine
3AX3	Limousine
3AX81	4-Light limousine

3AX91	Saloon
3AZ118	Limousine
3AZ116	Limousine
3AZ172	Allweather
3AZ220	Limousine
3AZ26	Sports saloon
3AZ56	Sedanca de ville
3AZ96	Saloon
3BT135	Landaulet
3BT191	Sedanca de ville
3BT77	Sports limousine
3BU146	Sports saloon
3BU200	Saloon with division
3BU4	Fixed-head cabriolet
3BU50	Landaulette
3BU62	Saloon
3BU86	Allweather
3CM139	Limousine
3CM141	Sedanca de ville
3CM163	Special saloon
3CM77	Sports limousine
3CP104	Sedanca de ville
3CP150	Sports limousine
3CP16	Limousine
3CP28	Limousine
3CP76	Limousine
3DL186	Touring limousine
3DL22	Touring limousine
3DL26	Cabriolet
3DL76	Touring limousine

Vanden Plas Ltd

3AX65	Sedanca de ville
3BT185	Cabriolet
3CM53	Limousine
3CP134	Drophead coupé

Vanvooren

3CM81	Sports cabriolet
3CP158	Sedanca de ville

Vester & Neirinck

3AX103	Saloon
3AZ216	Saloon
3BT131	Saloon
3BU194	Saloon
3AX103	Saloon
3CP144	2-Door saloon
3DL92	Saloon with division

Voll & Ruhrbeck

3BT187	Cabriolet

Atcherley of Birmingham

3CP38	Limousine

Wiklunds Nordbergs

3DL162	Limousine

William Arnold of Manchester

3BU38	Limousine

Windovers Ltd.

3AX163	Limousine
3AX173	Limousine
3AX175	Sedanca de ville
3AX181	Saloon
3AZ108	Limousine
3AZ110	Sedanca de ville
3AZ130	Limousine
3AZ150	Limousine de ville
3AZ40	Sedanca de ville
3AZ90	Saloon with division
3BT11	Limousine
3BT15	Limousine
3BT199	Limousine
3BT43	Limousine
3BT45	Limousine
3BT57	Limousine

3BT59	Sedanca de ville
3BT61	Sports saloon
3BT63	Landaulette
3BT75	7-passenger saloon
3BT83	Limousine
3BU12	Sedanca de ville
3BU120	Limousine
3BU152	Saloon
3BU158	Sedanca de ville
3BU180	Limousine de ville
3BU198	Sedanca de ville
3BU22	Limousine
BU54	Limousine
3BU74	Saloon with division
3BU98	Sedanca de ville
3CM1	Brougham de ville
3CM129	Saloon
3CM143	Limousine
3CM149	Limousine
3CM153	Limousine
3CM179	Limousine
3CM25	Limousine
3CM33	Limousine
3CM45	Saloon
3CP112	Sports saloon
3CP116	Cabriolet
3CP164	Limousine
3CP174	Limousine
3CP182	Limousine de ville
3CP190	Brougham de ville
3CP44	Limousine
3DH9	Limousine de ville
3DL12	Sedanca de ville
3DL166	Limousine

Titled Owners

The Phantom III was an expensive car. The price of the chassis
alone was about £2000, the equivalent of
$10,000 US, when a Ford sedan cost $800. The first owners were
necessarily wealthy persons, many of whom were titled.
A list of them, compiled by W. J. Oldham, follows.

3AZ43. *Another photograph of the Phantom III car built for HRH Prince George, Duke of Kent. He is shown arriving at the Old Folk's Home, Tunbridge, England, in 1938.*

The original order for the Duke of Kent's Barker limousine calls for a steering column 2 1/2 inches longer than standard, special bonnet 2 inches wider than standard, locking radiator cap, American police siren, French Marchal lamps, 3-note horn and chromium-plated instrument board and finishers, among its special features.

(Photo: RREC Photo Library).

Titled Owners

AX26	Ex-Trials, Earl of Carnavon	Thrupp & Maberly sports limousine
3AZ32	Viscountess Castlerosse	Gurney Nutting Sports saloon
3AZ43	H.R.H. Duke of Kent	Barker touring limousine
3AZ44	The Hon. Lloyd George	Abbott Ltd. enclosed limousine
3AZ46	Lord Doverdale	H. J. Mulliner Sedanca de Ville
3AZ47	Lord Linlithgow, Viceroy of India	Hooper enclosed limousine
3AZ50	H.M. The King of Romania	Gurney Nutting Sedanca Drop-head Coupé
3AZ58	Sir Edward Hammer, Bart.	H. J. Mulliner six-light saloon
3AZ62	The Hon. Seymour Berry	Gurney Nutting sedanca de ville
3AZ68	Sir John Leigh	Freestone & Webb sports saloon
3AZ76	Duke of Sutherland	Allweather Motor Bodies cabriolet
3AZ86	The Hon. A. C. Nivison	Arthur Mulliner coupé cabriolet
3AZ92	Earl Beatty	Barker limousine de ville
3AZ94	Viscount Bearsted	H. J. Mulliner sports saloon with division
3AZ96	Count C. Haugwitz Reventlow	Thrupp & Maberly sports saloon
3AZ100	Earl of Derby	Hooper enclosed drive landaulette
3AZ116	Sir William Firth	Barker limousine
3AZ118	Sir Edmund Davis	Thrupp & Maberly limousine
3AZ136	The Hon. P. Henderson	H. J. Mulliner sports saloon
3AZ142	Lord Brocket	Barker enclosed drive limousine
3AZ148	Sir Pomeroy Burton	Barker enclosed drive limousine
3AZ152	Sir Adrian Baillie	H. J. Mulliner sports saloon
3AZ154	The Hon. M. R. Samuel	Gurney Nutting sedanca de ville
3AZ156	Lord Glendyne	Park Ward sedanca de ville
3AZ158	Lord Roseberry	Gurney Nutting drop head sedanca coupé
3AZ168	Sir H. Smith, Bart.	Gurney Nutting sedanca de ville
3AZ172	Sir Norman Watson, Bart.	Thrupp & Maberly Allweather open tourer
3AZ176	Lady Buckland	H. J. Mulliner sedanca de ville
3AZ206	Princesse de Fancigny-Lucingo	Kellner town car
3AZ208	Contessa Freda Constantine	Kellner sedanca de ville
3AZ226	Sir Walter Rea	Hooper enclosed drive limousine
3AZ228	Sir Charles Craven	Gurney Nutting sports saloon
3AZ230	Sir Walter Forest	Park Ward sedanca de ville
3AZ232	The Duke of Devonshire	Hooper enclosed drive limousine
3AZ234	Lord Milton	Gurney Nutting sedanca de ville
3AX5	Sir H. White	Hooper sports saloon
3AX15	Sir Julian Cahn, Bart.	Sports saloon limousine by J. S. Woolley
3AX37	Sir Julian Cahn, Bart.	Enclosed drive limousine by J. S. Woolley
3AX49	The Duchess of Marlborough	Hooper sedanca de ville
3AX55	The Hon. Mrs. Brindsley-Plunkett	Gurney Nutting sedanca de ville
3AX83	Sir George Mellor	Park Ward limousine
3AX87	Ruler of Bahawlpur	Barker saloon limousine
3AX97	Sir John Latta	Barker landaulette
3AX99	Lt. Col. Sir J. Humphreys	Park Ward enclosed limousine
3AX107	Baron Hirst of Wilton	Park Ward limousine
3AX109	The Marquess of Queensbury	Gurney Nutting sedanca de ville
3AX111	Lord Moyne	Lancefield limousine
3AX123	Lord Aberconway	Cooper Motor Bodies open phaeton
3AX147	Maharajah Holker of Indore	Gurney Nutting enclosed drive limousine
3AX149	Sir David Milne Watson	Thrupp & Maberly enclosed limousine
3AX161	Sir Eric Geddes	Barker enclosed limousine

Titled Owners

3AX173	Lord Portal	Windovers enclosed limousine
3AX181	Sir Edmund Crane	Windovers saloon
3AX195	H.R.H. Duke of Gloucester	Enclosed limousine by Barker
3AX201	Maharajah of Baroda	Hooper enclosed limousine with sun roof
3BU14	Sir R. Milbourne	Hooper enclosed drive limousine
3BU16	Sir George Martin	Park Ward Sedanca de ville
3BU34	Sir Albert Bingham	Hooper sports saloon
3BU46	Sir Alfred Butt, Bart.	Hooper limousine
3BU52	The Lady King	Barker enclosed limousine
3BU68	The Aga Khan	Hooper sedanca de ville
3BU74	Lord Bradford	Windovers saloon with division
3BU76	Maharajah Jaipur	Barker sedanca de ville
3BU82	Maharanee of Nabba	Hooper sedanca de ville
3BU86	Ruler of Bhopal	Thrupp & Maberly sports saloon
3BU92	The Lady Buckland	Hooper enclosed limousine
3BU102	Maharajah of Jodhpur	Hooper enclosed limousine
3BU106	Maharanee of Baroda	Kellner enclosed drive limousine
3BU128	Sir Edgar Horne, Bart.	H. J. Mulliner sedanca de ville
3BU132	Lord Glanelly	Hooper enclosed drive limousine
3BU134	Maharajah of Kolhapur	Barker open tourer
3BU136	Sir John Leigh	Freestone & Webb drop head coupé
3BU144	Lord Somers	Barker enclosed limousine
3BU162	Lord Roseberry	Gurney Nutting sports sedanca de ville (cancelled)
3BU168	Lord Fairhaven	Barker sedanca
3BU172	Sir Abe Bailey, Bart	Hooper enclosed limousine
3BU174	Sir Montagu Burton	Barker landaulette
3BU176	The Lady Foley	Barker sedanca de ville
3BU196	Lord Plunket	Owen sedanca. Orig. for Marquis of Queensbury
3BU198	Maharajah Rajppla	Windovers sedanca de ville
3BU200	Countess Haugwitz Reventlow	Thrupp & Maberly saloon with division
3BT5	Duke of Alba	Hooper sports saloon
3BT11	Lord Portalington	Windovers limousine
3BT15	Lady Ward	Windovers enclosed drive limousine
3BT19	Lord Illiffe	Hooper enclosed drive limousine
3BT25	Sir Patrick Duncan, Bart. Governor	Hooper landaulette
3BT41	Lord Camrose	Hooper enclosed drive limousine
3BT43	Lady Grace Dance	Windovers enclosed limousine
3BT57	Sir A. Kay Muir	Windovers enclosed limousine
3BT61	Sir William Jeffrey	Windovers sports saloon
3BT63	Sir Robert Hadfield	Windovers enclosed limousine
3BT69	Sir Hugh Bray	James Young saloon with partition
3BT75	The Hon. Charles Fitzroy	Windovers seven-passenger saloon
3BT87	Lord Vesty	Hooper enclosed limousine
3BT95	Lord Ebbisham	Barker limousine
3BT99	Sir John Leigh	Freestone & Webb sports saloon
3BT167	Lord Londonderry	Barker enclosed limousine
3BT171	Sir H. Wernher	Barker enclosed limousine
3BT179	The Hon. William Bithell	H. J. Mulliner sedanca de ville
3BT181	Ruling Chief of Keonjhar State	Barker sports torpedo cabriolet
3BT193	Sir John Jervis	Hooper limousine
3CP2	Baroness von Einser	Freestone & Webb saloon with division
3CP6	Sir Cecil Rolls	Hooper standard enclosed limousine.
3CP12	Hon. S. Vesty	Hooper enclosed landaulette
3CP22	Sir Emsley Carr	H. J. Mulliner limousine de ville
3CP26	Mme La Duchess de Talleyrand	Barker standard touring limousine
3CP34	King of Roumania	Park Ward sports limousine
3CP54	Sir Charles Craven	Gurney Nutting sedanca de ville

The Titled Owners of Phantom III Cars

3CP86	Sir Philip Sassoon	Barker cabriolet de ville
3CP90	Count Maurice de Bosdari	Sedanca de ville by Fernandez & Darrin
3CP94	Sir Frederick Minter	Barker touring limousine
3CP100	Governor of Bombay	Hooper enclosed limousine
3CP108	Sir Francis Peel	H. J. Mulliner sports limousine
3CP110	Sir John Latta	Barker landaulette
3CP112	Prince of Baroda	Windovers saloon
3CP116	Prince Berar	Windovers cabriolet
3CP180	Countess of Inchcape	Hooper enclosed landaulette
3CP182	Sir Frederick Richmond	Windovers sedanca de ville
3CP190	Lord Portalington	Windovers enclosed limousine
3CM19	Lord Craigmyle	H. J. Mulliner limousine
3CM23	Sir H. Harmsworth	Park Ward sports saloon
3CM31	Sir Herbert Smith, Bart.	Gurney Nutting sedanca de ville
3CM37	The Rajah Baliadur of Panchakota	Park Ward Continental touring saloon
3CM51	Sir Richard Sykes	H. J. Mulliner limousine
3CM55	Lady Cora Fairhaven	Barker landaulette
3CM63	H. M. King of Egypt	Hooper enclosed limousine
3CM71	Lady Brumner	Barker landaulette
3CM85	Sir James Roberts	Hooper standard enclosed limousine
3CM92	Sir George Grant	Barker touring saloon
3CM97	Sir Hardman Lever	H. J. Mulliner enclosed limousine
3CM99	Earl of Dudley	Barker saloon with division
3CM115	Sir Ernest Cain	Gurney Nutting sports saloon
3CM121	Lady Ludlow	Barker enclosed limousine
3CM137	Lady Llewellyn	Hooper limousine
3CM139	Sir Robert Mc Alpine	Thrupp & Maberly enclosed limousine
3CM167	The Hon. Philip Henderson	James Young sports saloon
3CM171	Lord Cowdray	Park Ward enclosed limousine
3CM187	Princess Fancigney-Lucinge	Kellner sedanca de ville
3CM193	Viscountess Wimborne	Hooper sports saloon
3DL18	Sir John Lorden	Hooper limousine
3DL26	Maharajah Sadret of Barlakinadi	Thrupp & Maberly 4-door All Weather
3DL34	Sir Ernest Oppenheimer	Ex-stock H. J. Mulliner sedanca de ville
3DL52	Lord Craigmyle	Hooper standard enclosed drive limousine
3DL68	Lord Rothermere	Hooper enclosed drive limousine
3DL82	Lady Lindsay	H. J. Mulliner sports saloon
3DL84	Sir George Sutton, Bart.	Park Ward touring limousine
3DL92	Baron Brigman de Walzin	Vester & Neirinck interior drive with division
3DL96	Maharajah Shabeb of Moroi	Park Ward Phaeton
3DL104	Sir Herbert Smith	H. J. Mulliner sedanca de ville
3DL106	Lady Patricia Guiness	Hooper sedanca de ville
3DL118	The Hon. Peter Beatty	Park Ward convertible sedan
3DL130	Sir Edmund Crane	H. J. Mulliner 4-light touring saloon
3DL138	The Imperial Court of Iran	Park Ward touring limousine
3DL148	Lord Glanelly	Hooper touring limousine
3DL154	Sir John Leigh	Freestone & Webb touring saloon
3DL158	Prince Aditya of Siam	H. J. Mulliner limousine de ville
3DL166	Lord Inverforth	Windovers enclosed limousine
3DL182	G. M. King of Egypt	Body Card missing. Hooper limousine
3DL200	High Commissioner for India	Park Ward coupé cabriolet
3DH1	Marquise Marie Suzanne de Villory	Hooper sedanca de ville

The Gentlemen
of
The Society

The 157 members of
The Phantom III Technical Society
for the year 1994.

The Gentlemen of the Society

Altman, John D., Mr.
5 Struan Street
Toorak, Victoria 3142
Australia
Phone: (613) 827-9392
Chassis: 3DL154

Anderson, Laurence C., Mr.
1214 Tenth St.
Berkeley, CA. 94710
Phone: (510) 527-2938
Associate

Bannister, Hugh E., Mr.
11 Bridge Road
Park Gate, Southampton S03 7AD
Great Britain
Phone: 0489-572251
Chassis: 3BT201

Barrett III, Thomas W., Mr.
5601 E. Naui Valley Drive
Scottsdale, AZ 85253
Chassis: 3BT155

Bartlett, D. C. F., Mr.
Alma House
Skelton Road, Norfolk 1P22 3EX
DISS, Great Britain
Phone: 0379-642289
Associate

Barton, Eunice H., Mrs.
2801 Seabreeze Dr.
St. Petersburg, FL 33707
Phone: (813) 345-2227
Chassis: 3CM203

Beacham, Gregory, Mr.
P. O. Box 8533
Havelock North
New Zealand
Phone: (06) 878-8600
Associate

Beck, George, Mr.
5136 Sie Belmont
Portland, OR 97215
Chassis: 3AX75

Beers, Keith C., Mr.
701 S. Rogers
Waxahachie, TX 75165
Phone: (214) 937-7579
Chassis: 3BU30

Benham, Neal R., Dr.
3131 Stein Blvd.
Eau Claire, WI 54701
Phone: (715) 832-2056
Chassis: 3AX33

Bhogilal, Pranlal, Mr.
Das Chambers
Dalal Street
Bombay 400023
India
Phone: 273-661
Chassis: 3AZ47, 3BT75, 3BU82

Birkbeck, Benjamin H., Mr.
2701 Reeds Lake Blvd. S. E.
Grand Rapids, MI 49506
Chassis: 3BU60

Blaize, André L., Mr.
"La Closerie",
50290 Coudeville, Brehal
France
Associate

Blenko, Jr., Walter J., Mr.
4073 Middle Road
Allison Park, PA 15101
Phone: (412) 486-2017
Chassis: 3CP154

Bramer, F., Mr.
11211 Hunter Dr.
Hunter Classics, Inc.
Bridgeton, MO 63044
Associate

Brauer, Stephen F., Mr.
11250 Hunter Dr.
Bridgeton, MO 63044
Chassis: 3BT181

Butterworth, Charles, Mr.
P. O. Box 1286
West Perth 6872
Australia
Phone: (61) 9-321-5477
Chassis: 3AX121

Buzzi, Paul V., Mr.
P. O. Box 86
Moorestown, NJ 08057
Chassis: 3BT55

Campi, Thomas R., D.M.D.
2306 Ramshorn Drive
Box 23
Allenwood, NJ 08720
Phone: (908) 528-5020
Chassis: 3BU176

Canton Classic Car Museum, Inc.
104 Sixth St. S. W.
Canton, OH 44702
Associate

Casteel, James, M. D.
3310 E. Kirkwood Ave.
Orange, CA 92669
Phone: (714) 997-5354
Chassis: 3CM3

Chapler, R. Raymond, Mr.
3627 Mesa Lila Lane
Glendale, CA 91208
Phone: 249-0958
Chassis: 3CM141

Clarke, Tom, Mr.
77 Kitashirakawa Nishimachi
Sakyo-ku, Kyoto 606
Japan
Phone: (075) 213-4595
Associate

Cockayne, John J., Mr.
Codwell Lane
Sheffield, S10 5TJ
Great Britain
Phone: 0433-651488
Associate

The Gentlemen of the Society

Cook, Raymond A., Dr.
606 Georgia Avenue
Valdosta, GA 31602
Phone: (912) 244-4810
Chassis: 3CP184

Cooke, Frank, Mr.
59 Summer St.
North Brookfield, MA 01535
Associate

Coomber, Martin, Mr.
43 Tweedy Road
Bomley, Kent BR1 3PR
Great Britain
Phone: 0814-605671
Chassis: 3AX65

Crowley, B. J., Mr.
Egmont House
101A Pound Lane
Sonning on Thames, Berk. RG4 0GG
Great Britain
Associate

Cunny, Walter E., Mr.
1650 Oakland Dr.
Sycamore, IL 60178
Chassis: 3BT175

Curtin, Charles W., Mr.
25 Gardner Avenue
New London, CT 06320
Phone: (203) 443-1107
Chassis: 3BT123, 3DL190

Daniels, Lisa R., Mrs.
1609 Cherokee Trl.
Plano, TX 75023
Phone: (214) 517-8311
Chassis: 3DL170

Davis, William M., Mr.
P. O. Box 2491
Charleston, WV 25329
Phone: (304) 343-2955
Chassis: 3BT149

DeCampi, John, Mr.
Sprucehaven Farm
Chester Heights, PA 19017
Associate

Dennison, John, Mr.
322 South Concord Road
West Chester, PA 19382
Phone: (610) 436-8668
Associate

DeRees, Robert O., Mr.
6515 East 82nd Street
Suite 204
Indianapolis, IN 46250
Phone: (317) 849-5324
Chassis: 3AZ232

Dia, Amir, Mr.
2800 Via Campasina
Verdes Estates, CA 90274
Chassis: 3AZ74

Dorner, Violet, Mrs.
290 Shadowood Lane
Northfield, IL 60093
Chassis: 3AX79

Doyle, William H. W., Mr.
4350 La Jolla Village Dr.
Suite 700
San Diego, CA 92122
Phone: (619) 566-6287
Chassis: 3BU112

Durham, John, Mr.
2 Daws Lea
Daws Hill Lane
High Wycombe, Bucks. HP11 1QF
Great Britain
Phone: 0494-521714
Chassis: 3AX143

Ellerman, Garry H., Mr.
1226 Cardwell Road
Crozier, VA 23039
Phone: (804) 784-0011
Associate

Elzinga, Theodores, Mrs.
Chateau Sainte Radeyonde
LeLouroux, Bottereau 44430
France
Associate

Enzler, Hans, Mr.
Halden 39
Buechen 9422
Switzerland
Chassis: 3AZ44

Erbrecht, Claus F., Mr.
Zum Bahnhof 10
Brest 21698
West Germany
Phone: 49-4762-2930
Chassis: 3CP190

Estridge, M. N., M.D., F. PIIIT. S.
989 W. Marshall Blvd.
San Bernardino, CA 92405
Phone: (909) 883-9339
Founder/Editor

Fane, William J., Mr.
2851 Trillium
N. Vancover, V7H 1J3
British Columbia
Phone: (604) 929-4973
Chassis: 3BT69

Feller, Robert, Mr.
22 Westlake Court
Somerset, NJ 08873
Associate

Ferguson, John, Mr.
8 Main Road
Gourrnors Bay, Lytteilton
South Island, R. D. 1
New Zealand
Chassis: 3DL22

Field, George D., Mr.
399 Harwin Drive
Severna Park, MD 21146
Phone: (410) 544-9945
Associate

Fisher, John R., M. D.
P. O. Box 283
Herman, MO 65041
Phone: (314) 486-3565
Chassis: 3DL42, 3DL94

The Gentlemen of the Society

Fortenbach, Stanley J., Mr.
9470 El Tejado Rd.
La Mesa, CA 91941
Phone: (619) 465-3521
Chassis: 3BU196

Friedman, Harry, Mr.
1911 N. 2nd St.
Philadelphia, PA 19122
Chassis: 3BU108

Gabrielli, Frank P., Mr.
Relax Technology
3101 Whipple Road
Union City, CA 94587
Phone: (510) 736-9185
Chassis: 3BU190

Gehring, William M., Mr.
5390 Edgehill Dr.
Cleveland, OH 44130
Phone: (216) 886-1365
Chassis: 3BU4

Gilbert, Lamar, Mr.
198 Mt. Paran Road NW
Atlanta, GA 30327
Phone: (404) 252-7189
Associate

Gir, Srikant, Mr.
8250 Byre Hollow CV
Cordova, TN 38018
Phone: (901) 756-7765
Chassis: 3AX133

Goodman, John K., Mr.
283 N. Stone Ave.
Tucson, AZ 85701
Chassis: 3AZ40

Gorjat, Jean M., Mr.
P. O. Box 3608
Harrisburg, PA 17105
Phone: (717) 599-5853
Chassis: 3CP88

Gray, Judd J., Rev.
St. Anselm College
100 St. Anselm Drive
Manchester, NH 03102
Phone: (603) 641-7000
Chassis: 3AX111

Green, Edward H., Mr.
21 N. Wisconsin Ave.
Addison, IL 60101
Phone: (708) 833-7918
Chassis: 3AZ172

Griffiths, John H., Mr.
c/o Post Office
Wallington, Victoria 3221
Australia
Phone: (052) 54-2496
Chassis: 3DEX202 (32EX)

Guyton, Fred F., Mr.
200 N. Broadway
St. Louis, MO 63102
Chassis: 3CM67, 3DL86

Haimowitz, Ely, Mr.
2601 Solari Dr.
Reno, NV 89509
Chassis: 3BT53

Harwood, John, Mr.
3 Yon Road
Huntington, NY 11743
Chassis: 3AX177, 3BT103, 3BU14 3CM81

Hawk, Ronald L., Mr.
26045 Darmouth
Madison Heights, MI 48071
Phone: (810) 398-7756
Chassis: 3AX173

Hazzah, A. S., Dr.
4701 Willard Ave.
Chevy Chase, MD 20815
Chassis: 3CM177

Hemmingsen, John O., Mr.
22-881 Nicholson St.
Victoria V8X 5C5
BC, Canada
Phone: (604) 479-7338
Chassis: 3AX47

Hensley, David, Dr.
2415 Avenue K.
Galveston, TX 77550
Phone: (409) 762-1158
Associate

Heyn, Donald G., Mr.
4944 Golden Eagle Ave.
Palmdale, CA 93552
Phone: (805) 273-4827
Chassis: 3CP44

Hind, E., Mr.
3888 Wokineham Rd.
Earley, Reading R66 2HX
England
Chassis: 3CP32

Hooke, John A. L., Mr.
26 Buckingham Road
Killara, N. S. W. 2077
Australia
Phone: (61)2-498-3093
Chassis: 3AZ56

Jacobs, Philip L., Mr.
804 Manistee Court
Manitowoc, WI 54220
Phone: (414) 682-9447
Chassis: 3BT77

James, Ian, Mr.
16 Woodcote Close
Epsom, Surrey KT18 7QJ
Great Britain
Chassis: 3CP172

Jefferson, Robert T., Sr.
Sports Classic's Ltd.
Box 317 RFD
Brookfield, MA 01506
Phone: (508) 867-6288
Associate

Jens, Pilø, Mr.
Goldham Hall
Stanningfield, Suffolk 1P29 4SD
Great Britain
Phone: (0284) 827-072
Chassis: 3CM195

Jensen, Jr., Irving F., Mr.
4320 Perry Way
Sioux City, IO 51104
Phone: (712) 252-1891
Associate

Jessen, Philip L.
744 Panorama Dr.
Colorado Springs, CO 80904
Phone: (719) 634-6087
Chassis: 3CM71

Karger, Kenneth, F.PIII.T.S.
P. O. Box 707
Exton, PA 19341-0707
Phone: (215) 524-0424
Chassis: 3DL122

The Gentlemen of the Society

King, David M. Mr., F.PIII.T.S.
5 Brouwer Lane
Rockville Center, NY 11570
**Associate Compiler of Second
Edition of The Directory & Register**

Kinloch, Alastair G., Mr.
P. O. Box 73
Hawker, ACT 2614
Australia
Phone: 6-2542448
Chassis: 3DL150

Klein, Ann E. Mrs.
2650 Colombia Ave.
Lancaster, PA 17603
Phone: (717) 397-8328
Associate

Kroemer, J. Albert, Mr.
5508 Frankfort Court
Dallas, TX 75252
Phone: (214) 248-8847
Associate

Larson, Curtis L., Mr.
P. O. Box 650202
Dallas, TX 75265
Phone: 62-21-522-7425
Chassis: 3CP174

Larson, Willard A. E., M. D.
3802 Colby Avenue
Everett, WA 98201
Associate

Laska, Herbert, Mr.
Holtrasse 2
Linz., A-4020
Austria
Phone: 0043-7229-3138
Chassis: 3AX41

Lindquist, Ralph G., Mr.
800 Mandy Lane
Camp Hill, PA 17011
Phone: (717) 737-6422
Associate

Little, John, Mr.
The Mill
Cowbit, Spalding
Lincolnshire PE12 6AP
Great Britain
Phone: 0406-380455
Chassis: 34EX, 3AZ34, 3BU114

Long, T. M., Mr.
8025- 10th Ave. South
Seattle, WA 98108
Chassis: 3BT185, 3DL98

Lougee, Fred M., Mr.
161 Talcott Notch Rd.
Farmington, CT 06032
Associate

McCorkindale, Douglas H., Mr.
1132 Langley Lane
McLean, VA 22102
Phone: (703) 442-8750
Chassis: 3CP144

McIninch, Richard D., Mr.
21 Stoney Creek West
Nellysford, VA 22958
Phone: (804) 361-2568
Chassis: 3AZ174

McKee, Mark T., Mr.
64 Riverside Dr.
Mt. Clemens, MI 48043
Phone: (810) 469-7474
Chassis: 3AEX37 (37EX)

Meserow, Steven J., Mr.
346 Roger Williams
Highland Park, IL 60035
Phone: (708) 433-0517
Chassis: 3AX77, 3AZ46, 3CM89

Miller, Ralph E., Mr.
P. O. Box 316
Homer, AK 99603
Phone: (907) 235-8819
Associate

Mitchell, Anthony B.
1134 Valley View
St. Helena, CA 94574
Phone: (707) 963-7050
Chassis: 3AX107, 3BT163, 3CM183

Morey, Thomas J., Mr.
1075 Griffin St. W.
Dallas, TX 75215
Phone: (214) 353-9091
Chassis: 3BT157

Morris, Jean G., Mr.
1730 Christopher Dr.
Deerfield, IL 60015
Phone: (708) 945-9603
Associate

Morris, Sheldon A., Mr.
3991 St. Johns Ave.
Jacksonville, FL 32205
Chassis: 3AX93

Morrison, Roger, Mr.
210 Greenway Rd.
Salina, KS 67401
Phone: (913) 825-5461
Associate

Newton, Dennis, Mr.
Neweton Hall Lane
Mobberley, Cheshire WA16 7LL
Great Britain
Phone: 0565-873524
Chassis: 3BT145

Nydegger, Charles C., Dr.
1820 Lincoln Ave.
Wyomissing, PA 19610
Phone: (610) 796-9410
Associate

Parker, Richard T., Mr.
10910 Morrison St. #202
North Hollywood, CA 91601
Chassis: 3CP36

Patten, Joe G., Mr.
60 Ponce De Leon Ave. NE
Atlanta, GA 30308
Phone: (404) 892-5688
Chassis: 3BU160, 3BT33

Pickett, David, Mr.
c/o Dr. Christabel Barran
Woolhouse Farm
Stedham, Midhurst GU29 0QH
West Sussex, Great Britain
Chassis: 3BU88

Podsedly, William J., Mr.
13384 Fallen Leaf Rd.
Poway, CA 92064
Phone: (619) 451-3340
Chassis: 3BT5

The Gentlemen of the Society

Pollard, Gary B., F.PIII.T.S.
6030 Greenwood Plaza Blvd.
Greenwood Village, CO 80111
Phone: (303) 689-0100
Chassis: 3BU28, 3CM101

Pryer, Heather, Mrs.
340 Pennant Hills Rd.
P. O. Box 83
Pennant Hills N.S.W. 2120
Australia
Chassis: 3DL146

Raabe, Gale G., Mrs.
9334 Turner Ln.
Durham, CA 95938
Phone: (916) 343-3730
Chassis: 3CP182

Revere, J. J., Mr.
P. O. Box 2279
Oqunquit, ME 03907
Phone: (207) 646-8708
Chassis: 3AZ234

Reynolds, John, Mr.
The Old Vicarage
Bradley, Staffs. ST18 9DY
Great Britain
Phone: 01144-785-780413
Chassis: 3CP172

Richey, D. W. G. (Woodie), Mr.
Ivory Cottage
1819 Eleventh Avenue North
St. Peterburg, FL 33713-5703
Chassis: 3CP14

Rosenberg, Rudy, Mr.
68 Custer Ave.
Williston Park,.NY 11596
Chassis: 3DL20

Rossum Jr., John R., Mr.
26190 Bennie Lane
Fort Bragg, CA 95437
Phone: (707) 964-6361
Chassis: 3AZ110, 3DL70

Rusnak, Albert C., Mr.
2737 Range Rd.
Columbiana, OH 44408
Phone: (216) 594-3110
Chassis: 3AZ32

Sauzeau, Sarl Marc, Mr.
148 Q Rue De La Republique
Argenteuil, France 95100
Phone: (1) 34-10-12-44
Chassis: 3AZ208

Schofeild, John, Mr.
1 Everton Road
Potten, Beds. SG19 2PA
Phone: (44) 767-261986
Chassis: 3AZ176

Shaffner, Robert D., F. PIIIT. S.
c/o Flight Systems
I-83, Exit 16
Lewisburg, PA 17339
Phone: (717) 932-1950
Founder/Chairman
Chassis: 3AX163

Sherper, Kenneth H., Mr.
Route 1, Box 542
Bluemont, VA 22012
Chassis: 3BU86

Sinicki, Richard, Mr.
1841 Babcock Blvd.
Pittsburgh, PA 15209
Chassis: 3CP38

Smith, Brian P., Mr.
2 Short Road
Off Mount Street, Bryanston 2021
South Africa
Chassis: 3BT101

Smothers, Larry A., Mr.
6636 Barnhurst Drive
San Diego, CA 92117
Phone: (619) 279-1408
Associate

Spitzack, Gordon, Mr.
221 NW 11th St.
Fairbault, MN 55021
Chassis: 3CM99

Stevens, Everett S., Mr.
3619 Haverhill St.
Carlsbad, CA 92008
Phone: (618) 434-2532
Chassis: 3CP132

Stuckey, Steve, F.PIII.T.S.
7 Pindari Gardens
Condell Street
Belconnen ACT 2617
Australia
Compiler of The Directory

Sullivan Jr., Robert V., Mr.
2260 Orchard Home Drive
Medford, OR 97501
Phone: 779-9208
Chassis: 3AX3

Sysak, Matthew A., Mr.
27 Canal Run East
Washington Crossing, PA 18977
Phone: (215) 493-9119
Chassis: 3CM92

Thill, William, Mr.
1110 Langworthy
Dubuque, IO 52001
Phone: 582-1261
Chassis: 3DL184

Townsley, G. M., Mrs.
70 Edinburgh Dr.
Ickenham Uxbridge, Middelsex
UB 108 QZ
Great Britain
Chassis: 3CM5

Trapp, David M., Mr.
284 Bal Bay Dr.
Bal Harbour, FL 33154
Phone: (606) 231-0010
Chassis: 3AX25

Treworgy, Harry T., Mr.
P. O. Box 61
Castine, ME 04221
Phone: (207) 326-4193
Chassis: 3AZ146

Trotter, Richard R.
P. O. Box 1544
Bulawayo
Zimbabwe
Associate

Tuttle, Mark, F. PIIIT. S.
10646 Art St.
Shadow Hills, CA 91040
Phone: (818) 352-6081
Chassis: 3BU92, 3BT23, 3CP12,
3CP20, 3CM39, 3CM106

The Gentlemen of the Society

Vallis, James H., Mr.
1526 Simpson Street
Kingsburg, CA 93631
Phone: (209) 897-2939
Chassis: 3BT97

Waites, Lucius, Dr.
9245 Meadowbrook
Dallas, TX 75220
Phone: (214) 559-7525
Chassis: 3DL8

Walter, Julian A., Mr.
67 Walters Drive
Osborne Park 6017
W. Australia
Phone: 09-340-3500
Chassis: 3DL14

Weidemann, J., Mr.
17520 Revello Dr.
Pacific Palisades, CA 90272
Phone: (310) 454-5656
Chassis: 3CP114, 3DL186

Westlund, II, Bernard J., Mr.
20590 Arrowhead Dr.
Bend., OR 97701
Phone: (503) 383-4444
Chassis: 3BU100

Whyte, Peter, Mr.
Churchill Color Labratories
80 Churchhill Ave.
Sabiaco 6008
W. Australia
Phone: (61) 09-381-9688
Chassis: 3BT3

Wuesthoff, Herbert O., Mr.
6150 Dimm Way
Richmond, CA 94805
Phone: (510) 232-1146
Associate

Yardumian, Haig S., Mr.
113 Woodland Road
Malden, MA 02148
Phone: (617) 322-9772
Chassis: 3DL5

Yarwood, L., F.P.III.T.S.
Lynhurst
1 Wrights Lane
Sandbach, Cheshire CW11 OJX
Great Britain
Honorary

Late Entries

Due either to late registration
or error of our Registrar.

Albrecht, Harry, Mr.
Mannenvain
Duernten CH-8635
Switzerland
Associate

Bartz, H. J., Mr.
2589 Puesta Del Sol
Santa Barbara, CA 93109
Phone: (805) 682-4123
Associate

Bennett, Dana, Mr.
21843 Alamagordo Road
Saugus, CA 91359
Phone: (805) 297-1004
Chassis: 3DL46

Boode, Arthur, Mr.
1182 Elgin St.
San Leandro, CA 94578
Phone: (510) 481-8555
Chassis: 3AX131

Burkhardt, Gerard, Dr.
16 Bolt Court
Leasmundie, WA 6076
Perth
Australia
Phone: (61) 9-291-9615
Fax: (61) 9-291-8843
Chassis: 3CM49

Dewar, Murray, Mr.
17 Landcox Street
East Brighton, Victoria 3187
Australia
Phone: (613) 596-5061
Chassis: 3BU2

Gabrielli, Frank, Mr.
3870 Deer Trail Lane
Danville, CA 94506
Phone: (510) 736-9185
Chassis: 3BU190

Kapson, Norman J.
171 Mill Street
Ortonville, MI 48462
Phone: (810) 627-3241
Chassis: 3CM117

Leuthausel, Walter, Dr.
Fronhofstr, 6
6307 Linden
Germany
Phone: 06403-71791
Chassis: 3AX193, 3BT141

Montgomery, R. B., Mr.
76 Nuns Way
North Abbey
Cambridgeb CB4 2NR
England
Chassis: 3BT37

Neale, T. R., Mr.
11 Pembroke Road
Northwood, MIDDX HA6 2HD
Great Britain
Phone: 90923-822938
Chassis: 3BT37

Provencher, George, Mr.
4391 Casa Oro Dr.
Yorba Linda, CA 92686
Phone: (714) 961-8698
Chassis: 3BT99

Sangster, John, Mr.
Bix House, Windsor Road
Bray, Berks.   SL6 2EW
Great Britain
Phone: 0628-26833
Chassis: 3CM125

Spina, Joseph R., Mr .
15 Sinclair Street
Farmingdale, NY 11735
Phone: (516) 420-9613
Chassis: 3BU84

Teissier, Christian, Mr.
26-28 Rue Jeanne d'Arc
74300 Villeneuve/Lot
France
Phone: (33) 53-40-3000
Chassis: 3CM29

Wardley, Peter, Mr.
79 Church Street
Halesowen,
West Midlands B62 9LO
England
Phone: (021) 559-7732
Chassis: 3CP164

Wetzel, Donald A., Mr.
10 West Isle
The Woodlands, TX 77380
Chassis: 3AEX34 (34EX)

Photographing The Phantom III Car

Suggestions for Photographing Your Rolls-Royce Phantom III Car

by Ken Karger, F.PIII.T.S.

Photographing your Phantom III car to show it off at its best takes a bit of doing, but surely the finest Rolls-Royce deserves first-rate pictures.

1. Use at least a 35mm camera, preferably a name brand. Anything smaller than 35mm is a toy.

2. Put your camera on a tripod. The car will be rock steady (turn off the engine) but you probably aren't.

3. Work slowly. Take your time. Look at the car through the camera; look at the background and the light. If things don't look right through the camera, they won't look right on the film.

4. For film, you should use negative (for prints) rather than slide film. Kodak and Fuji make excellent films with ISO (film speeds) of 100 and 200. If you take the film to a lab, talk to the lab to find out what film they know best and recommend.

5. You need good light to make a good picture. An overcast day, even though the amount of light will be less, helps minimize reflections. Try shooting between 8 and 10 AM or 3 and 5 PM. Noon light is very harsh. Dawn and dusk can be wonderful.

6. To take an effective picture of a car, use a plain background. Keep it simple. Complex pictures of fancy cars with gorgeous houses in the background are for the professional. Emphasize the car by keeping the background virtually unnoticeable. Don't let anything come between you and your car, especially trees, bushes, fences or people. Location. Location. Location.

7. Once again, use a tripod. A tripod is the cheapest way to use a mediocre camera/lens and improve the pictures it takes. A tripod also forces you to slow down. Use a cable release to trip the shutter so you don't accidentally jar the camera when you take the picture. (Even the best tripods are something of a pain, but if you compare results between hand-held work and that taken on a tripod, you will be shocked at how unsteady you really are.)

8. Use a normal or somewhat longer focal length lens to photograph a whole car. For 35mm cameras, that means the lens should be at least 50mm. Wide-angle lenses tend to distort subjects; the wider the angle, the greater the distortion.

9. Emphasize the lines of the car, i.e., the bodywork. We all know what a Rolls-Royce radiator looks like. The distinctive part of these cars is their coachwork.

10. The original photographers of the cars, the men who were hired by Messrs. Rolls-Royce or the coach builders to take pictures of the cars when new, had a real eye for design. (They also had a representative of the company/coachbuilder on location to make sure everything on the car was right: e.g., door handles straight, wheels dead straight, etc.) You can be your own car stylist; look at the work of these photographers, for they are our guides.

11 Take pictures from several angles so you are really documenting the car. The standard reference view is a dead-on side view, a profile. This is usually taken from the driver's side – which typically has more interesting exterior features such as spare tire, mirrors, perhaps a radio antenna (sometimes under the running board on a PIII).

12. For the side profile view you need to put your camera in a very precise place in two planes. *Fore and aft:* line up the windscreen pillars so the one nearest you hides the other. You will be just slightly ahead of the middle of the car. *Up and down:* you want to see the far door capping rail just over the near one.

13. Now come forward and take a slight 3/4 front view. You should still be able to see most of the side view of the car, but you will also be able to see some three-dimensional modelling of the front and rear fenders.

14. Now go toward the rear of the car and take a 3/4 rear view. There are far too few pictures taken of these cars that show their tail-end treatment.

15. If there are any unusual special exterior features, come in close and catch them now.

16. If you need to move the car relative to the sun to take these various views, do so. You are in no hurry.

17. Look inside your car and document it, too. You will almost certainly need an electronic flash to give you enough light to photograph what's here. The inside of most closed Phantom III cars is dark! Record the instrument board, especially if it is not one of the R-R factory jobs, but is the work of the coachbuilder.

18. Record any special coachbuilder's plate, patent plates, etc., in particular items that may be present on only a few cars. This may prove tricky, especially moving in close enough, but it immeasurably enriches and expands our knowledge of these cars.

19. Do not be put off because you are not a flawless photographer. Nobody else is either. The major error owners make when taking pictures of their car is not to take enough.

20. Film. While you can shoot black & white (your camera doesn't care, doesn't even know that's what you loaded), getting black & white film developed and printed is not so easy nowadays. Really good black & white work is expensive because it is likely to be custom work. Talk to someone at your local camera store about b&w. If they aren't interested, go to another store. Good modern color films, if really carefully exposed, developed and printed, reproduce quite acceptably in black & white. *(We scanned many color prints for this Directory - Ed.)*

21. Take color prints (negative film). You can take slides (also called positives or transparencies) too, but a print will have to be made from them before use so an extra layer of degradation will be involved.

22. Color negative films vary widely. The slower films (with lower ISO numbers, e.g., 25, 100, 200) need more light but are typically sharper, have finer grain, and show better color saturation. Kodacolor 100 and 200 are excellent as are Fuji's equivalents. I particularly like Fuji's Reala which is also quite tolerant of flourescent lamps. If you are not familiar with these films, talk to the people who will process and print them for you. They probably know one film's idiosyncracies in depth and can do a better job with it even if the film is less good theoretically. Your goal is a good print of your car!

23. Order 4 x 6 prints (Kodak calls them 4R) not the 3R (3 1/2 x 5). The former includes the entire negative while the 3R, because they are not the same proportion as a 35mm negative, by definition must chop off some of your careful work. The cost of the larger print is only marginally higher.

24. When you are taking the picture, allow a bit of room around the edges so you do not cut off part of the car, especially wheels, bumpers, or roof.

25. Avoid the 1-hour photo labs unless you find one that does really good work. Most of them are just production outfits, though you may be able to speak directly with the person who works the machine to make corrections.

26. A fine print can only be made from a first rate negative, one that is sharp and well exposed. With your camera on the tripod, it is easy to take several different exposures so you have several differently exposed negatives. The one that prints best is the one to use. This taking of several different exposures is called bracketing (see below). It is cheap insurance. Most professional photographers do it if they can. It only costs you a few frames and film is cheap.

27. Bracket by one stop increments – that is, expose a frame at whatever your meter says, then take another at double the exposure (change the shutter speed dial to a smaller number; exposing at 1/30 gives twice as much light as one taken at 1/60), then another at half the exposure (1/125 gives half as much light as one taken at 1/60). This assumes that your camera has a meter and is set to manual operation.

28. Whatever film you use, buy rolls of 36 frames so you feel free to take lots of pictures. A full roll costs little more to buy, little more to process, and just a bit more to print.

29. When you have the finished prints in your hand, be ruthless. The image is all that people will use to evaluate the car. If the result does not please you, analyze why, then go back and take the picture again.

30. Within reason, Ned will gladly assist/advise you, and I will try to do the same. Reach me at P.O. Box 707, Exton, PA 19341, 610-524-0424.

Ken Karger, May 1994.

How This Book Was Produced

Page 268

How This Book Was Produced

OB SHAFFNER sent me a box of papers and a packet a few years ago. It included car photos he had accumulated and copies of pictures from the Ted Reich and John deCampi collections. With them was a note: "Let's print a new directory based on the accompanying compilation by Steve Stuckey and include a picture of each member's car." I thought this was not too big a task. Previously I had worked with the process camera, using half-tone screens for the photographs. With this method, I could make about 10 half-tones per day.

I started in the old way and found that I would never be able to finish the task. I had been interested in desk-top publishing, but had no experience. The last issue of **Spectre** had been set in a word processing program and printed out with a daisy-wheel printer capable of proportional spacing, but still didn't look right. So, I bought the Pagemaker® by Aldus and tried to use it, but quickly realized that it was a very complicated program. One of the local colleges offered a course in its use, so I signed up. After some 4 months of this, I was fairly proficient and began the typesetting.

At our local RROC Christmas Party, I ran into Mark Tuttle and we discussed this project. He was very interested, and agreed to help with it. What a blessing that turned out to be. He is a professional writer and was able to give tremendous help.

About this time, I began to look for someone to do the image setting, which produces a negative with the halftone photos in place with the text. I met Kwaku Boeting, who was just starting a company here for this purpose. He was having financial difficulties surviving until his customers paid up, so I loaned him some money as sort of a prepayment for his efforts. We tried a few pages and found that Pagemaker® was really not compatible with his form of work. He suggested that I buy Quark Xpress®, which he insisted was the top professional publishing program. I agreed. When the package came, it was even more complicated than Pagemaker®. How could I learn it in time to produce anything? An advertisement in one of the Southern California printing magazines informed me that I could learn the thing in three sessions of three days each. The school, New Horizons, was in Santa Ana. Classes started at 8:00 AM and lasted until 5:00 PM. This is the worst time to travel in our area, so I decided to stay at a local hotel while attending these classes. They were fascinating, well taught and complete in scope. I was able to begin work after this first series, although I did later return for the other two series.

Now, on planning the book. I consulted a designer, who recognized that the material was easily standardized to a form. He suggested the top banner and then we worked setting up the text boxes. This was a problem due to the first line with the chassis number being larger than the rest of the box. Eventually we set up two boxes, a left one for the title of the material, set in boldface type, left justified. The right one for the material was set plain and right justified. We set the leading (width between lines) at 12 points, except the space between the chassis number and engine number which is 11 points. After much manipulation with the master pages we were able to get the program into motion. We put together 24 pages copied from the Master page to make a signature. I hired a young woman from our local college as a part time worker. Myrna Esparza did not know the program, but was an excellent typist. She learned quickly and started entering the data. Soon, she could do one signature a day.

Each signature was either mailed or faxed to Mark, who would proofread it, note the errors and return them for correction or, later, travel here to input the changes directly. During this period we also had to rescan many photos and revise the Master page several times for alignment of the data and the text boxes. Every addition or change seemed to introduce new mistakes and, eventually, it added up to twenty or more revisions of each of the twelve signatures.

The photographs were scanned and processed with a Microtek IIXE desktop scanner and *Photoshop*®. That meant three more series of sessions at New Horizons in Santa Ana to learn it. We scanned the photographs in our possession, but found we had nothing for most of the cars. Letters to authors of the various books on Rolls~Royce cars yielded permission to scan pictures from their books, principally photographs made by the coachbuilders. Steve Stuckey loaned us his large collection and, as our search for photographs continued, we learned of other excellent sources mentioned earlier in *"About The Photographs"*.

It is now well over two years after we started our part, four years since Stuckey's start. We have been able to continuously upgrade the data as time has gone on.

How This Book Was Produced (Cont'd)

Each individual picture used (and there were over 550 of them) takes up about 3/4 of a megabyte of storage memory. I had installed a 1300 megabyte hard disk in my Quadra MacIntosh, but that was quickly filled. I bought a removable hard disk system, but these discs only hold 88 megabytes each, not enough capacity for a signature (the pictures and text for each signature must be on the same disk). Later I bought a 200 megabyte removable hard disk. This solved the problem. A MicroNet optical disk system which holds 256 megabytes on each of the disc's two sides is used for master storage, since it is more stable.

The main typeface is Cheltenham®, by Adobe. The text is in 10 point, chassis numbers in 12, titles in 14 point type. The title pages used Zapf Chancery Italic, 28 point. Nearly all the pictures required retouching and the screening patterns removed from photographs taken from books, as well as shadow and highlight details adjusted. Some pictures were computer sharpened. Many of the photos would not fit our picture boxes which are 3.75 x 2 inch size. They had to have sections filled in, usually by computer copying parts of the photograph and pasting them into the blank areas, then blending the area with the software's "cloning tool". The pictures were then imported into the appropriate box on each text page. When a signature, usually 24 pages was completed, it was stored on a 200 megabyte removable SyQuest disk to be taken to Quaku for image setting (at 175 lines per inch) on his Scitek imaging system.

Quaku delivered negatives with pictures and text for each page on one negative. After being 'stripped' into paper registration masks, printing plates were made from the negatives with a home-made device using a high-intensity light source. The negatives were placed in a carrier against a photo-sensitized aluminum plate and held in close contact by 30 pounds of vacuum. After a six minute exposure the plate was developed and dried. One plate for each two-page sheet was installed in the press and printing begun. The image from the plate was transferred (offset) to a rubber-faced drum which did the actual printing on each paper sheet. We used my Hamada 660 press which is just capable of covering 11x17 inches, the size of two pages.

Printing two-color pages required two passes through the press with a second plate made by masking off the page's printed area and exposing just the color section. In the press, several sheets were required to achieve alignment. Registration marks were imprinted on each second color plate to assure proper registration with the already-printed first sheet. When this was set, the marks were removed from the plate with a pencil eraser and the second pass through the press begun. The four-color title page, its reverse, and the picture of 3CM29 required eight passes through the press for the two sides. This also meant that the ink had to be changed and the press cleaned eight times - something of a dirty chore.

The paper we've used is 80 pound Tahoe® gloss stock (which costs $35.00 per 1000 sheets). The sheets were collected from the press in lots of 50 and stored on drying racks. This reduced the weight of the finished sheets to prevent offsetting (the transfer of ink from the drying sheet to one next to it). We allowed them to sit overnight before printing the reverse side. The completed pages were then taken to a folding company which folded the sheets in half. Following that, they were taken to Stauffer's Automated Bindery and transformed into books. The covers were imprinted from negatives we supplied..

The total cost for 500 books was about $15,000. We have received $4400 from membership, $2200 from the Society bank account. The hope is that the balance will be made up by selling the remaining books.

M. N. Estridge, M.D., F.PIII.T.S.,
Editor-Publisher
December 8, 1994

The Producers of the Directory and Register

The Chairman:
R. D. Shaffner, F.PIII.T.S.

Editor-Publisher:
M. N. Estridge, M. D., F.PIII.T.S.

Chief of Printing. Frank Klein at the Hamada 660 press checking the sheets being printed.

The Associate Editor:
Mark Tuttle, F.PIII.T.S.

The Compiler:
Steve Stuckey, F.PIII.T.S.

Gallery

*As space allows, some notable examples of the coachbuilder's
art on the Phantom III chassis.*

3DL86 *James Young coupé.*   (*Photo: RROC Foundation*).

3CP18 *Inskip coupé limousine.*   (*Photo: Automobile Quarterly*).

3CM91 *Franay Sedanca de ville.* (Photo: Coachwork On Rolls-Royce).

3AZ158 *Gurney Nutting drophead sedanca coupé.* (Photo: Those Elegant Rolls-Royce).

3CP124 *Inskip fixed head coupé.*   *(Photo: Mr. Thomas Kilbane).*

3CP116 *Windovers cabriolet, amended by Hooper, 1948.*
                    (Photo: Rolls-Royce, The Derby Phantoms).

3BU78 *Barker saloon.*   *(Photo: Those Elegant Rolls-Royce).*

3CP200 *Hooper sedanca de ville.*   *(Photo: Mr. Nicky Wright).*

3AX141 *Inskip convertible sedan.*   *(Photo: Mr. C. I. Schwartz).*

3DL84 *Park Ward touring limousine.*   *(Photo: Coachwork On Rolls-Royce).*

3DL122 *Gurney Nutting saloon.*   *(Photo: Mr. Ken Karger).*

3BT165 *Inskip coupé de ville.*   *(Photo: Rolls-Royce In America).*

3CP38 *Freestone & Webb sedanca de ville, coachwork circa 1946.* (Photo: Mr. R. Sinicki).

3CM81 *Van Vooren drophead coupé.* (Photo: Mr. Bill Dobson).

3DL96 *Park Ward tourer.* (Photo: Coachwork On Rolls-Royce).

3DL192 *James Young sedanca de ville.* (Photo: Bill Dobson Collection).

3BU76 *Barker sedanca coupé.*   *(Photo: Mr. Ken Karger).*

3AX193 *James Young drophead sedanca coupé.*   *(Photo: Mr. Klaus-Josef Rossfeldt).*

3CP20 *Inskip fixed head coupé.* *(Photo: Mr. Mark Tuttle).*

3CP192 *Park Ward sedanca de ville.* *(Photo: Bill Dobson Collection).*

3BT103 *H. J. Mulliner fixed head sedanca coupé.* (Photo: Bill Dobson Collection).

3BU76 *Barker sedanca de ville.* (Photo: RROC Foundation).

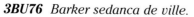

I'm a little wounded, but I am not slain;
I will lay me down for to bleed a while,
Then I'll rise and fight with you again.
Dryden, 1702 .

3AZ20. *It's final resting place? This photograph was sent to Bob Shaffner by Mr. Ludo C. Pivron and published in the PIII.T.S. Newsletter. The car was discovered in a Paris scrapyard in 1980 by Mr. Pivron. Whether he owned or eventually acquired the car is not clear. A letter to him at the address listed was returned unopened.*

3DL200. *As recently photographed in the now-open air wreckage of the royal Afghanistan garages in Kabul. Note the bullet holes in the door and the barely-worn pre-WWII Dunlop Fort tires. This overdrive Park Ward cabriolet was delivered with polished aluminum coachwork, its fitted luggage and interior leather dyed silver gray to match. Rescue attempts are underway but their outcome is highly uncertain.* (Photo: Select Photo Agency, England).

Some Final Editorial Comments

HIS finishes full-time, seven-days-a-week work getting this publication delivered. It has been very stressful at times, with budget and time worries always with us. Many mistakes required retypesetting and often reprinting pages, but we wanted it as perfect as possible.

These efforts on the part of our little team make responsiblities for the readers. A database form is enclosed, which we hope you will fill out fully and accurately and return promptly. The information will be entered into a computer where it will be privileged. Please keep us posted as to repairs with costs for both material and labor, and names of good mechanics in your area. Sources for parts, prices and adequate substitute parts should be sent to us, as well.

Notice all the missing pictures in this directory. Many of the last-known owners were in the U.S. If you have a lead on any of the cars, report it and send any photos you might have of them.

Lastly, supply us with photographs. Take your camera to all meets you attend and make a picture of any Phantom III cars there, following Ken Karger's instructions. Owners will usually move the car to a suitable location for a good picture if you promise them some prints. We would like to have more color pictures, since the next Directory edition will be larger with larger photographs and as many in color as possible. Lastly, photograph your own car at least once a year and send us the prints. Use a label, noting on it the chassis number, coachbuilder, your name, date taken and any other interesting details such as the occasion, and attach it to the back of the picture. This will be a record both for yourself and us.

Our overseas members will note that many photographs are missing from owners in several foreign countries. We need contacts in the Netherlands, Belgium, Spain and other countries to search for these missing cars. Please make some recommendations in this regard.

M. N,. Estridge, M.D., F.PIII.T.S.
Editor-Publisher
December 8, 1994

Additions and Corrections

Dedication: I was not aware of Mr. Larry Yarwood's death at the time of printing. It seems even more appropriate now to dedicate this Directory and Register to him and the late Mr. Ron Haynes.

Page 14; Page 102: 3BU174; Page 150: 3CP110; Page 159: 3CP180: Page 171: 3CM55; Page 172: 3CM71. 'Landaulet' should be spelled 'Landaulette'.

Page 24: 3AZ40. Correct body number is 6344.

Page 26: 3AZ52. The coachwork pictured is the second body on the chassis. Photo from Mr. Rance Bennett.

Page 34: 3AZ114. The photo contributor is an as-yet-unidentified dealer.

Page 69: 3AX137 now owned by member Mark Colona, 196H Templing Rd., Glen Moore, PA 19341. (610) 458-8334.

Page 74: 3AX179. Correct engine number L28P. Now converted to open two-door; current owner, S. Brunt Ltd.

    3AX197. Correct engine number V68F.

Page 81: 3BU2. The photo contributor is Mr. Klaus-Josef Rossfeldt.

Page 91: 3BU84. The photo contributor is Mr. David Kelly.

Page 103: 3BU184. The "aerodynamic coupé" now on this chassis is an original design, not a replica.

Page 143: 3CP50. For sale by Canadian dealer, November 1994.

Page 133: 3BT197. The car pictured for this chassis number may be incorrect.

Page 138: 3CP14. The photo contributor is Mr. Woody Richey.

Page 184: 3CM143 now owned by Mr. Emilio Arias, Spain.

Page 100: 3BU154. The photo contributor is Mr. Matti Schumacher.

Page 285: 3BU76. This photo is courtesy the RREC *Bulletin*.

A great deal of time and expense has gone into verifying the accuracy of the data contained in this publication; however, the Editor-Publisher and the PIII Technical Society take no responsibility for errors or omisions of any kind.

Further, it is to be understood that this publication's primary purpose shall be for use by the Phantom III Technical Society, such as information, convenience and interest of Members of the Society. Its use as a mailing list or for any other commercial purpose by any individual or organization is strictly forbidden and may be cause for legal action.

Notes

No Photo. *This is a color view of the decoration we used to indicate no photograph of a particular car was available. The elements of the decoration were scanned from illustrations in an original Phantom III sales catalog. The left half of the wreath arrangement was scanned, separated from its right half, copied to a computer file and colorized with two shades of green. It was then put in place in the final canvas. This half of the wreath was then flipped in the computer, copied and placed into position on the right-hand side as well. Next, the engine, a separate drawing, was scanned, enhanced, copied and placed into the composite. The right-hand lion figure was then copied from the catalog to a separate file. It was colorized gold with the Photoshop® 'spray can' tool after redrawing the black portions to intensify the outline and saved. At this point, the left-hand lion in the source drawing was found to be clearer than the right-hand version, so it was treated as above, then reversed, copied and placed in position on the right side. Finally, a single rose was hand-drawn, colorized with two shades of red and duplicated in the three positions selected for it. Due to the extensive manipulation, the final file for this small decoration occupies 4.9 megabytes of memory.*

Printing of this publication was completed on December 17, 1994.